CASES OF CONSCIENCE

Alternatives
open to Recusants and Puritans under
Elizabeth I and James I

ELLIOT ROSE

ASSOCIATE PROFESSOR, DEPARTMENT OF HISTORY
UNIVERSITY OF TORONTO

CAMBRIDGE UNIVERSITY PRESS

Published by the Syndics of the Cambridge University Press
Bentley House, 200 Euston Road, London NW1 2DB
American Branch: 32 East 57th Street, New York, N.Y.10022

© Cambridge University Press 1975

Library of Congress Catalogue Card Number: 74–76947

ISBN: 0 521 204623

First published 1975

Printed in Great Britain
at the University Printing House, Cambridge
(Euan Phillips, University Printer)

CONTENTS

ACKNOWLEDGEMENTS

Whatever the faults of this book, they are not the results of lack of help, nor yet of haste. Over the last eight years I have picked many brains, and am only too conscious that some whom I can only remember generally here ought to get particular mention in footnotes; I hope they will accept this as a sort of apology.

My heaviest and longest-standing debt, for encouragement and hospitality as well as advice, is to Geoffrey and Sheila Elton. My most complicated debt is to Sir John Neale, Joel Hurstfield and the members of their joint seminar at the Institute of Historical Research, London, in 1965–6; plus to Joel Hurstfield and the same seminar continued by him later. Fr A. J. Loomie, S.J., has probably forgotten I ever consulted him, it's so long ago, but Patrick Collinson, John Bossy, and Fr Thomas Clancy, S.J., have all allowed themselves to be pumped at length. Natalie Z. Davis, D. J. Guth and Norah Fuidge are people I have talked to too often for clear recollection. On the other hand, Alan Davidson (of the History of Parliament Trust) was generous with his time and notes so recently that I have not been able to incorporate all the material he offered; much the same is true of Millar MacLure, who lent me Bishop Robert Sanderson's *Eight Cases of Conscience* (edition of 1674) too late to mention anywhere but here.

Of my own graduate seminar at the University of Toronto I must single out Dr Ogbu U. Kalu. Parts of my argument have been tried out on the Canadian Society of Church History, the Toronto Renaissance and Reformation Colloquium, and, of course, on my colleagues.

Like anyone engaged in this sort of work, I am indebted to the efficiency and courtesy of the staff of the Institute of Historical Research, and those of the several libraries and archives that have supplied my material. Among these, the first place in terms of bulk of material belongs to the Public Record Office, London, and next to it the British Museum. I have also to thank (in no particular order) the staffs of Dr Williams' Library, the Guildhall Library, Lambeth Palace Library, the Catholic Central Library, the London Library, and the old London County Council and Middlesex Record Offices, all in London; the John Rylands Library, Manchester; the Cambridge University Library and the Ely Diocesan Record Office, Cambridge; the Hampshire Record Office, Winchester; and the Salisbury Diocesan division of the Wiltshire Record Office at Salisbury.

The Canada Council made this whole project possible by a Leave Fellowship in 1965–6; and my University gave me the leave. It still would not have seen the light of day without the Syndics, readers and staff of Cambridge University Press.

While these are the obligations I can recall at this time, I am sure there are others; some buried far in the past, some quite intangible. I can only hope there are no glaring omissions and say, for all such sins, *mea maxima culpa*.

Toronto, October 1973

ELLIOT ROSE

Introduction

I want to discuss the situation that confronted religious dissidents, both catholic and puritan, in the England of Elizabeth I and James I. I am chiefly interested in the situation of those members of either group who were law-abiding by inclination and who hoped to stay out of trouble so far as their principles would let them. Martyrs are conspicuous and prophets cry aloud. It can easily happen that the attention of historians becomes concentrated on those who seek attention, or those who compel admiration by the boldness of their stand. This is natural but it is surely unfortunate. The situation of the less militant catholic or puritan was much more typical of the ordinary human condition and has more to tell us about that condition. The less militant must have been the majority among catholics and puritans. If we include absolutely silent sympathizers with each group and add the two together they may well have been a majority of the English nation. By the later sixteenth century the country had suffered four official changes of religion, well within an ordinary lifetime. The number of people who were privately dissatisfied with the result must have been enormous, though it includes people who were dissatisfied for quite different reasons. Obviously most of them wanted to stay out of trouble; most people always want to, and most of these people actually did. Somewhere between those whose discontent was so strong that it drove them to martyrdom and those whose discontent was so weak that it did not drive them to do anything at all, lay the world of the common catholic and that of the common puritan – the rank-and-file membership of the party or the subculture that was to be. Life in those worlds involved difficult choices, all the more difficult because the individuals concerned were not temperamentally cut out for militant action. It was sustained by hopes, and threatened by temptations, which did not affect the natural zealots. Hopes could be realistic or unrealistic and still be part of the situation. The situation of the moderate dissenter in persecuting times could never be static;

he could be beaten down by it into full compliance with the official policy, or he could be driven by despair into immoderate courses. To stay on the tightrope was an agonizing problem in itself. It is the problem I want to look into.

It was a religious problem. It was in a religious context that Englishmen, these Englishmen, first had to confront the moral issue of principled civil disobedience. To a twentieth-century mind this is hard to credit. Our dealings with the supernatural order of things play such a minor part in our lives that when we find people talking as if their religion was central to them, or even behaving as if it was, we are inclined to suppose that there must be something more behind it. We simply have to accept that the sixteenth century was different. Religious questions were the central concern of the age, at least at the conscious intellectual level. Any idea that they were merely masks and disguises for something ulterior, for political or economic ambition for instance, must be handled with the greatest caution. Theories along those lines are not absurd but they are best left to psychologists who know what they mean by words like 'subconscious'.

Religious questions were the outstanding questions of serious public debate; political questions, such as the virtues of a strong monarchy, might be discussed in the universities as an academic exercise but church matters were disputed in the home, the tavern and the street. Religion was the mainstay of the printing presses. Busy men allotted hours of their day to meditation and prayer. Prayer, indeed, was still considered to be an important activity in the public interest, even though after the dissolution of the monasteries it was no longer regarded, by protestants, as an adequate whole-time profession. In its cultural context it is not surprising, and it is any-how the fact, that the Reformation created – in England and in every country where it caused serious divisions – the problem of 'conscientious objection'. Bold men had always thought it their privilege to disobey the laws they disapproved of. From now on, good men sometimes think it their duty.

Most of the people I am concerned with were not of the stuff that conscientious objectors are made of. The conscientious objector is already half a martyr. But, as is the case with pacifists in wartime today, there were a thousand degrees between full compliance and full defiance. Some solutions that fell short of full defiance were acceptable to a martyr like Sir Thomas More; some were permitted by the Pope. On the puritan side of the line, in the early days of puritanism, full defiance would be a hard thing to define. There was room for almost as many personal compromises as there were puritans.

It is this area that I want to explore. Several questions may profitably be asked: how hard did the government try to enforce its own legislation? How far was it able to? How far could the dissenter hope to further his cause by any means except disobedience? What kinds of evasion and half-compliance were possible? how much were they resorted to? and perhaps most important of all, what did either the Roman or the puritan religion teach about the morality of such evasions?

On the Roman side, this is the very age when casuistry grew up as a science. It immediately attracted to itself the bad name which it still bears in protestant circles. This could be a tribute to the effectiveness of the early casuists. In any case the catholic church definitely claimed to provide answers to moral questions, and its activity in that sphere was increasing in this period. As the period was the one that saw the beginning of puritanism, it is reasonable to suppose that it saw the beginning of puritan morality, of a specifically puritan kind of approach to conscientious problems. In discussing the problems of catholics, the developing science of casuistry or case-divinity needs to be taken into account. If there was a corresponding development on the puritan side it needs to be considered also.

It is no part of a historian's business to pass irrelevant judgements on the dead by projecting backwards in time the system of values that obtains in his own century. It seems to me that Reformation historians are more inclined than other historians to do this, as they are also inclined to project backwards to the sixteenth century the present-day attitudes and styles of different religious denominations (as if Luther had been a modern Lutheran, or as if Clement VII had been defending the indissolubility of marriage against a protestant Henry VIII). It is imperative, if we are to understand a past age at all, that we should understand the set of values by which that age judged. It is not necessary, it may even be a danger signal, that we should share the same set. We should be careful not to condemn men for acting as they thought right, nor to praise them for actions that they thought wrong. We should not impute modern attitudes to men of the past, either for praise or blame. This sounds obvious, and hardly worth saying, but to name one example it is a constant temptation for historians to talk as if Elizabethans who protested against persecution did so from a modern, liberal, conception of toleration. Another form of anachronistic error to avoid is the projecting on to Elizabethan England, not the ideas that we work with in our twentieth-century lives, but the romantic haze which hangs in imagination between those lives and Elizabethan England. We are failing to judge the men of that age by its own appropriate standard if we see them as engaged in picturesque high adventure. The fugitive priests of the English mission were heroes indeed, but not heroes of fiction; to hide in priests' holes and fly from the pursuivants was not a great romantic game.

Some of the questions I suggested above may be nearly impossible to answer. Most of them can only be answered impressionistically. On some aspects of those questions objective and statistical evidence can never have existed. On others, the survival of evidence has been scrappy and fortuitous. For others again, the statistical approach is feasible but will not be attempted by me. In the foreseeable future it will be possible to analyse in all its economic implications the financial pressure on the leading catholics. A reasonable quantity of material survives, and it is material of a kind that can be fed into computers. It is being collected, as I write, by people with the appropriate professional skills. Even this material survives only in part, and can throw light on only part of its subject. All catholics were liable to financial penalties; the majority were subject in practice to only such minor penalties as have vanished from the record and are past searching for. As for their non-financial sufferings, these for the most part cannot be fed into a computer at all.

An impressionistic approach to this problem is the only possible approach to parts of it. It carries with it the special danger that my impressions are bound to be affected by my subjective attitudes and feelings. I had better make these clear. Of the various religious groups whom I am considering, my sympathies (it is not a question of approval) lie mainly with the 'church-papists', that is to say with those catholics at heart who grumbled but conformed. I regard them in something like the way that, in the context of the Vietnam war, a Canadian over draft age could reasonably regard a troubled young American who trusted to luck and deferment rather than exile or jail to get him out of a horrible predicament. Of course when I draw this comparison I, too, am projecting the twentieth century back, but – I hasten to explain – not with the faculty of moral judgement. For moral judgements, if I need to make them at all, I hope to apply such moral theories as existed in the sixteenth century.

Comparisons can be drawn. Facts of the past can be organized

4

into contemporary models to see if they fit. For instance, if I was attempting a sociological approach to the dynamics of puritanism, one fashionable historical model that I should try is 'the revolution of rising expectations'. I think this handy, multi-purpose explanation does have some light to cast on how puritanism got started in the first place and what kind of a movement it was. My aversion to twentieth-century comparisons is a fairly narrow one, and is primarily an aversion to the kind of historical writing which awards good and bad marks for behaviour in circumstances that the marker never had to face. This is still a subjective attitude.

I cannot claim that my time-division is anything else. It is on impressionistic grounds, or call them intuitive, that I include the reign of James I with that of Elizabeth I. That is how the material, such as it is, seemed to carve up. There was no way to stop in 1603, in the middle of a developing and manifold complexity of problems for both catholic and puritan. The death of James did hardly anything to alter the situation, which could be regarded at that point as more or less static for the time being. At that point it was possible simply to stop. Later in Charles' reign my problem erupted and flowed over into every other problem, all boundaries gone. Confining myself to an earlier period than that, I hope I can confine the subject within definitions that make sense and will stick.

Two terms that need a certain amount of defining are 'catholic' and 'puritan'. There is some difficulty in each case, but the difficulty can be easily exaggerated. When I use the word 'catholic' I mean Roman Catholic. In a book that has to talk about them all the time, to use the shorter name without further explanation seems so obvious as to need no defending. There are objections to the usage but they belong in a different context and I shall not pause to consider them. In the context I am concerned with, the question does however arise, when is a catholic not a catholic? Strictly speaking, anyone who obeyed the Act of Uniformity, 1559, however unwillingly, was in a state of schism from Rome. He may not always have understood this, or, understanding, have accepted it. I imagine that often the 'church-papist' solution, mere outward conformity under compulsion, led to full conformity in the next generation. This was certainly what the government of Queen Elizabeth hoped for, and the Pope feared. But the church-papist must have thought of himself as a catholic and that is how I shall regard him. (Contemporary protestants would have agreed. They used the words 'papist' and 'catholic' interchangeably, and readily stretched them to include those who acquiesced in the official settlement while their hearts' allegiance remained elsewhere.)[1] Those who made their communion with Anglicans, however, even if they hankered for the Latin in their hearts, had decisively thrown in their lot with the new order if they did it under anything less than actual physical duress or the fear of death. Since such duress was never imposed, refusal to communicate, rather than to attend church, seems to be the most meaningful line of division. I do not believe anybody of ordinary intelligence could cross it without knowing what he was doing. Those who were fully committed, themselves, to the new regime, and wanted to commit others, were specially exercised about the problem of forcing people to commit themselves in this way – a very difficult problem while Elizabeth was on the throne.[2] The church-going non-communicant is probably to be set down as a church-papist. It is also usual to assume that if a man went to church and his wife did not, he was a church-papist. The assumption was made by contemporaries,[3] and doubtless it was often true, but by all the laws of probability it cannot have been always. However, when we are talking about the enforcement of laws, the man who is suspected of being a catholic by those in authority is in practically the same situation as a catholic. It matters less whether the Pope would agree.

As for puritans, Elizabethans who used the word in scorn and contempt doubtless exaggerated the unity of what they described; it is a temptation for historians, with seventeenth-century hindsight, to exaggerate the disunity. The word (sometimes varied by 'peevish precisian') entered the language about 1565, to describe an objectionable 'them-group' whose existence the common man began to be conscious of about that time. What made the group objectionable was its irritating claim to be more pure, or precise, than its neighbours in religious matters – which implies that there was no great difference between puritans and neighbours in the goals they were both supposed to be seeking, but only in their degree of devotion to those goals, or their readiness to make small points into major issues.

The word was used loosely (like 'communist' in our own day) to suggest a kind of conspiracy. In fact, it was at the most a very untidy movement within the Elizabethan church, which united at times, and at times failed to unite, around different issues and behind

---

1 E.g. Grindal, quoted by John Strype, *Annals of the Reformation*, vol. 1, Pt. 1, cap. 28 (p. 492 of Oxford ed. of 1824) and cf. Dr Williams' Library, Morrice MS, vol. 1, 129f.
2 E.g. Aylmer to Walsingham, SP 12.114.22 (21 June 1577) (see below, pp. 43–4) and and cf. J. E. Neale, *Elizabeth I and her Parliaments*, vol. 1, p. 192f.
3 E.g. John Earle, *Microcosmographie* (1628) s.v. 'Church papist'.

temporary leaders. Nevertheless there were English protestants who were in the movement and others who were not; when the name 'puritan' was bandied about there were those who applied it to themselves (at first resentfully; they preferred to be called 'the sincere sort', or sometimes, revealingly, 'the brethren'). All puritans wanted further reformation, of the Church and of everybody's morals. The most recognizable puritans were those who were working to bring in a reformation on Geneva lines – in religious ceremonial, in the structure of church government, and above all in 'Godly Discipline' – the reformation of morals by church courts themselves reformed on presbyterian lines.[1]

You could want all these things to come about without getting yourself into trouble. But to *deserve* the name 'puritan' a minister (not so clearly a layman) would have to drive his dislike of the Elizabethan settlement to the point where he must either risk trouble or swallow his principles. This is the point at which I become interested in him.

The earliest and easiest way the problem of conformity could arise for a puritan was over the ceremonial requirements of the Act of Uniformity and Queen's Injunctions and especially the prescribed dress of the minister, the surplice and square cap. I shall not, however, have much to say about this question, because it does not seem to have given rise to much serious controversy. Almost everybody seems to have thought that the surplice question was a triviality not worth a confrontation. The issue of 'Godly Discipline', however, and to a rather lesser extent the related issue of church government, belonged to the substance of reformation in that there could be no reformation worthy the name without them. I therefore would like to know how far the men of the movement had to go in seeking these if they wanted to satisfy their consciences, and how far ways of accommodation and half-compliance were open to them.

Already in Elizabeth's reign some extremists whose programme for reformation sounded very like the usual one despaired of the national church entirely and separated from it. In James' reign the General Baptists, first of the outright sects, organized themselves on a tiny scale. Extremists of any party, however, are outside my terms of reference. The puritans I am concerned with were still hoping to transform the national church from within; their brightest hope lay in 'discipline', and as an adjunct a new, Geneva-type polity. I shall hereafter generally use the word 'puritan' in this sense.

---

[1] See below, beginning of Part Two.

7

For another reason I shall ignore the 'Family of Love'. This metaphysical cult, rather than church, did gain some adherents in Elizabethan England; at least its literature circulated in English translation (it was Dutch in origin). It was a very minor complication of the religious picture. When Robert Parsons, the catholic apologist, wanted to make the reformation look ridiculous, he said there were four 'religions' in England: catholic, protestant (or 'Lutheran'), puritan, and familist.[1] Nobody else paid them much attention. Protestant apologists hardly bothered to confute familist errors, and though their existence was an irritation to tidy official minds they occasioned the government no anxiety.[2] This is easy to understand. Not only were they, presumably, very few in numbers but their principles permitted them to conform outwardly to the established religion of any country. While this qualifies them as moderates, it also made it childishly easy for them to avoid persecution, as outward conformity was all the government demanded. For Parsons' purposes there were four religions in England, and he was not including Brownists (his book came out before they existed). In practice, to any given Elizabethan, there were probably only two that mattered. For my purposes there were three.

One of these, the Anglican establishment, does not much concern me either. There were two main bodies of dissentients from it, and each can be regarded for some purposes as a unity though neither was without internal divisions. They quarrelled among themselves chiefly on how to carry on their larger quarrel with the official church. Each quarrelled with the official church on different grounds – on grounds almost diametrically opposed at least in appearance. The laws intended to enforce conformity did not always specify whether they were meant to hurt papists or puritans, but in effect the two were in danger of different laws. Certain aspects of their predicaments were similar, and furnish grounds for comparison, but both would have been horrified to think so. Though the moral problem of conscientious dissent was posed to both groups, not only the detailed circumstances differed but also the severity of the persecution each had to face differed greatly in degree. They were persecuted for different things, and one group was persecuted much harder than the other. It is therefore only reasonable to deal separately with each, and draw comparisons only as they happen to arise. From every point of view it seems just and appropriate to discuss the catholics first.

[1] *A Brief Discours*...('Reasons for Refusal'), Sig. ‡ iii.
[2] But see Neale, *Elizabeth I and her Parliaments*, vol. i, p. 410.

Part 1 – The Papists

Part 1 The Papers

I

The situation on paper

The Act of Uniformity, 1559,[1] required everybody to attend church on Sundays and holy days. The penalty for each absence was a fine of twelve pence to be levied by the churchwardens and applied to the poorbox. The act forbade all worship except that provided in the Book of Common Prayer; it was an offence to say or to hear Mass. By giving legal force to the Prayer Book it endorsed the rubric requiring communion three times a year, but for this it set no penalty, as authoritarians were later to complain. The Act of Supremacy[2] imposed the Oath of Supremacy on all clergy (and on holders of civil office). This was tightened by the 'Act for the Assurance of the Queen's Majesty's Royal Power...' (1563),[3] whereby a *second* refusal of the oath became treason. (This, however, was practically a dead letter.) More significant were two acts of 1571, inspired by the Northern rebellion of 1569 and the Bull *Regnans in Excelsis*. The Act against the Bringing in and Putting in Execution of Bulls and other Instruments from the See of Rome[4] made it high treason not only to bring in a papal Bull but to absolve anyone, or reconcile them to Rome, by virtue of such a bull, while to import objects, such as *Agnus dei*, blessed by a foreign bishop involved *praemunire*. All this of course was mainly aimed at priests. It was accompanied by an Act against Fugitives over the Sea, concerned mainly about their lands and rents. This act was tightened next year.[5]

The act of 1581, 'To Retain the Queen's Majesty's subjects in their due Obedience',[6] was likewise aimed at the richer catholics. It increased the penalties both for saying Mass and for hearing it said (to 200 and 100 marks fine plus one year's imprisonment) and

---

[1] 1 Eliz. I, cap. 2.   [2] 1 Eliz. I, cap. 1.
[3] 5 Eliz. I, cap. 1.   [4] 13 Eliz. I, cap. 2.
[5] 13 Eliz. I, cap. 3 and cf. 14 Eliz. I, cap. 6.
[6] 23 Eliz. I, cap. 1.

set penalties also on recusant schoolmasters and their employers; more famously it imposed a fine of £20 a month for a continuous month's absence from Common Prayer, which became indictable. In 1585 the 'Act against Jesuits . . .'[1] banished all Jesuits and seminary priests; it became treason for Englishmen ordained overseas to enter England at all; children might not be sent abroad without licence on pain of £100. From this time on, incidentally, the recusancy laws were routinely excepted from general pardons. In 1587 a new act[2] tightened up the act of 1581; cases could be heard at assizes instead of quarter sessions, one conviction would mean that the £20 would continue to fall due monthly until submission, the Crown had the choice of taking the fine or sequestrating two-thirds of the offender's property. In 1593 an Act against Popish Recusants[3] confined all persons over sixteen convicted under the earlier acts to a five-mile radius of their homes; copyhold tenements were forfeit for recusancy; those with less than 20 marks a year income were to abjure the realm (refusal was felony). All the later and tougher recusancy laws left the original twelvepenny fine unaffected.

Under James I, an act of 1604[4] consolidated previous legislation and clarified the point that a recusant who submitted could be excused fines already incurred. In 1606, after Gunpowder Plot, a new act[5] for the first time required those who had been convicted under the acts of 1581 and 1587 to make their communion yearly on pain of fines mounting to £60. Another[6] heaped on new disabilities; recusants were not to approach the Court (£100), could not practise law or serve as officers in Army or Navy (£100), must have their children baptized in the parish church (£100) and be buried in its graveyard (£20); no *husband* of a recusant could hold any public office, and no actual recusant could act as executor or guardian, present to a living or own weapons except for self-defence. From now on, civil disabilities continue to multiply beyond our period; eventually it would be illegal for a catholic to live in London, lease land or bequeath it by will or own a horse above a fixed low value.

Apart from statute, life could be made uncomfortable for catholics, and the practice of their religion hampered, in at least two other ways. In the first place, the vast and vaguely defined powers of the

[1] 27 Eliz. I, cap. 2.
[2] 29 Eliz. I, cap. 6, 'An Act for the more speedy and due execution of certain branches of the statute...entitled an Act to retain the Queen's Majesty's subjects in their due obedience'.
[3] 35 Eliz. I, cap. 2.   [4] 1, 2 Jas. I, cap. 4.
[5] 3 Jas. I, cap. 4.   [6] 3 Jas. I, cap. 5.

Royal Prerogative could be turned against them. Besides the more or less regular prerogative powers, the sphere of executive discretion which lawyers knew all about and which is still with us today – the authority whereby somebody in the government commutes heavy sentences to light sentences, the right to choose the design on the money and so on – there was a higher and more mystical prerogative, roughly corresponding to what we would now call emergency powers except that it was definitely conferred on the Prince by God. Both kinds of prerogative, in practice, were wielded throughout this period and especially under Elizabeth by the Privy Council more often than by the Prince in person, and the Privy Council was consistently protestant whatever the sovereign might be feeling at a given moment. The prerogative definitely included, for instance, the power to imprison without trial; it was also the only authority, in England, for the use of judicial torture. However, it was more useful against key individuals than against catholics as a class (or any other class). For one thing, such enormous powers could not, in their nature, be delegated except to officials working closely under the sovereign's eye; Prince or Council had to consider every case. For another, while nobody would venture to say what the prerogative could not do, it was pretty clear (except to James I) that it could not make new law. Actually, except for cases where state security was involved – a very large exception – the prerogative was not often invoked against catholics. Puritans complained of it more.

In the second place, there were always the canon law and the ecclesiastical courts. Even when deprived, the Marian clergy remained subject to them. For some purposes, so was everybody. Side by side with the new legislation designed by Parliament to make everybody go to church, or to catch and isolate those who did not, there were old, pre-Reformation rules of the church itself which were designed to do much more, and which were still part of the law of the land and still backed by coercive machinery if the machinery would only work. Despite the 'erastian' character of the English reformation, it had made little difference, formally, to the medieval system of spiritual jurisdiction. Laymen were still judiciable in the church courts for such offences as fornication, slander, and non-payment of tithe. (I may add, as a curiosity, that tithe was the first of these to be removed into the secular courts, because it concerned property and land and attracted the ambitions of secular lawyers and judges.) Proctors and apparitors and Officials-Principal and Vicars-General – all the tribe of tonsured vultures that anti-catholic propaganda had been so scathing about – were still there, though without the tonsure, and catholics were still subject to this jurisdiction until partly relieved under Charles I. This provided plenty of opportunities for harassment. The ability of such courts to harass went beyond their capacity to punish. To catholics who despised the protestant establishment its excommunications might be a *brutum fulmen* but they carried civil inconveniences. In theory the church courts possessed that weapon against the non-communicant which the Elizabethan statutes had failed to provide. How it worked in practice I shall discuss in a moment.

Another kind of pressure deserves a bare mention at this point. In an age of personal government what the law said on paper might be more than it meant or could make effective but it was not all that it said. Quite apart from the claims of prerogative, a ruler could enforce his policy by the unequal distribution of his favours; he could demand proofs of loyalty, beyond the call of strict duty, from those whom he chose to regard as possibly disloyal, and it would be hard for them to refuse; he could demand of those who wanted to enjoy his favours that they enforce the same policy by the same kinds of informal sanction on those beneath them all down the social scale. In a hierarchical society not only are there endless opportunities for such pressures from above but they are entirely respectable. They are hardly outside the law. Rather, they and the law form a seamless web, a cloak to Majesty and a muffle for dissent.

2

The situation in practice;
the chance of not getting caught

On paper, catholicism ought not to have survived the reign of Elizabeth I. Martyrdom, lifelong imprisonment or exile should have been the only alternatives open to the catholic who was unable to compromise, and the catholic who *was* able to compromise should have been easily led into the bland comprehensiveness of the Anglican settlement. We all know that this did not happen. The policy of repression did produce results; almost certainly the great majority of Elizabethans who were catholic in sympathy eventually conformed, in round figures two hundred were martyred and many others died in exile.[1] But catholicism in England was neither stamped out nor coaxed out of existence. There have been catholics, and wealthy catholics, in England from that day to this. This is the more remarkable because the catholic was not usually threatened with punishment for performing a forbidden action, which might be done in secret, but for not performing a compulsory action, which the entire nation was supposed to perform regularly and publicly, and which was supposed to be regularly checked up on.

At this point we must turn our attention to the mechanics of law enforcement. I am not thinking only of the well-known idea that the Tudor government cannot have been a despotism because it relied on unpaid justices of the peace and had no standing army. It is obviously difficult to run a police state without police. But there were, in fact, ways of ensuring that unpaid officials did their duty or that somebody else did it for them. Moreover the government's lack of force was only relative. There *was* a catholic rebellion in Elizabeth's reign and it was suppressed. We need to consider more in detail the question of how effective the government could be, and, if it actually was less effective than it could be, why this was so. Both the efficacy of the machinery itself and the motivations of its

[1] Patrick McGrath, *Papists and Puritans under Elizabeth I* gives the most recent figures; and cf. Fr A. J. Loomie, *The Spanish Elizabethans, passim.*

human agents need to be considered. I shall here give first attention to the machinery.

First, because it applies across the board to all law enforcement, there is the factor of the law's delays. Hamlet was right to use the plural. Any court case was liable to run into several delays, and different kinds of delays were characteristic of different courts. The only prompt justice available in Elizabethan England was the rough kind meted out by justices of the peace to rogues and vagabonds. It was a simple enough matter to put a drunkard in the stocks, but at any higher level all the courts, Common Law, Canon Law, or Prerogative, including Star Chamber, were agonizingly slow. It is true that Star Chamber had something of a name for speedy decisions. The problem there was to make the decision stick and to collect the fine. In Common Law, most delays were the result of competitive legal ingenuity, and the arts of evasion had been elaborated with loving care over centuries. In a Consistory or Archdeacon's court the thing that took the most time was to get the parties to appear in the first place. The numerous opportunities for spinning out proceedings, and the exercise of the art, or sport, of dodging the process server, must have considerably alleviated the plight of the Elizabethan on the wrong side of the law, provided he was on the right side of the prison wall. On prisoners the slowness of the judicial machinery had a different effect.

Coming down to the particular laws catholics had to fear, the basic burden applying to everyone (over sixteen) was the twelve-penny fine for single absences from church. Although imposed by statute, this was administered as part of the ecclesiastical law. The responsibility for enforcement lay primarily on the churchwardens. The office of warden, being an office 'of burden', normally rotated among the parishioners; since the burden involved could well be financial, the poorest would be excused, but it was certainly sometimes discharged by men who were only just not paupers, and it might even happen that a man whose duty it was to distribute poor relief one year was himself in need of it the next. A number of consequences. The catholic recusant would sometimes be a churchwarden himself, and if he was fairly prosperous he would often be a man on whom a warden was economically dependent, or to whom he was socially inferior. On the other hand, many wardens had a strong personal interest in the state of the poorbox, to which the fines were applied. In any parish where it was thought improper to elect recusants (and it is a fairly obvious thought) the fact that the office was one of burden meant that those excluded from it were in the popular mind 'excused', in which case the fines would look like an alternative form of public service. These considerations cut both ways. It is clear that no *a priori* argument can be erected except for the inherent probability that practice varied a good deal according to local, temporary and personal circumstances, which is a generalization (and not at first sight a very useful one) which would apply to Tudor government in just about all its aspects.

The wardens had to detect the offender and collect the fine, and they also had the spending of it, pretty much at discretion. Such an arrangement, which would appal us today, was reasonable enough given the extreme publicity of rural and small-town life; it was a basic assumption of the whole parochial system that everybody knew his neighbour's business. It meant that unless the offender made trouble about paying, there was no necessity for anybody to account to anybody, or for the transaction to be recorded in any way, shape or form. Parish accounts survive in some places, but were not always kept. Thus not nearly enough records exist which could provide for the beginnings of a basis for a statistical study of the enforcement of the Act of Uniformity on catholic recusants. Since later acts were directed much more against the landed classes and the clergy than against the common man, our ignorance here is particularly serious. When we come to ask how the great majority of catholic sympathizers were treated we have nothing but inference to go on. The outcome suggests that over a large part of England the law was taken seriously, since eventually the common people abandoned catholicism completely except for little pockets of tenants and servants on the estates of recusant squires – a pattern establishing itself in our period, and which lasted to the nineteenth century. This need not have been the result of the twelve-penny fine (the availability of priests is another obvious factor in determining the pattern), but the trouble is we can never know what part the fine played.

The wardens did not always collect easily, and they did not always try very hard. In either case, the principal official remedy lay in the Visitation – the Archdeacon's, every year, or the Bishop's, every three or four years. These traditional tours of inspection were not apt to be very searching. Despite the efforts of some reforming bishops (notably Hooper in Edward's reign) and the regrets of others at a great opportunity lost, the late-medieval routines for making Visitations painless still largely prevailed. Few bishops attended in person; they were more likely to send their chancellor as Vicar-General, and he (to the scandal of puritans) might well be a layman. The Archdeacon, the *oculus episcopi*, normally did visit in person but few at this time were very eagle-eyed. The Visitor summoned all the clergy and wardens of a rural deanery (say ten parishes)[1] to meet him together, and addressed to them a list of prepared questions. (The questions did vary from Visitation to Visitation, according to the personality of the Visitor or directives from the Privy Council.) To all questions it was notoriously the custom of clergy and wardens alike to answer *omnia bene*. Where they were allowed to get away with this, the Visitation Book might end up containing no information beyond the names of the persons present, deanery by deanery. In fact, this is not uncommon. However, this was the chance if the wardens liked to take it to 'detect' an offender. This would result in an 'office' case in the Consistory – i.e. one where the cause was promoted by an official, as distinct from an 'instance' case – one between parties – which was a possible but very unlikely recourse for church-wardens. The Visitation was equally the clergyman's opportunity to report any slackness in the wardens. Nobody else was likely to report it, and my impression is that parsons very seldom complained of wardens except by way of counter-attack when they themselves were in trouble of some kind (this seems to be a recurrent pattern in Visitation books, in contrast to the much more usual pattern of *omnia bene*.)[2]

If a non-paying recusant was finally summoned to the Consistory, the delay mentioned above operated. There was one such court to a diocese, though some archdeaconries and all 'peculiars' had separate courts of similar powers, under Commissaries or Deans of Peculiar. In a large diocese the court had to move about. The sessions varied according to local custom, but in most of the country the consistory would not be in session for much of the year. When it was, it met about once a week. It would normally take four weeks to bring a refractory party to a hearing – three weeks before the apparitor was authorized to fetch him *vi et armis*, which usually did the trick. I imagine this procedure was successful not so much because the armed force employed was formidable but because actual assault on an ecclesiastical official would involve excommunication rather earlier in the proceedings than was convenient. After appearing, the culprit

---

[1] As a unit of administration the Rural Deanery was on its last legs at this time; in every modern diocese except Exeter it is a nineteenth century revival.

[2] The visitation books searched by me are those for the dioceses of London, Ely, Winchester and Salisbury. Cf. R. A. Marchant, *The Puritans and the Church Courts in the Diocese of York*.

could spin things out as best he knew how but would probably, in the end, be sentenced to a money 'penance', which he would then omit to pay. After another routine delay, he would be declared 'contumacious' and formally excommunicated. The 'Act Books' which are the records of consistorial proceedings very often record nothing about a case except the delays, the one essential being to determine at what point a man became so contumacious as to incur excommunication. Excommunication was inconvenient in the same sort of way that outlawry was – for instance, one could not do anything which required taking an oath – but no more than outlawry did it drive an Elizabethan to take refuge in Sherwood Forest. It was one of the recurrent hazards of an active life and of course for catholics it held no spiritual terrors.

Eventually, either the inconveniences or a writ *de excommunicato capiendo* and the discomforts of the county jail would persuade the offender to submit to penance – that is, to pay his fine which by now would be more than 12d. It was uncommon for a recusancy case to be driven this far. In theory of course it might go further, for a prisoner could still refuse to pay. This should produce simple deadlock, but there was a more serious possibility: the man who went so far out of his way to emphasize his catholicism was in danger of being proffered the Oath of Supremacy, though as this was suggested as an improved procedure as late as 1592[1] we cannot count it among the major hazards run.

The £20 fine was a different matter entirely. Not only was this real money, but it was the Treasury's money, accountable in the Exchequer, a source of revenue that came to be depended upon and might be anticipated. The offence here involved was indictable, and the procedure was the Common Law routine of presentment, Grand Jury, and Quarter Session or (after 1587) Assize. While this means that we are much better off in the matter of records – by the end of the century there were 'recusant rolls' for each county[2] by whose means the Exchequer could compare the statistics of non-compliance, in the classes affected, year by year – on the other hand this method of enforcement ran into its own characteristic set of difficulties. The offence was that of not attending one's parish church or any other church, chapel, or ordinary place of Common Prayer for a whole month without reasonable excuse. This was a very great deal for

[1] BM Lansdowne 72, 41 (Chief Justice Popham).
[2] These are Exchequer documents in the Public Record Office. County Record Offices also frequently hold judicial records produced by this legislation.

a witness to take his oath on. It amounted to an extremely elaborate negative proposition, which all had to go in the indictment. The Clerk of the Peace for Hampshire about 1585 complained that the paper-work expended on recusants was hindering all other business at Quarter Sessions, and that he had not the staff to handle it. He also pointed out the peculiarity of this offence in being cumulative; until you actually got your man convicted, every month that elapsed constituted a new offence and needed a new indictment, which as he said was quite pointless but the inevitable result of applying Common Law procedure to a law drawn up in those terms. (*After* a recusant was convicted under the act of 1587 the £20 just went on falling due every month until he conformed.) The clerk is perhaps worth quoting on the burden of bringing people to justice, bearing in mind that he was piling it on to make a case:

If the parties indited be present and doe appeare & answere to their Inditements, then must the Clerke of the peace drawe in paper and enter in parchment severally all the first iudgements given against them.
(3) If they wch doe appeare & answere doe not satisfie their forfeitures or re-concile them selfes w^thin three monethes after the inditement fownd, then must the Clerke of the peace likewise severally drawe and enter a second iudgement given against them.
(4) If the parties indicted be at large then must the Clerke of the peace make first a *venire facias* then a *distresse*, a *capias* and an *exigent* against them if they doe not appeare.

There is more to it, but more office work rather than more delays. The last stage meant calling out the sheriff's posse.[1]

The Clerk of the Peace, the Justices of the Peace, the Grand Jury and the sheriff were all virtually unpaid officers discharging a public duty. It was the policy of Elizabeth's government to employ catholics in local office as little as possible, but in some localities it could not be avoided. It should therefore be mentioned at this point that Star Chamber existed to discipline irresponsible juries and the Privy Council at least tried to supervise justices of the peace and remind them periodically of their duties.[2]

The same machinery of enforcement was applicable to all further statutory burdens on catholics except those that were extensions of the law of treason, but in practice a difference came in when by the act of 1587 sequestration of two-thirds of a man's land could be substituted for the £20 fine. This transformed the situation

1 SP 12.185.83. Undated (1585).
2 The process is described by Sir Thomas Smith, *De Republica Anglorum* (1565), p. 89.

by greatly increasing the number and importance of interested third parties, tenants or would-be tenants or grantees of the two-thirds. The catholics' difficulties must have been greatly increased when it became possible to make a regular income out of them.[1]

When crimes were assimilated to treason they became a little easier to prove because of the greater acceptability of the evidence of accomplices. Also, although no law said so, suspects in treason cases could be softened up by torture. This required a special act of the prerogative, and even so evidence extracted by torture was inadmissible. It was used primarily to extract actual information, and is perhaps best looked upon as a counter-espionage device.

This brings me to the subject of spies, who of course played a large part in harassing catholics. To those who view this age in a romantic light the English government was already famous for the elaboration and deviousness of its secret service. In cold fact, Cecil, Walsingham, Leicester and every self-respecting statesman employed spies but they hardly amounted to an espionage system. Nor did busy ministers employ agents to smell out mere non-compliance with the Act of Uniformity. Spies could hope for reward only if they revealed threats to the security of the state. Quite possibly some such threats were invented by them and others abetted. In isolated instances the activities of an *agent provocateur* may come to light, and more often we may feel grounds of suspicion. However, these agents were not guardians of the ordinary law and were not, except by accident, a danger to the catholic who wanted a quiet life, with whom I am mainly concerned. On the other hand, since the main business of secret agents and 'pursuivants' was to track down priests, their activities did bear directly upon the chances that a catholic might have of going on practising his religion, as distinct from his chances of avoiding punishment for not practising another religion. The catholic situation had the dilemma built into it that the priest who carried with him the keys of salvation, who alone could nourish the faithful with the sacraments and without whom they might as

---

[1] The machinery set in motion by these acts is described by Dom Hugh Bowler in his edition of the *Recusant Roll No. 2* (Catholic Record Society vol. 57, 1965); cf. his *Recusant Rolls Nos. 3 & 4* (CRS vol. 61, 1970). See also F. X. Walker, *The Implementation of the Elizabethan Statutes against Recusants 1581–1603* (unpublished Ph.D. thesis, London 1961). Other relevant theses include: John Paul, *The Hampshire Recusants in the reign of Elizabeth I*...(Ph.D., Southampton 1958); Michael O'Dwyer, *Catholic Recusants in Essex c. 1580 to c. 1600* (M.A., London 1961); Alan Davidson, *Roman Catholicism in Oxfordshire 1580–1640* (Ph.D., Bristol 1970); V. Burke, *Catholic Recusants in Elizabethan Worcestershire* (M.A., Birmingham 1972), cf. Wark, K. R. *Elizabethan Recusancy in Cheshire*.

well not be catholic and not be in danger, also brought danger with him. A man could hardly refuse to harbour a priest on the run and still call himself a son of the church. The catholic squire virtually had to make his house a local centre for something that the government chose to regard as sedition, if a seminary priest was referred to him along the grapevine and came and urged it.[1]

If there were two horns to the dilemma, there were two ways you might hope to dodge it – the usual two ways: you might not attract the attention of anybody in authority, or the people in authority whose attention you attracted might be people with some reason for feeling sympathetic towards you. The secret agents and pursuivants just mentioned existed to block the first of these, but there were not many of them and they were not well organized. Spies, as I have said, were usually in some politician's private employ. Pursuivants were rather to be described as self-employed. There was nothing secret about them but they were not regular officials either. They were men armed with some kind of warrant, in search of some kind of reward; there was not, in other words, a trained staff of pursuivants, still less a nationwide network. They shade off into the class of 'common informers' who supplied the place of a detective force until the nineteenth century, and who brought actions against law-breakers in return for half the fine. Along this line the chance of simply being overlooked by the amateur policemen was quite high although there was absolutely nothing you could do to bring it about. The other chance – the chance of a private understanding of some kind with people who ought, in accordance with their duty, to have enforced the law against you and who might or might not do so in actuality – brings up the whole question of private arrangements.

---

[1] The situation of the catholic squire can certainly be seen in a different perspective, and is so by John Bossy, 'The Character of Elizabethan Catholicism', in *Past and Present* vol. 21 (1962).

3
Private arrangements

Given the personal character of Tudor rule already referred to, indeed given the necessarily personal character of all government in a society at that or an earlier stage of technical civilization, the ultimate severities of the law were never going to be applied uniformly to all categories of persons, and contemporaries never expected that they would. What this kind of observation suggests to a twentieth-century mind is that a privileged class, an elite, were exempted from the normal operation of the law and could live in safety while the common ruck of mankind, the little people, had to suffer. This is by no means necessarily the way it worked. Another possibility is that a prominent few were selected for special attention, and the heaviest pressures brought to bear on them, while the obscure majority escaped. This appears to be more or less what the people who drew up the Elizabethan statutes, and the senior officials who had to implement them, expected and wanted to happen. This is not necessarily the way it worked, either. And, further on the point of what contemporaries expected to happen, they could be right in general and wrong in detail. I think the discrepancy, between public expectations and reality, was perhaps more marked in the treatment of puritans than in the treatment of papists, but it is hard to be sure.

The laws paid much more attention to rich recusants than to poor ones. The tiny proportion of the total national population who owned land in substantial quantity – not even their family members – were the only people affected by the act of 1581, and they were the main people affected by every act except the original Act of Uniformity. Not only was Parliament's attention confined to heads of families, and of landed families; it was pretty well confined to heads of families whose land was worth one hundred and twenty times the property qualifications for the county franchise. However unfair this Parliament may have been, at least it is free of the imputation of passing 'class legislation' in the usual sense. In another sense it was expressing a class-bound attitude to society. Parliament only really represented the landed class, and a high proportion of all its legislation, regardless of subject, reflected the concerns of that class as did the whole corpus of the Common Law. In this matter the sixteenth century compares quite favourably with the thirteenth or the eighteenth, but it remains true, as how should it not, that the 'political nation' tended to identify itself as constituting the people who mattered. Nobody was trying to draw up a perfectly even-handed law that would somehow have imposed an equivalent penalty for the equated offence whether it was committed by a peer or by a ploughman. The intention seems to have been rather that the aristocrat alone should suffer (though as a matter of fact the government was remarkably tender of the privileges of peers).[1] In documents of the period, wherever the word 'recusant' occurs, it is usually possible to gather from the context that this means not only 'popish recusant' but also 'rich recusant'.

There was an obvious rationale for such an approach. In Tudor England it was a natural assumption, and very largely a correct one, that a dissident movement could not last and cause any trouble unless it had great men to lead it and to protect lesser men. Remove the great men, or render them in some way incapable of serious mischief, and you solve the problem of dissension in your society. It was a standard, classical, maxim of political wisdom to lop off the heads of the tall weeds, and many a noble house had been made to feel its force in the most literal way. It remains to be seen whether the actual behaviour of government reflects this rationale.

I think it did only up to a point. Any policy of discriminating between one kind of case and another, within a general rule, falls into an unhappy area of borderland between consistent policy and mere caprice; it could be called an inconsistent policy. When personal factors enter, they enter in a personal way. What happened was that the question whether personal factors entered into your case or not depended on how high you were on the social ladder; but the question whether they operated for you or against you depended on what they were. Friendship with the Queen, or great prominence in the public service, could cut both ways, whereas humble poverty did not cut at all.

Elizabeth demanded token compliance, at least, with her religious settlement from everybody whom she favoured. At the outset of her

---

[1] This emerges from the thesis of Dr Walker (above, note 1, 21) and is explicit in the 1571 Act against fugitives. But see below, p. 37, for a case of pressure being exerted on peers.

reign she offered high favour, so far as she could without great expense, to her own cousins the Howards (and other, more protestant, cousins such as Lord Hunsdon). From most of them she got at least token compliance. Sir William Petre, kept on as co-Secretary from the previous regime, was required to conform. Both Howards and Petres were to become traditionally catholic families, and the tradition was established in this period, not by the family heads but by their wives and children. When the £20 fine was first imposed it was imposed on a select group, a mere handful of individuals; most of them had recently been Elizabeth's hosts on a progress.[1] In 1558 and 1559, great efforts of persuasion were used on particularly respected figures in the old church, such as Cuthbert Tunstall of Durham or Abbot Feckenham of Westminster. Tunstall died shortly after the government had proceeded, very reluctantly, to deprive him of his see for refusing the Oath of Supremacy. Otherwise it is likely that his fate would have been similar to Feckenham's, who died many years afterwards in Wisbech Castle, an honoured and even an affluent prisoner but still a prisoner. On this occasion as on the accession of Mary, no difficulty was put in the way of the smaller fry if they wanted to leave. Dr Caius was allowed, in spite of undisguised popery, to remain as head of his Cambridge college, a favour shown to nobody else, but in that position he had to endure much petty persecution. No great man in Elizabeth's reign was singled out for special disfavour in the way that her father had shocked all Europe by singling out Sir Thomas More, but by contemporary standards of judgement one woman was. Whether it was Elizabeth's fault or not, whether it could have been avoided or not, special rules were invented for Mary Queen of Scots and some of them were invented for the purpose of killing her.

Among very important people such as these the decision rested with the Queen herself or the Council, and the determinant was the relationship that existed between the Queen and them. (It may be worth adding here that the special relationship and the fact of special treatment that flowed from it were unaffected if the very important person went to jail.) A worse problem for the implementation of national policy arose from the private relationships, or private views on the policy, of subordinate agents of government or law. This is where the justices of the peace come in. The reign of Elizabeth saw a serious attempt, beginning in the late 1560s and to be described later,[2] to eliminate known catholics from the Commission of the

---

[1] Walker, *Implementation of Elizabethan Statutes.*   [2] See below, pp. 37–9.

Peace. The justices of a county by this time normally included all its greater landowners who were past middle age – dozens, rather than the earlier three or four – and while only those who were likely to attend could be appointed to the *quorum* it was habitual to include in the commission the names of peers and privy councillors whose presence there was merely honorary. The position, in fact, without ceasing to be highly functional in most cases, had become a mark – at its own level almost *the* mark – of status in the county community. It was thus easier to include a really prominent person than to exclude him, whatever his suitability. Catholics *were* weeded out, with some difficulty, but nothing much could be done, across the country, to prevent an outwardly conforming 'church-papist' from ever being appointed, and there were places where ideological purity could only be insisted on at the cost of seriously weakening the commission.

The obvious example is Lancashire. It was notorious for the strength of its recusancy and it remained largely catholic until the industrial revolution; it has never been Anglican territory at all. It was more notorious for recusancy than the other Northern counties, but it is not clear how far it was actually more recusant. The priests of the English mission boasted of the freedom and the welcome they enjoyed everywhere North of Trent,[1] and it was the Border country that rose for Mary Queen of Scots in 1569. Still, Lancashire had the reputation. It was the classic case of a district where the government could not govern without the co-operation of the recusant gentry except by relying on the church-papist gentry, though even here it did try. The Crown itself, through the Duchy of Lancaster, was the greatest landowner in the county, which lacked great magnates except the Stanley family and was dominated socially by a class of modest and rustic squires, the kind of gentleman whose ancestors had always been lords of the same single manor and whose surname was the same as the name of his estate. The Duchy was a mere legal abstraction, commanding no such loyalty as a Percy or a Dacre or a Neville further North, but its officials were people of considerable local influence and its economic power was at least enough to keep the estate village of Manchester smugly Anglican and safe for anti-catholic operations.[2] Incidentally, the Chancery of the Duchy, then

---

1 But see A. G. Dickens, *The English Reformation*, p. 312 and references there given.
2 F. Peck, *Desiderata Curiosa* ed. 1779, vol. 1, Bk. 3, No. 42, p. 110 (For a quite different picture of religion in Manchester, see R. C. Richardson, *Puritanism in North-West England, passim*).

as now, made the appointments of JPs for Lancashire and Cheshire. No catholic would be appointed if his religion was known; it was not always easy to be sure.

A report on Lancashire (actually mainly confined to the region around Liverpool), 'a vewe... bothe for Religion, and Civill government', survives from 1590.[1] It lists the magistrates; after praising two peers it comments that Sir Richard Molyneux

> maketh shew of good Conformitie, but many
> of his companie ar in evell note
> Peter Leigh, esquire
> of great good hope
> Thomas Holecross
> for himselfe well professed in religion:
> but not so forwarde in the publique actions
> for religion as were meete
> John Atherton of Atherton, esquire
> not of good goverment for his privat state
> but well affected in religion, and forwarde
> Richard Boulde of Boulde, esquire
> maketh shew of good conformitie: but not
> gretely forwarde in yᵉ publique actions
> for religion
> Edward Scarisbrick of Scarisbrick esquire
> Conformable he: but his wife a recusant
> Edward Halsall of Halsall, esquire
> Conformable, but otherwise of no good note
> in religion
> Another Richard Molyneux
> Of verie bad note in religion: his wife
> a Recusant
> Robert Langton
> well affected in religion but he hath
> spoiled his estate, & useth bad company.

Going on to knights and esquires not in the commission, one

> hathe made shewe of conformitie in our
> Countrie

sixteen

> All of them, thoughe in som degree of
> conformitie: yet in generall note of
> evell affection in religion: no

[1] SP 12.235.4 (?1590).

27

> Communicantes: and the wives of y^e
> most of them recusantes

besides nine

> More usuall commers to the churche: but
> not Communicantes

and three 'soundly affected in religion', plus one in jail for harbouring a seminary priest. Among the officers of the county palatine, the procurator at Lancaster was

> Backwarde in religion his wife a Rescusant
> or lately reformed, & so his mother also

the clerk of the Crown

> Evell geven in religion no Communicant:
> his wife never at the Church in Lanc

The clerk of the peace 'of the same disposition in religion', the deputy Vice-Chancellor 'of the like disposition in religion', and so on down the line to the three Receivers of the Duchy, of whom two were 'better geven then the rest', and the third 'As badde as any'.

The parson of Wigan was mentioned among the few preaching ministers of the county. This parson, Edward Fleetwood by name, was quite possibly the source of much of the information. He pressed similar information on Burghley in a letter of 1590.[1] He complained that out of seven hundred recusants whose names had duly been given in by the bishop only about three hundred had actually been indicted; in the other cases no indictment was drawn up on the ground that the names had not been given in their proper legal form on the bishop's list.

The supplie wherof beinge referred to Certaine of the Justices of peace some happelie of them not of the soundest affection in stead of such addition, they used rather subtraction eich one of his frend, but litle or noe goode done withall for ye helpe of ye defectes of ye presentmentes. But for those which stand presented heretofore at ye assises and sessions to the number of 900 there was nothinge done at all, wherof I knowe not what reason can be alledged, but partlie that which was given to your honor: when I was in presence to witte the Backerdnes of the Attourney and Clarke of the Crown Contrarie to your honors directions in that behalfe. And more especiallie the backwardnes of the Justices of assisse him selfe

---

[1] BM. Add. 48064, f. 68.

who, apart from the plain evidence of his slackness at these assizes (at which he made a speech, pretending to disbelieve that the country was as full of recusants as the bishop had just told him it was), was reputed to keep a catholic wife and family. This judge (Walmsley) was well known locally for his leniency in such cases

> in particular when some came before him hertofore Comitted uppon the good behaviour, for Recusancie, or some other more speciall lewdnes, he thought good to graunt them baile for Conference sake with their pastors (wheras for one of them)...he hath had that favour from assisse to Assisse this 3 Assises paste

Walmsley was much more inclined to enforce conformity on the puritan clergy of the district than on the recusant gentry, in fact he was anxious to get Fleetwood into trouble. This document is not an unbiassed source but there is no reason to doubt its general tenor. In the next reign several local puritans did get into trouble; by then there were twelve J.P.s sufficiently puritan in sympathy to sign a petition in their favour. It put the religious state of the country this way: 'And whereas the disposition & state of this Contrey is knowne to be such y^t where they be protestantes thei have all remembrance of poperie, & where thei be papistes thei reioyce greatelie in the least monument thereof if it be but a palme Cross.'[1] It is clear that though even in Lancashire outward conformity was a condition of public office the government could set its standards no higher, so that in fact the conformists were a cloak of protection to the non-conformists. A recusant could rely on a good deal of public support, some of it from the bench. It would still be a mistake to think of Lancashire as sanctuary. No part of England was as far beyond the reach of the laws as the Scots region of Morar where catholics could boast that no protestant sermon had ever been heard.[2] Lancashire was a danger spot that had to be watched, and if only a minority of its enormous throng of recusants ever got indicted the number was still great enough to overflow its jails.

No other county was notorious in the same way, but in several the Commission of the Peace was hard to make up without including anybody who was suspect in religion. Sussex has been studied in detail by R. B. Manning.[3] A county so close to London, and one

[1] BM. Add. 38492, no. 96; cf. Cotton Titus B III, f. 65.
[2] G. Hay, *Architecture of Scottish Post-Reformation Churches* (Oxford, 1957), p. 152.
[3] R. B. Manning, *Religion and Society in Elizabethan Sussex* (Leicester, 1969), esp. caps 11, 12; cf. his article, 'Catholics and local office-holding in Elizabethan Sussex', in *Bulletin of the Institute of Historical Research* 1962.

of the few counties that was also a diocese (by the same token one of the few dioceses that were of manageable size), it should surely have been more conformable than most. Until studies such as Manning's have covered more ground we cannot say that it was not. It is clear, though, that at least in the early years of Elizabeth there was a good deal of crypto-catholicism in high places in Sussex. This is not particularly surprising since its principal nobleman was Lord Arundel. Here the purge of the commission was probably successful. At the county level it had a very good chance of success, eventually.

At the city and borough level a different problem arose. The magistrates of incorporated towns were normally magistrates *ex officio*, officers of the corporation, and therefore elected. Municipal democracy was on the decline in the sixteenth century compared with the middle ages, but still the choice of mayor and aldermen did not rest with the Crown, and typically that meant that the Crown had at best a very indirect control over the authority mainly responsible for local law enforcement. For instance, the Bishop of Hereford complained to Cecil in 1561 of his helplessness in his own cathedral city; the town authorities, backed by a couple of county justices, maintained the old religion to such a point that

upon thursdaie last past ther was not on bocher in heref' that durst open shis [*sic*.] shopp to seel on peace of fleshe: and the next daie being friday ther was not on in the holl citei gospellar nor other that durst be knowen to worke in his occupation, or to open his shop to sell any thing. So dewly and precisely was that abrogate fast & holydaie ther keapt.[1]

According to the bishop the whole county was a hotbed of popery, only kept in some sort of order by the vigilance of the Council in the Marches. He seems to have thought that the county gentry were the chief problem, though two ex-mayors of Hereford were noted as recusants when the main drive on J.P.s was undertaken. Clearly the civic elite was permeated by the old religion in a way that made it highly untrustworthy from the Council's point of view. Tudor governments, for all their large claims, and despite the fact that town charters were revocable acts of royal grace, seem to have been less inclined to interfere with established civic oligarchies than their successors in the late seventeenth century. Crypto-catholics were at times in a position to control a town corporation. Besides Hereford

---

[1] SP 12.19.24 (17 August 1561).

there were examples at York and Lincoln.[1] It is probably significant that all three places were cathedral towns and not major commercial centres. The old religious attitudes would naturally penetrate more deeply into the oligarchies of such places than into any other section of the upper and middle classes. By the same token, continuous protestant grip on the main sources of local patronage would be bound in time to cure the problem. The case hardly arose in such 'cathedral' towns as London and Norwich.[2] The loophole remained; until the sacramental test for municipal office was introduced after 1660 there was always the chance of the odd catholic magistrate in a borough. An entrenched succession of catholic magistrates was possible in theory, but the government would surely have had to do something about it. The heaviest responsibility for law-enforcement rested with justices of the peace, and with mayors and so on, because they usually were justices of the peace. There were no great feudal immunities left, with judicial powers, except the Bishopric of Durham. The machinery, such as it was, was under the central government's control, and judges at every level were appointed by it although some people were appointed, and more people expected to be appointed, as a tribute to their importance. The same general picture would hold good if we were to consider sheriffs or other local officers above the parish level. The catholic steward of a catholic Lord of the Manor could no doubt persuade the Leet jury to name a parish constable of suitable opinions but it would not matter very much, the informal power of the lord would remain the decisive factor whether that happened or not.

One kind of private arrangement that a moderate catholic might hope to make for himself did not depend entirely on the benevolence towards him that those in authority might feel. It was sometimes possible for a catholic to do the government a good turn. At one end of the scale this was why Dr Caius was left in charge of Caius College – it did not do to discourage major benefactors to the University. At the other end are the catholic exiles of the 'Scotch' party who may have hoped to purchase favour for themselves or their families by spying on catholic exiles of the 'Spanish' party for the

[1] See J. W. F. Hill, *Tudor and Stuart Lincoln*, cap. 5. For York: J. C. H. Aveling, *Catholic Recusancy in the City of York* (notably the cases of Lords Mayor Allen, in 1572, and Cripling in 1579); Wark, *Elizabethan Recusancy in Cheshire*, notes a doubtful case in Chester, p. 52.

[2] A borderline case would be Exeter, where cathedral patronage was declining but had hardly been replaced, economically, by the rise of the 'new draperies'. I know of no evidence for the attitude of the corporation.

Privy Council. I would like to suggest that this was a perfectly legitimate option, given what the 'Scotch' and 'Spanish' parties were separately hoping to bring about.[1] Somewhere in between comes the government's own proposals, in 1584 and 1585–6, to let prominent recusants off part of their fines in return for a prompt and handsome offer of light horse. As this was only to exchange one kind of economic liability for another, it is not surprising that nobody seems to have responded with much enthusiasm. Such as it was, the concession was tied to an expression of patriotic loyalty, and the same gesture was demanded from other people in a poor position to refuse it (the senior Anglican clergy) on grounds of patriotism alone.[2] Catholics and the clergy for one reason or another were sufficiently in the government's power that they could be asked to show themselves super-patriots. Such a demand is itself a form of pressure. The catholic who could earn grace by earning gratitude was in a very dangerous position morally, and not exactly a happy one from any point of view. This, however, is the characteristic situation of the moderate in the times that try men's souls.

1 And thus I feel that the attitude adopted by Roland Mathias, *Whitsun Riot*, cap. 8 is more balanced than that of Fr L. Hicks in *An Elizabethan Problem*.
2 On the whole light horse question see W. R. Trimble, *The Catholic Laity in Elizabethan England* esp. p. 177f.

4
Pressure:
how it increased and where it hurt

Elizabethan nearly died in 1562. If she had died then, or at any time before the rebellion of the Northern Earls, it is likely that her reputation among historians in the catholic, and continental European, traditions would be the opposite of what it is now. She had sat on the throne for as long as her brother and sister put together before she ordered an execution for religion or for high treason. Mary's early clemency had seemed dangerous to her advisers, but Elizabeth's far exceeded it, and contemporaries acknowledged this freely. Whether a change would have come about without the rebellion none can say; there is some reason to suppose that it might. Elizabeth was not the woman to accept continuous flat disregard of her wishes by catholics or by anybody. For a decade however she seems to have imagined that this was not a domestic problem, and that the settlement of 1559 (which the Queen may have been alone in regarding as permanent) would eventually gain universal acceptance without the necessity of harsh and rigid implementation.

Abroad she pursued something which could just qualify as a 'forward' protestant policy. The English intervened in Scotland and in Le Havre; there were efforts to send delegations to the Colloquy of Poissy and the last session of the Council of Trent.[1] At home there was a small flurry of official energy in 1561, provoked by nonconformity in high places, apparently linked in the official mind with political fears. When it turned out not to involve the Spanish Ambassador or the Queen of Scots it was allowed to calm down. Since it illustrates both the attitude of Elizabeth's ministers at this early stage and the attitude of crypto-catholics it may be worth while to take a look at it.

A massing priest (of course one of the old clergy who refused the

---

[1] This was an assertion of the equal rights of the English church to take part in a 'general council', which the Council – which might have admitted ambassadors – would not allow.

33

Oath of Supremacy; the Douai seminary was not even founded yet), a man called John Coxe or Devon, was arrested in Kent in April 1561, after the Council had heard some kind of rumour about him. He was examined by a local magistrate and then sent up to London and examined again, by Bishop Grindal. Grindal, reporting to Cecil, was very excited: 'Surelye for this Magicke & Coniuration yo[r] hono[rs] of the Counsell maye apoynte some extraordinarie punisshemente for example. My L. cheiffe Justice sayeth the temporall lawe will nott medle wth this. O[r] ecclesiasticall punisshemente is to slender for so grevouse offense.'[1] While the bishop's concern to make sure the offender was adequately punished reflects a constant preoccupation of Tudor government, on this occasion it was not the matter uppermost in the minds of his colleagues and superiors. They were not looking for a reason to do something specially unpleasant to Devon, but for information of a political nature. It is not clear from Grindal's interrogatory or Devon's surviving answers how magic came into it, though Grindal's suggestion was followed up at least to the point of searching the legal authorities for precedents of burning sorcerers.[2] Devon's importance was that he incriminated Sir Thomas Wharton of New Hall in Essex (who maintained a secret chapel) and Sir Edward Waldegrave of Borley in the same county, and looked as if he could lead to evidence against Sir Francis Englefield (already in exile) and foreign catholic governments. Nothing much beyond clandestine masses ever actually emerged. The council took it so seriously that Lord Oxford went in person to supervise the searches and arrests, but he expressed doubts in his report:

[Wharton] in verie humble maner submitted hymself to the gret clemencies of the quenes ma[tie] even of hymself declaringe unto me howe that onely towchinge the masse he was an offend[r], but (sayth he) concernynge my duetie besides if ye shall finde any suche matter againste me I do utterly renounce all mercie and favo[r], and so I toke hym wth me and made serche in all partes of his house so nere as I coulde for the things by yo[r] LL sp'ially noted unto me, and besides the trompery w[ch] in a scedule shall appere unto you, I colde neither in caskettes chistes or other places fynde any cause or presumpcon wherby his faithe and allegiaunce to the State was any whit impayred.[3]

(The trumpery was the furniture of the chapel.) Waldegrave looked a more promising suspect. Both men were lodged in the Tower,

[1] SP 12.16.49 (17 April 1561).
[2] SP 12.16.56 (20 April 1561). (The only precedents they could find were rather antiquated.)   [3] SP 12.16.50 (19 April 1561).

together with several of their servants and Lord Hastings of Lough-borough whose name occurs in none of the papers relating to John Devon. Later interrogatories allow us a clearer sight of the council's mind. It wanted to know about the forthcoming General Council (i.e., the third session of Trent); about conferences with the Spanish Ambassador; about possible marriages for the Queen of Scots, who at Candlemas, when Devon visited Wharton, had been a widow for a month. The most loaded questions concerned past loyalty to the Queen:

1. Whatt confference have yow hadde in the tyme of q. mary wth eny off her counsaillors towching her successor in the crown of the realme w^h whom where & when.

2. Whom thought or judgyd yow in such yor confference ffor y^r welth & suer contynuance off religion establyshed by q. mary [most, *inserted*] mete to be placed if [god, *inserted*] callyd her.

3. Whatt meanes was agreyd apon to use to bryng the same passe.

4. Ffor whatt cause was yt^{yt} the q. ma^{tie} y^t now is commytted to the tower off london in ye tyme of q. mary [*inserted* and kept in woodstok as a prisoner].

5. Who was agreyd to be apoynted her apparate successor to ye sayd q. if the q. yt now is hadde either dyed in prison or otherwyse by law as was then thought.

6. Whatt were the meanys devysyd to atteint her grecyus m' to deprive her off her possibilitie to ye crown.

7. In private & secret confferences att divers tymes in the late cardinalles house att lambeth towching the succes [*torn*] to the Crown & in sondry other metyngs sp'ally [*torn*] last yere of q. mary who was there thought good for ye welth of ye realm (as ye termyd itt) to s. q. mary & whatt were e meanes agreyd apon to bryng ye same to passe.[1]

The trend of these questions can speak for itself. After the suspicions here revealed it is remarkable that the main suspects were at liberty again by the end of July, having taken the Oath of Supremacy and entered bond to pay a fine of a hundred marks each (£66. 13s. 4d.). The fact that Lord Hastings was discharged on the same terms as the others seems to be the only reason for connecting him with the affair. His reactions are highly revealing of the man and the age.

My Lord Hastinges of Loughborowe yelded to the Oth willingly and followed the woordes of the reader wth soch a good courage as mought appere he ment frankely as ha spake. But being required to entre into a bande for his good abearing he became mavelously appalled therat and falling on

[1] SP 12.16.67 (? April 1561).

his knees wth weeping eyes he desyrd us for Gods sake to consydere the qualetye of his offence And therw[th] to waye that he was not of the basyst sorte of the Realme. But that that most troobled him was that yt shoulde ever appere by recorde that a companyon of the Garter shoulde for an offence of that nature bee bounde to good abearing wherby he sayed he shoulde bee a sclaundre to soch an honno[r]able compannye as all the worlde bothe for th'auncyentnes and thono[r] of that degree hadd in most honno[r]able estimacon. And therefore he desyred for the love of Godde wee woolde not requyre that at his handes, as wherbye that blotte mought remayne on his Cote which in opynion he shoulde never bee hable to skrape oughte.[1]

The Commissioners for the oath were favourably impressed, and urged that Lord Hastings should be spared this last indignity. He had been a Privy Councillor in the previous reign, and Professor W. K. Jordan describes him as a catholic on account of his will (which can never have been executed),[2] but it is clear that the word needs some qualification. Not only is this whole transaction in itself a lapse, but his obviously greater concern for the Order of the Garter than for the papacy – an even more ancient institution – gives him the look of a 'Henrician' conservative. If this was the sort of dissidence they were faced with, the authorities could afford to relax, and relax they evidently did. While they were about it, though, they did make Lord Hastings enter into a bond. Here we have an unusually neat example of a prominent man talking as if his prominence entitled him to specially favourable treatment, but being required to give special proofs of his loyalty – equally because of his prominence. (Hastings had been a close associate of Englefield, and Englefield was only technically not a traitor to Elizabeth, for lack of opportunity. Notoriously, he had plotted against her before she came to the throne, and her accession was followed by his immediate flight; he died a pensioner of the King of Spain. When Hastings was offered the chance of declaring himself a true subject, at the price of a little apostasy, he *was* actually being given the consideration due to his rank and previous good public service. But it is quite likely that he did not think so.)

Through the sixties protestantism in England continued to consolidate, without much in the way of organized opposition. William Allen founded the seminary at Douai, with four students, in 1568. In the same year Mary Queen of Scots arrived in England as a fugitive. The Duke of Norfolk – one of Elizabeth's cousins, and formerly

[1] SP 12.18.19 (16 July 1561).
[2] W. K. Jordan, *The Charities of Rural England*, p. 43.

in favour despite a reputation for clinging to the old religion – became involved in plots to marry him to Mary, and went to the Tower. At the end of 1569 the Northern Earls, of Northumberland and Westmorland, rose in Mary's support and ushered in a whole new phase in the government's attitude to surviving catholicism. A matter of days before the rising actually broke out, but in the shadow of its approach, the government took action which clearly showed it was no longer prepared to treat merely old-fashioned catholicism as nonpolitical and harmless in the style of the fifteen-sixties.

In November 1569 the Privy Council sent letters[1] to the justices of the peace in several counties, requiring them to sign a declaration that they assented to the form of common prayer established by the Act of Uniformity, and that they themselves would attend church *and communicate*: '...and shall also receve the holye sacramentes from tyme to tyme according to the teno^r of the said acte of parlament'. Having subscribed themselves, they were furthermore to collect signatures from former justices, and from peers and leading magnates in the county. Clearly this order was not solely designed to exclude catholics from office but also to single out for notice and disfavour every catholic rich and important enough to be a protection to other catholics. The demand for a blanket endorsement of the prayer book might have been aimed at puritans as well. At a later stage, or if the clergy had been included in the classes from whom subscription was required on this occasion, that is what it would have looked like. On this occasion, however, it is clear from the returns to the council's circular that it was catholics who refused, at least wherever it is possible to check. Thus, in Sussex the two who refused to subscribe are identifiable as catholics, and three who managed to subscribe were described as catholics as well.[2] In Hampshire the only magistrate to refuse was Lord Chideock Paulet, though his fellow-justices admitted '...that there are divers persounes within this Countie of greate liveloode, creadite & estimacon, nether presentlie, nor heretofore in Commission, vehementlie to be suspected of contempte to her ma^{tes} proceadinges (although diverslie they maye seeme to cover their hypocrisie)'.[3] Against such snakes in the grass the loyal justices asked for an extension of their own powers. In Essex the chief refuser was Lord Morley who was to become an exile and

---

[1] SP 12.48.69 (undated ?1568 or 9); SP 12.60.39 (16 December 1569); SP 12.60.47 (22 December 1569).

[2] Manning, *Religion and Society in Elizabethan Sussex* cap. 12.

[3] SP 12.59.46 (28 November 1569).

a somewhat inactive political leader of the 'Scotch' party; he was not a justice, and objected on the ground that peers were not named specifically.[1] In Berkshire another famous catholic refused: the great lawyer, Edmund Plowden, who was a landowner and magistrate in that county. Plowden stuck at subscription although he had actually been going to church. He first argued that he would need time to examine the whole book, and not only the Act of Uniformity, to understand how far he was binding himself or could bind himself by subscription; and his colleagues duly allowed him till the next justice day to make up his mind. On that day (a week later) he said that his actual practice in the matter of church-going since the Act of Uniformity came in had been as regular as could be expected of a man as busy as he was, and he thought the members of the Temple, and others, could testify in his favour on that point.

And therefor saide that towching that point he hitherto hathe not been any of those that y^r honours letters seeme to towche. But sithens the subscription required is not only to that poynte, but is generallie to all things in the acte and booke as he seithe. And suche subscription premysseth allowans not only presentlie but in tyme to come of alle things in the said boke.... And for that upon consideration of the boke and acte he conceiveth some scruple in conscience in some things in the said boke w^h he said he would have declared to us...And therefor he said he could not wth save conscience subscribe the said [letter] Ye he saide he could not subscribe, butt beleiff must precede his subscription And therefor he saide grete impietie should be in hym if he should subscribe in full approvance or beleiff of those things in which he was scrupulous in beleiff. And prayed us to certifie his sayeing to yr honours to thend you might understand that he did not upon stubbornness or wilfulness forbear to subscribe...[2]

Plowden is the first example I know in English history in any context of a man basing his refusal to comply with the law of the government's orders simply and solely on a scruple of conscience. Coming from a famous lawyer, the lack of any attempt at legal argument is the more striking. Whether Plowden was doing exactly the same as a modern conscientious objector is another question.

No other county produced anything quite as interesting. In Herefordshire, as might have been expected, the protestant justices had trouble with their catholic colleagues, who did not use Plowden's careful moderation of manner and language. In particular one John Scudamore of Kenchurch (of a noted local catholic family)

---

1 SP 12.60.53 (25 December 1569).
2 SP 12.60.47 (22 December 1569).

did there and then expreslye & more earnestlye than became hym refuse
to subscribe...and bothe the said Scudamore of Kenchurche and Havarde,
beinge required by us to be bounde accordinge to the tenure of your said
honourable letters did refuse so to be, and for asmuche as your honours did
not expresse your meaninge in your said letters unto us, howe we should
deale wth suche recusants, we were muche perplexed what to do[1]

Another Scudamore and this same Havard had been particularly
mentioned in the bishop's complaint to Cecil about the Herefordshire
justices, quoted earlier.[2] In Devonshire one James Courtney, not a
justice, protested that he was not really an important person enough
to be called on to subscribe, and refused to do so

nevertheless protestinge that he is readie...as his bounden dutie is to serve
the Quenes ma[tie] her heirs and successors with all that he can make to the
uttermoste of his power agaynste all persons whatsoever they be and dothe
also acknowledge and will depose that the Quene's majestie is the very true
lawfull quene and governor of this Realme and that no other person or
persons hathe any righte to the imperiall crowne of this Realme but onlie
the Quene's majestie her heirs and successors and will also stand bounde
as it shall please the quenes ma[is] most honorable councell for the accom-
plisshinge and performance of the premisses...[3]

It is not clear whether James Courtney drew up this fairly sweeping
declaration of allegiance or whether the Devonshire magistrates
composed it for him. It is the only statement of its kind that this
particular drive for conformity produced, at least the only one to
get on the record, but the record is in any case not complete. Returns
were only received, broadly speaking, from Southern counties; the
Council's original letter was dated 6 November 1569, and the rebellion
broke out openly on the 12th or thereabouts. The demand for subscription was formulated in the shadow of approaching rebellion and
the answers to the demand had to be formulated after that rebellion
had become a fact.

The government at the same time was making other demands,
determined by the emergency but relevant to the catholic situation.
The danger from the North made it necessary to circulate appeals
to loyal magnates to contribute troops, especially light horse, to serve
at the contributor's expense in the Queen's cause. It followed that
the Council was demanding two proofs of loyalty at once from the
most important people in the counties outside rebel hands. On this

---

[1] SP 12.60.22 (6 December 1569).
[2] SP 12.19.24 (17 August 1561) (above, p. 30, n. 1).
[3] SP 12.60.39. schedule 2 (12 December 1569).

occasion there was no close connexion between the two, but there could be later. The returns of recusant gentry and the returns of offers of light horse lie cheek by jowl in the State Papers, and this could well account for the fact that later on, in the fifteen-eighties, recusants were asked to prove their loyalty by contributing light horse.

The rebellion caused the government to take a more serious view of catholicism in high places; or, more probably, it induced Elizabeth herself to share the serious view that her advisers had always taken. It was still assumed that the only danger to public tranquillity stemmed from non-conforming aristocrats, and it was still apparently assumed that they could be dealt with individually. It was a full decade before any new general legislation was directed against lay catholics as such, and the new legislation when it came only applied to the rich. In the meantime the practice of arresting prominent catholics as a cautionary measure or as a way of exerting pressure on them and their friends began without benefit of statute, by an exercise of prerogative. It hardly proves anything when people whose sympathies are doubtful are taken and held in custody during a rebellion, but after the rebellion was over the government never went back to the easy-going ways of the fifteen-sixties.

There was, of course, an obvious reason why they should not. The rebellion of the Northern Earls shook Elizabeth's regime more than any other domestic trouble but it was soon over and never came near its main object. Its decline did more than its upsurge to bind a yoke on the necks of moderate catholics. It now seems clear that the Bull of Excommunication, *Regnans in Excelsis*, was issued in full knowledge that the cause was almost hopeless, as a last desperate plea to English catholics to rise and to foreign catholics to come to their aid. In this it failed. It succeeded in making sure that if the English catholics did not rise, and if foreign catholics did not come to their aid, their life would become almost intolerable. Even this only happened slowly, but surely it was bound to happen. It still seems curiously difficult for some catholic historians to understand that the Pope's intervention left Elizabeth's government with no option but to regard every popish recusant as a potential subversive until he gave special proof of his loyalty; 'toleration' without stringent conditions was simply no longer a real alternative for the Queen's councillors to contemplate. This consideration does not of itself make the measures actually taken any more palatable but it is a consideration.

For the time being the measures were still mild, and the government was anxious to make them seem milder. Mopping-up operations in the district actually affected by the rising were drastic. Outside it, the emergency had given a sort of opportunity to those whose sympathies might be suspect to demonstrate the falsity of such suspicions. Lord Morley, after refusing or dodging the question of whether he approved of the prayer book, was active in mustering militia and counting arms in Essex, as late as May 1570. About the beginning of June he fled, and wrote the Queen from Bruges protesting his loyalty. His son was eventually taken into custody; he himself spent what remained of his life (he died in 1577) in ineffectual plotting, on Spanish soil but not exactly in the Spanish interest.[1] Morley was the greatest recusant to flee *after* the rebellion, from fear of new severities. A few, whose only fault was their religion, were taken up and interrogated by the Council. To the councillors assembled in Star Chamber, about 15 June, Cecil made a prepared speech which reads like a proclamation but was apparently not used as one.

Where certen rumors are caried and spredd amonst sundry hir Ma[tes] subiectes, that hir Ma[ty] hath caused or will herafter cause inquisition and examination to be had of mens consciences in matters of Relligion: Hir Ma[ty] wold have it knowen that such reportes are utterly untrue and grounded ether of malice or of some feare more than there is cause.

For although certen parsons have ben lately convented before her Ma[tes] Counsell upon iust causes, and that some of them have ben treated wth all upon some matters of Relligion; yet the cause therof hath growen merely of them selves, in that they have first manifestly broken the lawes established for relligion in not comming at all to the Chirch to common prayers and divine service as of late tyme before they were accustomed and had used for the space of *ix* or *x* wholl yeres together: So as if they had not given therby manifest occasion by their open and wilfull contempt of breaking of hir Ma[tes] lawes, they had not ben any wise molested or deld w[t] all. Wherefore hir Ma[ty] wold have all hir loving subiectes to understand, that as long as they shall openly continew in the observation of hir lawes and shall not wilfully and manifestly breake them by their open actes, Hir Ma[tes] meaning is not to have any of them molested by any Inquisition or examination of their consciences in causes of Relligion...[2]

This assurance that so long as they obeyed the Act of Uniformity they would not be badgered to say whether they liked it or not may not seem a very generous measure of relief for troubled consciences. It is also not wholly in accord with the same government's acts of the previous November. It does express the classical Elizabethan policy, of bothering about outward conformity and not bothering about

[1] SP 12.70.13 (May 1570); SP 12.71. 6 (8 June 1570).
[2] SP 12.71. 16, 17 (15 June 1570).

inward dispositions of mind, and a semi-official assurance to that effect no doubt would relieve tensions for many catholics. Unfortunately for them, it did not square with the official thinking of their own church that they should be relieved from tensions.

The Bull *Regnans in Excelsis* declared Elizabeth to be no queen, and not only absorbed her catholic subjects from their allegiance but required them to withdraw it: 'We charge and command all and singular the nobles, subjects, peoples and others aforesaid that they do not dare obey her orders, mandates and laws. Those who shall act to the contrary we include in the like sentence of excommunication.'[1] Very few catholics paid any attention to this. Few seem to have made any bones about saying, if asked, that they intended to disregard it and did not feel bound by it. The text, of course, was not generally available. For legalistic minds there existed the out that the bull had not been promulgated in the usual form (though it is rather hard to imagine how a bull deposing a monarch ever could be). Even in the high middle ages no bull deposing a King of England had ever actually resulted in the end of his reign. John Felton, the militant who nailed a copy of the bull to the Bishop of London's door, was executed without protest from the catholic community and probably without regret. Nobody took that sort of thing literally; few people ever had. All the same, nothing – no amount of unprovocative behaviour, no protestations of innocence – could alter the fact that the catholic community had been hailed as a friend by the Queen's enemy. The Pope, who had a claim on the obedience of all catholics, had ordered all catholics not to obey Elizabeth. Any actual disobedience, such as not going to church, could now acquire a sinister significance if the government ever happened to be thinking along those lines, which it was almost bound to do if it felt at all nervous.

The next session of Parliament, in 1571, extended the law of treason so as to take account of the situation created by the Bull. As Tudor treason laws go it was not savage. The Act itself correctly stated that all the things that now became treason had previously been violations of *præmunire*, and *præmunire* itself was further defined rather than further extended (to cover recognition of beads, etc., blessed by a bishop overseas in his episcopal capacity). Although the act made it treason to be reconciled to Rome, in context it is clear that this was only intended to cover the case of one who sought to be absolved, by the Pope's agent, from the excommunication pronounced in the Bull – an absolution which, in the terms of the

[1] Trans. G. R. Elton, *Tudor Constitution* doc. 197, p. 418.

42

Bull, could only be purchased by disobedience to Elizabeth. The agents of reconciliation of course were traitors also. The Act was to be used against the seminary priests, but in 1571 no seminary priest had yet arrived in the country. The first of them began to slip over the Narrow Seas three years later. We may agree that, whatever the Privy Council thought, their mission was a spiritual one and not political. It inevitably had political implications. Their primary task was not so much to convert protestants as to rally and reorganize the scattered catholics, and in particular to persuade catholics to stand firm and refuse to go to church at the Queen's bidding. Their presence in the country was thus extremely inconvenient to the moderate or secret catholic, for the same reason that it was alarming to the government. It forced confrontation.

The Douai priests began to arrive in 1574. In 1577 the first Douai martyr, Cuthbert Mayne, was hanged under the Act of 1571. He had done nothing specially treasonable, he was merely careless. Perhaps the local authorities in Cornwall, where he was taken, were particularly vigilant or nervous for some reason. But 1577 in any case can be regarded as the turn of the tide. It seems to have marked, across the board, an intensification of the government's concern. Vague and sporadic searches for priests, occasional preventive detentions of lay recusants, occasional alarmist rumours fill the earlier fifteen-seventies; the first missionaries to become established in England wrote back to Douai in terms of glowing confidence. The rebellion, the Bull of Excommunication, and the Act against the Bull seemed not to be producing any real consequences. From 1577 or thereabouts however there are several indications of official anxiety, amounting to what looks like an actual policy of stepping up the heat. It is a neat coincidence that John Aylmer wrote his much-quoted letter to Walsingham a month before Mayne was arrested, on 21 June (he had just become Bishop of London). His main point was that imprisoning recusants did no good; such a policy 'hathe not onlie little avayled, but also hathe bin a meanes by sparinge of their howsekeepinge greatlie to enrich them'.[1] In other words imprisonment is no problem but something more than imprisonment is required.

Wherfore wth Conference had wth the rest of o^r Colleage we have thought good to forbeare the imprisoninge of the richer sorte, and to punishe them by round fynes, to be imposed for contemptuose refusinge of receaving the Communion accordinge to o^r order & Commaundementes, for if we

[1] SP 12.114.22 (22 June 1577).

43

should directlie punishe them for not comeinge to the Churche, they have to alleadge that the penaltie beinge alreadie sett downe by statute (wch is *xij* d. for every such offence) is not by us to be altered, nor aggravated. This maner of fininge of them will procure the Queene a thowsand poundes by yeare to hir Coffers whatsoever it doe more, it will weakne the enymie, and touche him much nerer, then any paine heretofore inflicted hath done.

Aylmer's ingenious use of the silence of the law as to a penalty for refusing communion, and his anticipation of an argument from the fixed penalty for ordinary recusancy, reveal a more legal mind than that of the average religious zealot, as does his reference to contemptuous refusal which was not accidental. Or perhaps they all reveal the mind of a religious zealot who has been consulting a lawyer. He obviously thought very highly of his own shrewdness, as witness his concluding piece of political advice, addressed, let us remember, to the Secretary of State, on how to handle Elizabeth:

In conferringe wth hir Matie about it, *ij* thinges are to be observed, first that hir Matie he geven to understand that it is mente hereby aswell to touche the one side, as the other indifferentlie, or els you can gesse what will followe, secondarilie if hir ma^tie by importunate seutes of courtiers for their friendes be easilie drawne to forgive the forfeytures, then o^r labor will be lost, we shalbe brought into hatred, the enimie shalbe encouraged and all o^r travile turned to a mockerie. Therefore hir Matie must be made herein to be *animo obfirmato* or els nothing wilbe done

On the economics of fining *versus* imprisonment Aylmer's judgement seems at first sight incredibly callous, considering the way in which sixteenth-century prisons were run for the profit of the jailor. But given that he was only thinking of the very wealthy he was probably right. This is at least the impression conveyed by Miss Mary Finch's study of Sir Thomas Tresham's finances, taken in conjunction with G. R. Batho's work on Henry Percy, ninth Earl of Northumberland.[1] Tresham, who lived like a peer, had an opportunity to cut down the ostentatious scale of his establishment, had he wished it, when he was lodged in the Fleet for religion from 1581 and was unable to entertain his Northamptonshire tenants and neighbours in person. The fact that he insisted on going on dazzling the county by remote control helped to prepare the eventual ruin of his vast estate (which incidentally was partly based on monastic lands). Miss Finch rates his financial burdens as a recusant as no more than a contributory

[1] Mary E. Finch, *The Wealth of Five Northamptonshire Families 1540–1640* (Oxford, 1956); G. R. Batho, 'The finances of an Elizabethan nobleman; Henry Percy, Ninth Earl of Northumberland (1564–1632)' in *Economic History Review* 2nd series IX, no. 3 (1957).

cause, though as a matter of fact Tresham was one of the most heavily fined individuals. Mr Batho suggests that his long imprisonment under James I (not for recusancy) helped to save Henry Percy's fortune by sparing him the personal ostentation expected of a nobleman – though not so much his 'housekeeping', for Percy also kept up his customary local hospitalities so far as was feasible while he himself was in the Tower.

It was also in 1577 that new moves were taken against the most prominent surviving refusers of the Oath of Supremacy, headed by Abbot Feckenham and Bishop Watson. Though technically under arrest and not pardoned, they had been living at liberty; they were now rearrested and committed to the custody of bishops under specially stringent regulations designed to prevent them from having access to their fellow-catholics. These may have proved to be too stringent to be workable in a bishop's palace. Anyway, the following year it was proposed to isolate them in some maximum-security castle. This was one of a number of proposals in a paper, *Howe such as are backwards and corrupte in relligion maie be reduced to conformitie and others staied from the like corruption.*[1] This seems to be only a sketch, a narrowing down of official ideas which were still pretty vague and general; thus, the desired degree of security may be achieved

ffirste in makinge choice of some apt place for the kepinge of them as *St. Johns Dertforde, Lumboroughe*
Secondly in appointinge some man of truste to take charge of them.

Nevertheless it does seem to indicate the direction that official thinking was taking, both in this matter of security measures for the leading catholic clergy (who in the end were permanently confined in Wisbech Castle) and in the matter of lay recusants. It was urged that the bishops should make up a list of recusants in each county

especiallie suche as are of countenaunce and qualitie and so offende in example.
Secondlarily to take order y^t the saide persons so offendinge may be conferred w^{t}all by the space of *ii* moneths by men sufficiently learned after a charitable sorte.
Thirdly: that not takinge effecte then to proceade by degrees w^t the obstinate. firste in restrayninge them of their libertes and punishinge them by way of *Multe* according to their habilities providinge that duringe the tyme of their restrainte they may be conferred w^{t}all. And in case by these saide meanes they shall not be reduced to conformitie after the space of *three months* then to proceede to the offeringe of them the othe according to the lawes of the realme

[1] SP 12.127.6 (? December 1578).

45

The author is concerned only with the very great and wealthy, with men capable of being a real menace and not likely to be deterred by a twelvepenny fine. He expects the government to take great trouble in individual cases, to arrange for learned protestants to wrestle for their souls. This paper makes an early suggestion that a watch be kept on the way recusants educate their children. No doubt the security problem was becoming more important and might justify an exertion of effort by the central government which it was barely equipped to sustain, and could not contemplate except in time of danger. It would be possible to claim that there was such a danger in 1578, though the rational basis for public alarm was slim; Thomas Stukely set sail early in the year under the Pope's standard and supposedly bent on the Pope's business, the *Impresa*, to subdue England by force of arms and put into effect the bull *Regnans in Excelsis*. Stukely's expedition was a token gesture and a fiasco but it advertised the fact that the *Impresa* was still the official policy of the Roman church and demanded the support of England's catholics. Later efforts were more serious.

The author of the advice just mentioned was more anxious to persuade catholics of their error than to collect large sums of money from them. In his scheme of things heavy fines figure as a pressure device, midway between gentlemanly debate and a really grave criminal charge (*præmunire* or treason). Perhaps because he did not think the actual money very important he paid no attention to the legalities of fining a man up to what his fortune would bear. Aylmer had noticed that this might turn out to be a problem, and had come up with a fairly deft solution for a legal amateur. Later in 1578 the attorney-general bent his more professional talents to it. He wrote to Walsingham on the 3 December:[1]

I have caused all the iudges and other of her ma^tes learned councell y^t were then in london to assemble together and to consider what is to be donne by lawe against suche as be recusantes to come to the churche and uppon conference by them had together with Mr. Dr. Lewes they thinke y^t by the statute of Ao. 1. of the Queenes ma^tes the commissioners for ecclesiasticall causes have authority to inflicte anie punishement by multe or otherwise wch the ecclesiasticall lawe dothe allowe of...it seameth that the lawe ecclesiasticall is plaine y^t a pecuniarie paine may be putt uppon suche recusantes...And for the manner of the levyinge of suche pecuniarie paines if it be estreated into the escheaquer the ordinarie course there is well knowen that suche thinges as be there estreated are to be levied of landes and goodes and also of the bodie if there be neither landes nor goodes.

1 SP 12.127.7 (3 December 1578).

In a postscript or endnote to the same letter:

And it is certain y^t by the same lawe th' ordinarie may punishe by pecuniarie paine suche as abstaine from goinge to the churche to heare divine service wthout reasonable cause of excuse especiallie if it be of contempte.
It is also noted by some of writers uppon that lawe that the Bishoppe may make a statute or ordonaunce that an excommunicate person shall paie x.£ for everie moneth he hathe contempteously remayned excommunicate.

The proposal is not merely to introduce higher fines for richer offenders but to toughen up the enforcing process both by using Exchequer machinery and by reviving the half-forgotten clause in the Act of Supremacy which set up a body of commissioners to exercise the royal supremacy on the Queen's behalf, but reviving it in such a way that what was meant in 1559 as a sop to clerical feeling made the church more than ever subject to bureaucracy. In broad outline the government's policy towards the recusant problem for the rest of the reign was in the spirit of these proposals.

This policy was crystallized into law in the act of the parliament of 1581.

By that time it was rational enough to take a grim view of the papal *Impresa* and of the connexion between it and the activities of missionary priests in England. In 1579 the task which Thomas Stukely had dropped with almost comic alacrity was taken up by James Fitzmaurice Fitzgerald. The Desmond rising to which he brought support and stiffening nearly succeeded in setting up catholic rule across Munster, and brought back to the soil of the British Isles, as a papal legate, the notorious Nicholas Sander, 'Dr Slander', the most violent of anti-Elizabethan propagandists. The author of *De origine et progressa Schismatis Anglicani* was an enemy agent and no bones about it, an emissary from the Pope to a rebel army. This was not true of the missionaries in England – though the government had no means of being sure of this – but the mission began to look more alarming at this precise moment, because the Jesuits joined it.

Robert Parsons and Edmund Campion – the 'Pope's white boys' of the sinister new society – arrived in England in 1580, the first of their order. To the government this may genuinely have looked like 'escalation'; in any case it was to be so represented. Campion inadvertently helped to put the new development in a bad, aggressive light by his challenge to disputation, 'Campion's Brag' as the protestants called it. Actually the 'brag' was a quite modest and courteous offer, not meant for general publication, that Campion was prepared

47

to debate about religious differences if any protestant wished it.[1] It was less aggressive than Jewel's *Apologie*. It was however denounced as an act of gratuitous provocation. It could not be represented, on its own, as an act of treason (though it was used against Campion at this trial), but the Jesuits had given their enemies a handle there too, without in the least meaning to. They had taken special pains to secure from the Pope (Gregory XIII) his 'Explication' of Pope Pius' unfortunate bull, and they evidently thought that this would prove that their mission was – as no doubt it was in fact – quite apolitical. Two things have to be realized about the Explication. First, from the Pope's point of view it was not designed diplomatically to soothe the government's fears – the Pope had not abandoned the *Impresa* and did not wish the government to feel any safer – but pastorally to reassure the consciences of catholics that it was not their immediate personal duty to depose the queen (which was still the ultimate objective). Secondly, from the government's point of view, the fact of circulating such a document involved indirectly publicizing the contents of the earlier one which this modified, thus bringing the colporteurs immediately and legitimately in the danger of the Act against Bulls from Rome. Parsons and Campion were probably the two ablest disputants ever employed on the English mission, and Campion one of the most attractive characters. They were phenomenally successful in the brief time before Campion's capture and Parsons' flight, and so they drew down the unwelcome light of their own publicity not on one or two hosts but on the catholic community – you can begin to call it that – as a whole. You can begin to call it that because the mission was welding the scattered groups of recusants to which it ministered into a self-conscious body. This it did directly by exhortations and by constant use of the grapevine, and indirectly by involving the recusants in new sufferings borne in common. The years 1580–1 saw a burst of debate on the churchgoing question, a girding of the loins for ideological battle, and an increase in the catholic prison population.

The debate will be discussed later. This is perhaps the moment to say a word about prisons. The complaint was constantly made that the recusants were overcrowding the prisons, or that they had to be left at liberty for lack of prison space. It must be remembered that prisons, though apparently numerous, were tiny; few had more accommodation than a private house. Apart from such mainly political places of restraint as the Tower or Wisbech Castle, the jails available

1 See Patrick McGrath, *Papists and Puritans*, pp. 168–9.

48

were of three types: felons' prisons, 'free' prisons and those in the jurisdiction of bishops. A 'free' prison held those arrested for debt or trespass; restrictions were minimal and very little social odium was incurred by a sojourn there. All prisons were expensive, since the keeper invariably lived off the profits of catering for his charges and was very seldom given an allowance for them from the government (or, in the case of debtors, the creditor, who was theoretically liable). All were insanitary, uncomfortable, and in plague times dangerous, but by the standards of today or at least yesterday the regime was easygoing (unless higher authority, such as the Privy Council, stepped in and imposed special severities), and not all prisons were equally shameful. It would be a complete error to suppose that before the recusancy laws gentlemen never went to jail; but in our period it did become an added grief for catholics that owing to the large number of them under restraint they were on occasion committed to any prison that chanced to have a vacancy. Moreover, the priests were usually held under an extension of the law of treason, and for them a felons' prison or a fortress were the natural places of incarceration. In London in Elizabeth's reign the prisons were, besides the Tower, the Fleet and Newgate (city of London), the Gatehouse (Westminster), the King's Bench and Marshalsea (serving the central courts and Middlesex, though physically in Surrey), the Clink in Southwark (Winchester diocese) and the White Lion (also ecclesiastical), plus the two little lockups in the City, the Poultry and Wood Street Counters. All the prisons named housed catholics, prisoners for religion, at one time or another, sometimes all of them simultaneously, and the two last, which were only intended to be used as short term 'bullpens', held catholics for extensive periods.

The concentration of catholics which was the inevitable result of holding them in custody in an age which lacked either the heart or the equipment to make wide use of solitary confinement, had everything in it to make the government nervous. It was a positive invitation to clandestine masses and subversive conference, and you could not have spies everywhere.[1] A little of the atmosphere comes alive in the awkward business of Morris Pickering, the tender-hearted jailer, in late 1580. He was keeper of the Gatehouse, and got into trouble with the Council through a report that he was being kind, beyond the call of duty, to his catholic charges. The story is perhaps best told in his ill-ordered but ingenuous words (to Burghley):[2]

[1] SP 12.155.29 (? 25 August 1582).
[2] SP 12.144.56 (20 December 1580).

49

Most Lamentable and dutiful wise wth Teares that as I remember a fortnighte afor micellmas I was wth Sir George peckham beinge Justis of peace wthin midellsekes wth a prisoner whom was disordered wthin the Towne of westmester for strikinge a Constable to be delte wthall acording to Justis and assonne as he hadde donne his suppere being broughte in williede me to tarye suppere and sittinge at suppere my Ladye sayde unto me you have mayneye prisoners for religgion I heare say I answerede that I have 2 maneye poore peopell for that cause and for restrente of theire frendes I feare the will starve I have no alowance for them and my Ladye saide Sir George I praye you geve them some money and after suppere as I have saide Sire George gave me *ii* angelles and desired me to geve it to those poore prisoners . . . for my part righte honorable I doe and ever have prayed for hir maigesties prosperas Raigne over us whom hath most godly & verteously maintined the Gospille among us hire poore and obediente subiectes whom hathe defended us from the Tearenye of the devell the poope and all his Ravninge wollves . . .

Both he and Sir George were in trouble. They were interrogated, on their own doings and each other's,[1] and Pickering was required to submit a detailed return of the visitors to his prisoners and the supplies sent in to them. Such a return survives for the period 25 October–21 November 1581. It records each individual visit and letter, and the visitor's authority, from which it appears that the Gatehouse was being much more strictly kept than would then be normal. We learn that James Braybroke received from his wife on the 30 October a pheasant hen, two geese, two capons, two chickens and 14s., of which he gave a capon and a goose to the poor prisoners of his religion. On 31 October his sister sent him a cake. Five flesh pies arrived on 11 November. All these were brought by his servant; he had various visitors, all apparently on business. John Corworth received 30s. on 31 October. Robert Dubdeale's father sent him two cheeses, a loaf of bread and 5s. on 3 November. Polydore Morgan on the 5 November got a leg of mutton, three pies and a bottle of wine; on the 12th, a leg of mutton, two mutton pies and a pudding pie; on the 19th, another leg of mutton and three more pies. His brother had permission to see him. Thomas Edwards' wife sent him a cheese and a featherbed on 10 November. On 14 November Humphrey Comberford received £4. 10s.; this was not a gift, but rent. Ambrose Edmunds similarly collected 33s. 4d. on the 15th. One other named prisoner, John Towneley, received numerous business visits and letters but no gifts, but as he was the richest recusant in Lancashire he doubtless bought what he needed from Pickering. Braybroke's gift to the poor prisoners

[1] SP 12.144.57 (20 December); 58 (21 December 1580).

is the only one mentioned, and could well be the only one that Pickering was obliged to report, because the only one that came from outside. In the circumstances, the more substantial inmates would be under considerable moral pressure to look after their poorer companions. If the government had deliberately planned to weld the rich and poor catholics together in indissoluble ties of mutual obligation, they could hardly have done more.[1]

(If it is asked, what option had they in this case? the answer is, legally very little, except that here the Council seems to have actually discouraged visitors and gifts. Poor prisoners, besides having an accepted claim on the casual charity of passer-by, were the responsibility of their native parishes, and the essentially makeshift character of parish relief at this date was of course compounded when it had to operate over a distance. The Council could have intervened, requiring the Middlesex General Session to take action, but its efforts in that kind sometimes only created new confusion.)[2]

The close watch on the Gatehouse began in December 1580. At that time the Privy Council was chiefly exercised about Parsons and Campion, who were still at large and making much more public stir, among catholics and protestants, than any seminary priest, or party of seminary priests, had previously done. The watch was still being kept up a year later. In the meantime, Parliament had met and passed the new act of 1581 against recusants (in March), and Campion had been captured (in June) and Parsons had fled. Sir Thomas Tresham, that greatest of recusant gentry, was in the prison population though not in the Gatehouse; his offence was harbouring Campion, or rather this was the occasion of his arrest; the Council also had, and was prepared to use, the handle against him that he could not take the Oath of Supremacy. He petitioned to the Council from the Fleet, in elegant style and tiny beautiful handwriting:[3]

...Which said offence of myne in any sorte to kindle her highness' displeasure against mee, doth by a thowsande of thowsand tymes, much deeper dentt, and wownde my subiect harte then doth my great fine, wch but to my Undowinge I shall not be able to paye: Or then doth my grevous, and perpetuall imprisonmentt, wch my decayed bodie cannot longe endure: Not desiering to live one houre wthowt her Maties grace, and favour, nor one minute of one howre, if I at any tyme have practised, or had intencion to practise any thinge against her Ma's person, and dignitie: Or against my deare and native contrie...

[1] SP 12.150.65 (21 November 1581).
[2] SP 12.155.1 (4 August 1582).
[3] SP 12.150.66 (22 November 1581).

This kind of eloquence was fairly standard with well-educated prisoners; so was the special care taken with the manuscript. The Council was to take Tresham at his word, perhaps rather more than he literally intended, when he suggested that he hardly minded being ruined by heavy fines compared with the pain he felt at displeasing the Queen.

Tresham was, of course, liable for the new fine, the twenty pounds a month, imposed by the act of 1581. It is easy to see this act as ushering in a new and darker phase of the pressure on catholics. In a sense it was so, though three things need to be remembered: most of the elements of the new exactions had been shots in the government's locker already; the machinery was still very loose and creaking and needed to be tightened up by the supplementary act of 1587; and both of these acts, like many other Tudor acts, were meant to be held *in terrorem* – no effort was made to apply them automatically and even-handedly to all cases. It had been possible, as Aylmer pointed out in 1577, to impose a heavy penalty on a selected recusant if you were prepared to go to the trouble; the Act of Uniformity, 1559, was admittedly inadequate but there was always 'contempt'; and others suggested the Oath of Supremacy and, following from it, *præmunire*. The awkward machinery of the new law was what the Hampshire Clerk of the Peace was complaining about.[1] After 1581 as well as before, and indeed after 1587, it was still the case in practice that the Queen's pound of flesh could only be extracted, at the cost of some trouble, from selected victims.

This is one aspect of the catholics' troubles that is capable of a statistical treatment, at least in principle. Until such treatment is forthcoming, judgement is premature. Some indications are already available, for instance the doctoral dissertation of Dr F. X. Walker,[2] which is concerned specifically with the enforcement of statutes from 1581 on. Dr Walker brings out strongly the highly selective nature of the government's pressure. In the reign of Elizabeth the number paying full fine was never more than seventeen, very disproportionately distributed, and later acts that seemed designed to affect more people seem in fact more often to have simply gouged more out of the same unlucky few. These supplied between half and two thirds of the total revenue from recusant fines, and it would seem in every case that the persons concerned had done something or other to attract the government's hostile notice apart from just not going to church. Dr Walker sees a nucleus for the most victimized group in Elizabeth's

[1] SP 12.185.83 (?1585).   [2] See above, note 1, p. 21.

recusant hosts on her progress through East Anglia in 1578; of sixteen who paid in full in the whole country in the early years, three were of Suffolk (and one, John Townley already mentioned, from Lancashire). Although the act of 1587 strengthened its predecessor by making recusancy an offence in King's Bench and the assizes rather than Quarter Sessions, and therefore more directly under the hands of the central government, this seems to have made little difference, reckoning in pounds, shillings and pence. There are, however, other ways to measure severity. While there is every reason to suppose that such men as Townley or Tresham resented their expensive prominence,[1] many lesser men suffered to some degree. The £20 a month class could only ever have been a small one, though it is surprising to observe how small it was. Many more suffered the alternative penalty of sequestration, which apart from the direct loss furnished opportunities for dishonest dealing for the government's lessees. However, probably only a minority of those indicted payed anything in to the Exchequer.

Only a few of the richest were called on to pay the full price. They were not called on with complete consistency and regularity; payments were allowed to fall behind, and a temporary shift in policy gave the victims a chance to compound for the penalty (a policy which might have been continued had the recusants been less parsimonious in the compositions offered). But harassment, at least, was the common lot. The execution of Mary, Queen of Scots, though it ended the only real chance of a catholic rebellion, did nothing to lessen the government's suspicion of a papist's loyalty. Since, in fact, some catholics (mainly exiles) *were* working for the King of Spain, and many more were up to a variety of plots, this attitude is hardly surprising. Official displeasure, however, was apt to fall on the just and the unjust. Moreover it must never be forgotten that the primary purpose of all the legislation was not to raise revenue or quell potential rebels but to persuade people to go to church, and to many of those who were involved in the enforcement processes this was genuinely a consideration of the greatest importance.

A document of nearly the end of Elizabeth's reign shows the ecclesiastical authorities still harrying catholics for all they were worth. This is a Winchester diocesan court book wholly devoted to '*Processus contra recusantes*', of 1598.[2] It appears to refer only to Hampshire, whose recusants have been studied by Dr John

---

[1] Trimble, *The Catholic Laity*... pp. 212–13.
[2] Hampshire County Record Office, Winchester Consistory Court Book 66A.

Paul.[1] (Surrey was also in the diocese.) It shows what seems to be a transitional pattern, for though one or two places (Otterbourn, West Boarhunt) clearly had concentrations of recusants there is a thin scatter more or less all over – one family in this village, two old ladies in that. Most of the accused were women; remarkably few bore the names of what were later to be known as the old catholic families of the county. (Thus, Mrs Francis Titchborne of Sherfield English was the only Titchborne.) Several were servants, not always servants to other recusants though the connexion was so likely that all the servants of a given offender might be summoned, and apparently even excommunicated, *en bloc* and unnamed.[2] Those cited were of all social classes except the peerage and the destitute, and several of them, when after much ado they appeared in court, answered by what was evidently a formula: that they had not been in church for such-a-number of years, and 'their conscience would not serve them to go'. One lady, a recusant of twelve years' standing, added that her health had greatly improved since she gave up church-going.

There is little sign here of the catholic enclave, the community dependent on the manor house with its priest's hole. That pattern was indeed developing, and it was in this latter end of Elizabeth's reign that most priest's holes were built. But many of these people were outside that world. Did they ever have a chance to hear Mass? There have been instances – in Indochina, in Japan, and in France in the *'petite église'* – where catholicism of a kind has nourished itself for generations on *paters* and *aves* and a rejection of the official religion, without the sacraments. It might have happened in England, but not, I imagine, without severe attrition of numbers – severer than what actually occurred. What this document seems to show is surviving Marian catholicism in its last days, touched but not transformed by the militancy of the missions.

The future lay with the new, tough, counter-reformation catholicism of Douai and St Omer. The religious conservatism that looked back to Queen Mary's days had nowhere to look but back. In the course of the fifteen-eighties the danger, if not the actual experience, of real persecution was an ever-present fact to be reckoned with, while the

---

1 J. E. Paul, 'Hampshire Recusants in the time of Elizabeth I, with special reference to Winchester', in *Proceedings of the Hampshire Field Club* XXI, Pt. 2 (1959). Note that since Dr Paul wrote this article and his Ph.D. Thesis (above, note 1, p. 21) the diocesan records have been moved and rearranged, and some MS references may now be out of date.
2 Winchester Consistory Court Book 66A f. 63, 65 ('*ancillam suam*'), 67 ('*servos quorum nomina non specificantur*').

hopes of 'better times' faded except for those who were prepared to bring in better times by violent means. In these circumstances it might seem that the problems of moderate men in the religious minority must soon cease to trouble them, for the religious minority was no place for moderate men. The new breed of catholic were fully committed men and women who knew exactly where they stood and had been tempered by adversity. But the desire for a quiet life springs eternal. Catholics saw the accession of James with high hopes of toleration. Their history in the seventeenth century is the history of the successive disappointments of that hope. It was a perfectly reasonable hope, even of James I; while some romantics indulged in fantasies about the son of Mary Stuart who would avenge his martyred mother, it remained true that James had been tolerant in Scotland, he was anxious for peace with Spain, and the Pope had not tried to depose him (though Father Parsons was quite prepared to). A certain relaxation of vigilance was to be expected, at the very least, a corresponding relaxation of tension on the part of catholics would make them think eagerly of some honourable arrangement they might come to, as it was said, for instance, Lord Huntley had done in Scotland. Even the Archpriest was thinking on these lines;[1] it was not just an aberration of the weaker brethren.

Those who had hopes of the new reign had underestimated the intransigence of Parliament and Privy Council, and of course they had reckoned without Gunpowder Plot. They had not wholly misread James. The catholic community in the early Stuart period does give an impression, at first sight, of shaking down into an unspoken, unguaranteed but tolerable *modus vivendi* with the forces that had earlier sought to crush it. Fines mounted; it now for the first time became finable to miss communion, though as I shall argue later it is not certain that this new action really made matters worse.[2] A constantly impecunious crown was not going to let slip the opportunities for profit that the recusancy laws afforded, but neither was it tempted to kill the goose that laid the golden eggs. The church-papist with his recusant wife and children and his 'steward' or 'tutor' from Douai became a familiar feature of the rural scene. Few priests were hanged at Tyburn.

This is probably as sound as most first impressions, but it underplays the very real dangers that remained. For instance, the risk for seminary priests was much less than it had been, but merely to be

---

[1] SP 14.28.5 (7 July 1607); 6 (undated – ? July 1607).
[2] This brought non-communion into the category of 'penal law'; see below, p. 69.

a seminary priest was still treason, and however little anxious the authorities might be to enforce a piece of panic legislation out of context, to the mob every priest was a Father Parsons and the flock he served was made up of Fawkeses and Catesbys. Life may have been tolerable enough in the recusant country houses whose squires, with no taste for Court life to make them regret the frugality and rustic isolation which allowed them to pay their fines, lived at ease with their neighbours, hunted and hawked and enjoyed the ordinary social amenities of the class from which sheriffs and justices were drawn. The servants and tenants of such a house had locally the protection of numbers and of the squire's good 'county' name. Even if there was no resident priest, fairly regular Mass and Confession could be counted on. If a daughter wanted to become a nun, there were obstacles in the way but they were not insuperable. But while this is true enough up to a point, the idyllic picture of simple faith and simple plenty in the old manor house on a fine hunting morning looks suspiciously like the pictures on biscuit tins and complimentary calendars. Side by side with the undoubtedly very tolerable life of the upper classes[1] there was, equally undoubtedly, much petty harassment, especially of those cottagers and common servants who were born to be bullied by their betters according to the social theory of the time – a peck-order theory which endured, in that same idyllic English countryside of the calendar art, to within living memory. What happened to catholic servants out of a place, or catholic paupers in a mainly protestant parish? For a full answer we must wait for a great deal more detailed archival work by local historians. A partial answer can be inferred from the pattern of catholic enclaves that eventually became almost universal outside Lancashire. Life for such people was simply impossible, and if they could not find a privileged recusant to protect them they became church-papists and from there, inevitably, churchmen. The condition of the recusant community as a whole has been aptly called a state of siege.[2] As in a siege, the

[1] One problem that specially concerned the upper classes, and may be mentioned here, was the education of their sons in schools and institutions of their choice. A. C. F. Beales, *Education under Penalty*, discusses the problem and the specifically catholic answers; he has naturally little to say on the extent to which catholics used protestant institutions. He does speak of virtually catholic grammar schools; it is clear that at Oxford and even Cambridge there were easy-going colleges and sympathetic tutors, though this could hardly be more than a 'church-papist' solution. No full study of this subject is known to me; for Oxford I have had the advantage of discussing it with Dr Allan Davidson. The *forcible* protestant education of catholic children never became legal (except for those sent overseas without licence); it could happen, in exceptional cases, by an exercise of the prerogative.

[2] By Philip Caraman, *The Years of Siege: Catholic life from James I to Cromwell* (1966).

poor could only survive with the help of the rich, and the community could only look after its own by severely controlling its numbers.

Looking back over the whole period, it must be stressed again that after real persecution started nobody was safe except by conformity. With all the allowances we must make for the inefficiency of the enforcement machinery and the habitual and avowed interference of considerations of personal friendship and favour in the execution of laws, we must still admit that every catholic potentially risked financial loss and imprisonment if nothing worse. The greatness of the Howards, and their closeness to Elizabeth, did not save them scatheless. Sir William Petre, with his entrenched position at Court and his transparent loyalty, could keep an undisguised chapel at Ingatestone and his family were apparently never fined, but Sir William himself had to conform. Elizabeth's later years were war years; the danger of catholic plots was real (there were, after all, several catholic plots), and as in all wars the danger was exaggerated. No man was too great or too small to have his letters intercepted, to be imprisoned and interrogated about casual encounters and trivial conversations. Some were too great to be tortured, but a prison was a prison whether it was Wisbech Castle or Little Ease.

If the accession of James brought about any improvement, it was of the nature of a settling down, a routinization of practices that had been essentially experimental. As such it gave the catholics a chance to feel that they now knew the worst that they needed to expect, which must have been a relief, but this relief was in large measure an illusion. In fact the state's treatment of the recusants remained fluid and provisional throughout the century, never very much changing (except under the Commonwealth) but repeatedly just about to change, or changed on paper, or mitigated or intensified for a brief uncharacteristic interval. The hopes and alarms broke out anew under Charles (which is my reason for stopping at this point). New elements entered into the situation – on the one hand the colonization of Maryland, for instance, and on the other the Test Act. But catholics were already familiar in this earlier period with all the problems of conscience, all the hard moral choices, that the century had in store for them. I now wish to consider the problems of the catholic conscience.

5

Legal means against the law

For men who do not want to be martyrs, and perhaps especially for Englishmen, it is natural to try the possibilities of legal evasion first, and only in the last resort stand on principle. Sir Thomas More, to whom I suppose nobody nowadays would deny the name of martyr, put his legal knowledge to the greatest effect in avoiding every danger of a treason charge except the one that he was morally bound to undergo. Edmund Bonner, who was not executed in the end, defended his life when he was charged with treason on the ground of twice refusing the oath to Elizabeth, by a highly ingenious line of argument resting entirely on English statute law, and so – some might have felt – conceding the authority of statute to rule on religious questions. (Bonner argued that he had not been tendered the oath, as the Act of Supremacy required, *by the bishop of the diocese* – and his argument that the person who did tender it was not the bishop turned, in part, not on any of the reasons later used by catholics for doubting Anglican orders, but on an act of Henry VIII which required four consecrators instead of the usual canonical three when none of them was an archbishop.)[1]

There were dedicated souls who scorned to protect themselves by legalism, or even by their just rights at law, when opportunity was offered them to confess the faith. This book is not about them. Margaret Clitherow, at York in 1586, was accused of habouring priests and refused to plead to the indictment; under the standard procedure at that date for such inconvenient prisoners, she suffered death by the *peine forte et dure* – pressing to death. She could have avoided this fate by pleading either 'guilty' or 'not guilty', whichever she chose, and in a district which was not very protestant in 1586 she might have found a sympathetic jury although of course the government tried to prevent that so far as was possible. She might

---

[1] *Dictionary of National Biography* s.v. Edmund Bonner.

58

have lived, a confessor instead of a martyr, or died a less lingering death, and it is hard to see what principle she would have sacrificed.[1] To her, obviously, the issue seemed clear-cut, and so it did, more comprehensibly, in the case of the hundreds of priests of the English mission who, being priests, had no option but martyrdom or apostasy once they were caught – if any third thing could happen to them, such as a lesser penalty than death, it was not in their control.

But for the vast majority of catholics it was possible and permissible, as well as natural and human, to try to avoid the worst severities of the law, when they threatened, by any honest means including those that were provided by the law itself. I have already mentioned as a rather singular fact that Edmund Plowden did not attempt to find a legal escape when asked to subscribe the prayer book in 1569. In the context this was not altogether surprising, since the worst thing that could happen to him as a direct consequence of refusal was dismissal as a justice of the peace; to do that the government did not need a legal handle, they merely needed to be dissatisfied with him, since nobody has a right to be a J.P. (unlike judges, they can be dismissed even today). As an indirect consequence of refusal, of course, he could draw down unfavourable attention on himself, but there was no way of avoiding that; legalistic hair-splitting certainly would not avoid it. Plowden did try to mitigate the bluntness of his refusal, so far as possible, by professions of loyalty and pointing to his own previous good conduct. In this he may be said to have behaved in a manner which was lawyerlike rather than legalistic. He may be compared to Lord Morley, on the same occasion, who tried to pick holes in the Privy Council's letter because peers were not named specifically and who fled the country six months later.

The most pressing legal danger on ordinary catholics was the danger of beggary by ruinous fines. Aylmer had realized in 1577 that the old twelvepenny fine of 1559, for those who could pay it, was itself a legal argument against further exactions. (He also probably recognized that another argument lay beyond that one – a moral claim, *in foro conscientiae*, that concerned laws 'merely penal', about which I shall say a bit more later.) That problem was met, up to a point, by the act of 1581; or at least that was what the act of 1581 was trying do to, though as we have said it was cumbersome to administer and proved less effective than Parliament had presumably hoped.

Some of the difficulties that were to emerge in enforcing the act

[1] *Ibid.* s.v. Margaret Clitherow.

59

were foreseen by a catholic writer who tried to arrange that his coreligionists would make full use of them. *A briefe advertisement howe to aunswere unto the Statute for not cominge to churche both in lawe and conscience*[1] got into the State Papers for 1580 but must in fact belong to the following year since it deals with a situation in which recusancy is an indictable offence but it is not yet clear how the law is going to be interpreted. There is thus room for those accused under it to defend themselves on legal grounds in the hope that it may be interpreted their way, and the author handles the question of conscience (which will concern us later) only in case these manoeuvres fail. I am not sure whether he is writing from the background of a proper legal training, or whether he is an amateur advising amateurs; he is, of course, advising legal laymen who might have to conduct their own defence (you were not allowed counsel when you were tried on indictment until the nineteenth century). I think he was an amateur and that a professional would not have thought all his suggestions worth trying. His style is exceedingly prolix and he labours small points at length in a way that would have been very antagonizing in court. Certainly the *advertisement* does not deserve to be called 'brief'.

He breaks the subject up three ways:

The firste what is to be said in Lawe to that commondement [*Sic*, for(?) common demand] doe you, or will you goe to the church.
The seconde whether the matter of the statute for not cominge to Churche can be founde by Inquisition of a Jurie.
Thirdelie if any person beinge denied the advantage of all exceptions by Lawe, howe to aunswere wth most salfetie accordinge to the dutie of a Catholicke.

To advise fitly on the last of these the author would need to be a priest; in the event, though, his advice on this point is still trying to establish an 'exception by law', still a matter of coaching the prisoner in what to say from the dock, rather than a consideration intended to weigh with a man's private conscience. Coming back to the first point, the catholic who is asked 'do you, or will you come to church?' is to make no answer at all. Such questions were asked by churchwardens attempting to do their duty under the Act of Uniformity, and though that act was an act of the secular legislature its consequences were in the realm of ecclesiastical law and those who administered it were ecclesiastical officers. In that system of

[1] SP 12.136.15. 'January 1580' in the Calendar.

law such questions were proper, or anyhow not very improper, and the author accepts that the positive duty of confessing the faith applied. But now that we are dealing with a Common-law crime under Common-law procedure, things are very different. That law is completely unconcerned, or it should be, about your future intentions, and it cannot require you to accuse yourself out of your own mouth. If you are guilty at Common Law, for instance, of refusing to go to church, the *onus probandi* rests with the prosecution to bring evidence that you refuse to go to church, and you are not obliged to help them in any way to find that evidence.

First because the verie wordes of the statute doe designe and limitt a iust proofe to be made by due order of Lawe for every person refusinge to frequent to devine service whiche proofe is to be made of a personall and voluntarie acte pretermitted and past...And is no due coᵣse of Lawe for any person to accuse him selfe. Therefore every subiecte livinge under protection of the lawes, is in this point to crave the benefytte of the lawe; that according to the purporte of that statute iust proofs might be made of his refusall or recusance

The 'secondly' and 'thirdly' that follow this 'firstly' are points of casuistry rather than law: a man is not obliged to accuse himself in this case, thereby arming his enemies against him, because the penalty is such a heavy one – 'so greate, that it importeth the losse of all his goodes and fortunes, and the utter undoinge of him selfe his wife and Children for ever' which we shall meet again as the argument from mortal fear, *metus iustus*; and he is not obliged to confess the faith, to his own damage, in this merely secular legal transaction. Further arguments, very ingenious, treat of the positive duty of not endangering the soul of your heretical neighbour by inducing him to think more uncharitably of you than he has to. The catholic is here definitely advised *not* to answer the question 'do you come to church?' etc., by stating his excellent theological reasons why he does not:

These sound speches and reasons and such like maie perhaps be considered within the danger of the statute.
And therefore aswell for the avoydinge of these peremptorie dangers, by the preiudice of a mans owne wordes as allso to stoppe the mouthes of a penall lawe, and to preclude the adversarie of all advantage to be taken by impeachinge of him self: It is best in my opinion for every person whollie to relie upon the benefite of the statutes eyther by due proofe therein limited to be convicted [i.e. only by such proofs as were normally acceptable in common law courts] wᵗʰout accusinge of him sealf

or, failing that, he could suffer with a quiet mind whatever penalties were inflicted on him arbitrarily, in the serene certainty that he had done nothing to provoke them.

Coming to his second main point, whether a jury could possibly convict under the statute, the author explains that the indictment has to be phrased in the exact terms by which the act defines the new offence, neither more nor less,

upon wch wordes the indictment must accordinglie by formed in this wise That he of the age of sixtene yeres from such a daie to such a daie vz. for the space of many moneths hath not frequented into any churche chappel or usuall place of praier not havinge any lawfull excuse . . .

Nowe for any inquest or jurie of any one county to finde this generall matter of Indictment upon ther certain knolledges and proofe of lawe accordinge to ther othes to be true, ageinst any person is impossible and inconvenient.

We are now talking about the Grand Jury, the jury of presentment that has to find a 'true bill' on the basis (theoretically) of its members' personal knowledge. They had actually done so, no doubt, in the twelfth century; in the sixteenth this was as much a fiction as it is today in those countries where the Grand Jury still survives. Most of the argument that follows and elaborates on this point is academic; the writer, who has no respect for the way the act was drafted and very little for his readers' intelligence, explains over and over again how impossible it would be to know the complex general negative that A.B., not having been to church for so many months in the parish church of D., county of S., had not gone to church anywhere else either, *and* had not got a lawful excuse. His reasoning appears to be sound in the abstract, but it takes little account of the way Grand Juries normally operated and therefore as an argument to be put up in court it had little chance of success. The author is, however, entirely in accord with the legal thinking of his age in seeing the wording of the indictment as the defence's opportunity to make a stand if at all possible, and this is his concluding advice in this section:

In particular there maie be diverse exceptions, both accordinge to the imperfections of the indictment and allso accordinge to every mans necessarie causes of lawfull excuses allowable by the statute, as by absence, by sickness, by imprisonment, by non resiancie, excommunication and the like.

It did not follow that all these would be accepted as excuses; they were worth trying. Another possible excuse had occurred to his ingenious mind, though it certainly had not occurred to those who drafted the act of Parliament.

What he was aiming to prove by all his philosophical nitpicking about general negative propositions was a supposition of his own about the future and the government's intentions. In the light of the event it cannot be claimed that he succeeded, but he tried to demonstrate by sheer incontrovertible logic that the difficulty of working the act was going to destroy due process. Ultimately to secure their object the persecutors are going to be forced to disregard the proprieties of their own laws and extort by fair means or foul an answer to the original question, 'do you, or will you come to church?' In that eventuality (we are now into the third main section)

Yf any person eyther in respect of his owne perfection be resolved and willinge [i.e. as a matter of heroic virtue, since it has already been argued that there is no positive obligation to behave in this way] or by any enforced and preposterous proceadinge beinge precluded of the former benefittes and advantages geven him by statute lawe reason and conscience, shuld be compelled to make aunswere directlie to the same question Then by the grace of god it shall not be amisse to crave favourable audience and free libertie not onlie to shewe what he doth in this kinde of dutie to god ward and by godes assistance is minded to doe. But allso to declare the weighty causes movinge him thereunto in Christian dutie and conscience

The catholic, thus driven to the wall, is to answer in a manner which the author proceeds to set out in considerable detail. He is to explain why it is absolutely impossible for him, in conscience, to attend the official form of service. In so doing of course he has to denounce protestantism, but only in the last resort, when the protestants themselves have left him no other option but to tell them what he really thinks of their newfangled religion. They thus cannot take him to task for wilful or provocative trouble-making. Finally, he is to plead that his conscientious scruples ought to be accepted as a 'reasonable excuse' within the meaning of the act.

And therefore to conclude every Catholik beinge perswaded in conscience by the former reasons or the like that the service nowe used is not that uniforme and Catholick service wch all Christendome hath receyved wth ther first faith, is to demaund iudgement.
That wheras the Lawes and statutes of this realme, or of any Christian countrie do not intend that any persone by any act shall willfullie and wittinglie damne his owne soule, whether therefore he shalbe compelled by lawe to goe to the Churche beinge perswaded in conscience by the reasons aforesaid, that his goinge thether is to the dishono^r of god, and so most wicked and damnable to him Or whether the same perswasion in conscience maie not be a reasonable excuse accordinge to the Statute.

Naturally it was unlikely that any judge would agree to take such a very convenient view of the law. It was unlikely that any judge would allow a prisoner to make a set speech, denouncing the Church of England, which ran to sixteen hundred words – and getting the speech delivered seems to have been the matter finally uppermost in its author's mind, rather than getting his man off.

It really was difficult to frame indictments under the act of 1581, and there were other reasons why it was hard to get convictions. When the number of potential offenders was large and socially prestigious there was every likelihood that all but the most dedicated of sheriffs, clerks, jurors and magistrates would succumb to the temptation to avoid a fuss and make use of the standard loopholes of the law, such exceptions to indictments as that a gentleman was described as a yeoman or his address was wrong. This was the sort of thing the Judge of Assize at Lancaster so improperly allowed to happen in 1590 – after the procedure had been strengthened by the act of 1587; before that these cases never went to an assize judge at all, but were left to the free operation of local influence and mutual backscratching at Quarter Sessions.[1]

The maintainers of lawful authority continued to be worried by the fact that when the law laid down a stated penalty it limited the freedom of government to treat delinquents according to their deserts. We find the Privy Council consulting Chief Justice Popham on this subject in 1592.[2] After conferring with his brother judges Popham replied in an ultra-authoritarian spirit but had to admit, reluctantly, that the law did set limits to what could be done by way of putting pressure on recusants. He suggested that there was no need to despair, there was still plenty that could be done, and he revived the idea (actually quite impracticable because of the Queen's known and rooted objection to it) that selected individuals could be deliberately put in danger of the death penalty by tendering them the oath of Supremacy twice over 'and by y^t ensample executed towardes some, others happelie may reforme them selves' – where, since he is talking about making an example, he presumably does literally mean to hang somebody. He was proposing that this treatment would be appropriate for young men who had not yet come to their inheritance and therefore could not have their lands sequestered for not paying the £20 fine, and had not goods enough to make the penalty of *præmunire* (incurred by refusing the oath once) worth the government's while. Catholic servants out of a place could be

---

[1] F. X. Walker, n. 1, p. 21 above.   [2] BM. Lansdowne 72 41, f. 117f.

handled in the same way. Even Popham in this rigorist document allows that those who could pay the fines could not be stung for further exactions 'for the bare recusancie', but their liberty could be restrained and other occasions sought against them; it could be treated as a suspicious circumstance if they sued a writ of *habeas corpus*, which is what Popham reasonably expected they would do. On the whole the document is a confession of weakness, of the deplorable fact that, within the terms of the existing law, it was impossible to be as harsh as one would have wished.

Popham incidentally mentions that one great problem, and apparently an insoluble one, was the barefaced nonconformity of the Inns of Court. These communities of lawyers were almost unamenable to law; their vast but undefined liberties and exemptions, extraparochial and extra-almost-everything-else, made them asylums for recusants as for puritans; for Abbot Feckenham, for instance, in his periods of semi-liberty, and later for the puritan Walter Travers at the height of his controversial fame. The Inns as institutions were of course directly under the eye of the judges, who by reason of their office were all ex-members of them, but there was nothing they could do to control them. Popham did recommend a special commission to reform them, but against the embattled might of the entire legal profession, what could it have availed?

On a question of that kind, where the privileges of their own order were involved, you could expect the legal profession as a body to back the recusants or at least to back the professional institutions that harboured them. In any case the legal profession was riddled with recusants. Plowden, for instance, was by reputation the most formidable barrister of his day, and we have seen a crypto-papist holding the assizes in Lancashire of all places. From 1606 onwards papists were excluded from the Inns, and confined to the lower branches of the law, by religious tests. Even that could not prevent the Roper family – Thomas More's relations – from being practically hereditary clerks of the Court of King's Bench.[1] Recusancy was a form of delinquency that took place within the 'establishment'.

In dealing with it, the government was faced with a legal dilemma. It was very unfair, considering that what it was trying to enforce, and what the delinquents were refusing to perform, was the virtuous action of going to church and joining in public prayers; but almost nobody would agree with the bishops and see this refusal as involving

---

[1] M. Blatcher, 'Touching the writ of Latitat: an act "of no great moment"', in S. T. Bindoff *et al.*, *Elizabethan Government and Society: essays presented to Sir John Neale.*

moral turpitude. Granted that recusancy did not involve moral turpitude, although it was a breach of the law, those whose business it was to enforce the law were caught one of two ways: either there was a set penalty or for all ordinary intents and purposes there was no penalty at all, and therefore no inducement to obey the law if you did not feel morally bound by it. If there was a set penalty then that made the law a 'penal' law, and payment of the penalty completely obliterated all obligation under it.

The concept of a 'penal law' was recognized alike by common law, canon law and moral theology. It lies on the borderline between matter of law and matter of conscience, and might just as well have come up in the next chapter. The phrase, at this date, meant the kind of law – assuming there is such a kind of law – which is concerned, as a police measure, to discourage an essentially indifferent action. It therefore attaches a penalty to the action, which you can pay if you would rather not obey the law. The legislator is deemed not to mind which of these options you take – the advantage to the revenue, from the fines, is supposed to be as important a consideration to the State as exact performance would have been. And since the action is not in itself morally wrong, God is deemed not to mind either.

It might be questioned whether there really exists such a category of laws. It is true that we can all think of examples, but they are not clear examples of an absolute indifference on the legislator's part; rather they are instances where it is possible to suspect that the fine is more attractive to the fining authority than compliance with the law would have been. Examples from our period are the penalties imposed in corporate towns on citizens who refused chargeable office such as sheriff or mayor. At times in the history of the City of London, and doubtless many others, such penalties were counted on as revenue. Examples from our own day are automatic parking fines. Certainly by the time of James I recusancy fines operated in this way – the king counted on them for revenue. This suggests he would not have been equally pleased if all the recusants had suddenly started going to church. From the point of view of people who were trying to extend the concept of 'penal law', however, this doubt would not matter – a law 'merely penal' or a law 'at most penal' would equally serve their turn. (The first of these phrases was the one they used, and they used it to mean that the legislator's intention was fully and equally satisfied by payment of the fine.)

Examples are available to hand of 'penal laws' as near as makes no

difference. The case is clear when revenue from this source is anticipated; when Queen Elizabeth, for instance, rewards a courtier by
bestowing on him the profits of recusancy fines not yet incurred.
It is clear when the North American municipality issues its police
with quotas of tickets and instructions to impose them on violators
by a set time. What is not clear is that any and every law with a fixed
penalty falls into this class. This, however, was what the recusants
were going to claim. This is why the phrase, 'penal law', was used
so habitually by catholics with special reference to the laws against
catholics that in the end that came to be its meaning in the English
language, and the sense, for instance, that it bears in the ballad 'The
Vicar of Bray'. Conventional moral theology allowed you to argue
from the fact that a law had a set penalty to the inference that it
had no higher purpose, and so if you were prepared to accept the
penalty you could consider that you were obeying the law according
to its real intention. This was allowed by the textbook on moral
theology used in the seminary at Douai, Navarrus' *Enchiridion*;
Navarrus got it from canon law and it was a highly respectable
opinion. The leading puritan authority on casuistry, William Perkins,
would be horrified to think that he was agreeing with a Romanist
on such a subject, but he also admits the law 'merely penal'. He does
not, indeed, admit in so many words the inference I have just stated
– that *every* law with a set penalty was 'merely penal' – but he does
allow that some laws bear this character on their face and that the
subject – not only his judge – can discern which laws are which.[1]

In the Common Law the expression 'penal law' was not well
established, but there was a rule, or tradition of interpretation,
closely allied to it. In that system, a law with set penalty had to be
narrowly interpreted; the definition of the offence could not be
extended by analogy, and such laws forbade only what they forbade
in express words. They also, of course, imposed by way of penalty
only what they imposed in express words. This tradition probably
reflects the professional lawyers' distrust of statute in comparison with
case-law, for penal laws could only be statutes, which meant to a
good Inn-of-Court man that they were inferior laws – mere petty
regulations rather than grand principles. By the time a good Inn-of-
Court man became a good Serjeants'-Inn man, and began advising
the government, he might want to take a higher view of statute,

---

[1] Martin de Azpilcueta, called Navarrus: *Enchiridion sive Manuale Confessariorum et
Poenitentium* (Antwerp, 1581), cap. 23. No. 56; William Perkins, *A Discourse of Conscience*
(Cambridge, 1596), p. 59.

3-2

and statute certainly could extend the definition of a major crime, felony or treason, but all agreed that statute could only do this by saying that it was doing it. The fact of fixing the punishment normally had the opposite implication – that the offence so punished was not being assimilated with a catch-all class of offences but was being treated in isolation. Either this principle of narrow interpretation, which was rooted in English law, or the more international and academic principle of a 'penal law' (that wherever there is a set fine that fine constitutes the limit of the citizen's obligation towards the law) offered opportunities to the recusant.[1] They left him very heavily liable; his case was still not one to be envied. But if this way of looking at his liabilities was allowed to prevail, it would follow for instance that there could be no talk of 'contempt' or 'contumacy' or 'wilful and persistent refusal to conform'. A penal law – this was its great and crucial advantage for the lawbreaker – did not admit of aggravating circumstances, and breach of it was not itself an aggravating circumstance for anything else. This would have been more use to the recusants if the society they lived in had had a high and meticulous regard for civil rights, and it cannot really be claimed that this was the case. But it was a legal-minded society with a legal-minded government, and the recusants themselves – the ones we hear about, and the ones the government cared about – were drawn from a legal-minded class. To a remarkable extent the law remained their protection, notwithstanding the possibilities of official and authorized violence and injustice which they always had to take into account and sometimes had to suffer.

Faced with the hampering limitations on penal laws, the government was thrown back on the laws without a set penalty. The most serious were those where disobedience was assimilated by statute to an existing major crime – refusing the Oath of Supremacy, or anything covered by the Act against Bulls from Rome, and the main clauses of the Act against Jesuits. Despite Popham's suggestion, these were not used regularly as a matter of policy against any class of catholics – not even priests, though no priest of the Mission was ever safe for a moment from the danger that the Act against Bulls or against Jesuits would be used against him if he was caught – and the first of them was nearly unenforceable against anybody in Elizabeth's reign because of Elizabeth's own distaste for it.

[1] Hence the pretended indignation of Daniel Defoe in *The Shortest Way with the Dissenters* (London, 1702), where Defoe is assuming the rôle of an 'Establishment' man: 'To talk of... 1s. per Week for not coming to Church, this is such a way of converting People as was never known, this is selling them a Liberty to transgress for so much Money...'

There remained the least serious laws. A fairly large class lacked all power to terrify, and for catholics this would include all ecclesiastical laws unless for some special reason it was temporarily inconvenient to be excommunicated. I think the one absolutely unenforceable law bearing on catholicism was the rubric which required three communions a year but was silent on the consequences of failure. The loophole was always a grievance to the more zealous protestants though it passes imagination what good they thought it could do to force people to communicate. (They cannot have merely wanted to use the rule to detect crypto-papists, because the rule without a penalty was enough to do that if it could do nothing else. They really wanted to punish people.) Sometimes the advocates of severity might put a bold face on it and behave as if sanctions were available after all. Lists of non-communicants were demanded by Visitation articles quite as if something was going to be done about them, and the puritanizing magistrates of Bury St Edmunds could airily order in 1579: 'If anie persons shall refuse to communicate in the prayers of the churche or sermons to be partakers of the Lordes table so often as by the order of this churche is appointed, he is to be punished accordinge to the Statute'[1] – where, to judge by the rest of the document, if the magistrates could have been more precise they would have said something about jail, whipping post and stocks. We have seen Bishop Aylmer, thinking about recusants of a quite different rank and station, trying to build a contempt charge on top of non-communion so that the combination would deserve a 'round fine'.[2] This proposal went no further; Aylmer himself expected it to run into trouble with the Queen and no doubt it did. The need for a stiffer law on the subject continued to be pressed, down to the Hampton Court Conference, and in the end a penalty was imposed[3] – thus converting the duty of regular communion into another 'penal law'. The most conspicuous result of that was the new custom – described in a famous and much-quoted passage of Earle's *Microcosmographie*[4] – whereby the 'church-papist' contrived to be 'out of charity' with some of his neighbours, and therefore unable to communicate, as Easter drew near. Theoretically this did not let him out, but unless a consistory or similar ecclesiastical court could force him to be reconciled to his neighbour, and then immediately

[1] BM. Lansdowne 27, no. 70 (f. 154–5).
[2] SP 12.114.22 (21 June 1577).
[3] By the act of 1606, 3 Jas. I, cap. 4.
[4] Earle, *Microcosmographie* (1628). The character of a church-papist was widely copied in MS and has been read as referring to Elizabeth's reign.

furnish an opportunity to make communion, it would be very hard to do anything more than let matters hang over till next Easter. The only certain way to catch a non-communicant was to offer him the sacrament on the spot, and the hottest zealot would surely hesitate before treating the sacrament in such a way.

6

Internal debate – 'casuistry'

'Casuistry' in modern English is a dirty word. It means whatever is sneaky, devious and jesuitical, 'jesuitical' meaning whatever is sneaky, devious and casuistic. To those who like to be a little more precise, it is a technique, evolved by the Jesuits, for finding excuses for not doing what you ought to do. Protestants, and good catholics, do not use casuistry. They face their moral problems like a man, and do what is obviously right. In view of this widespread misconception it is necessary to begin any discussion of the subject with not so much an explanation as a protest.

Casuistry is a respectable, and indeed a useful, branch of theology; it is the science of moral theology applied to cases, an alternative expression formerly favoured in Anglican circles being 'case-divinity'. As a separate academic discipline it took its rise in the counter-reformation period, and grew out of canon law, though the schoolmen had discussed cases and laid down principles which the new casuists adopted, a notable instance being the question of usury which was a favourite in the schools from St Thomas Aquinas onwards. Until the late sixteenth century there were hardly any systematic treatises or works of reference available, and this was a serious inconvenience to the parish priest in the confessional. Pretty well the only manuals of penance in existence were either vast compendia of canons or early medieval *poenitentialia* dating back to Theodore of Tarsus which provided a kind of tariff of sins and their penalties, like the laws of the Anglo-Saxons with which they were contemporary.[1] It is strange that it was not until the time of the Council of Trent that the church woke up to the necessity of providing confessors with better and more modern guidance, but it is of course quite typical and the same observation would apply to many other long-felt wants.

Casuistry, on the Roman side (for protestants had their own), was

[1] J. T. McNeill and H. M. Gamer, eds., *Mediaeval Handbooks of Penance* (New York, 1938).

primarily concerned with the confessional. Most early systematic texts classify sins in the manner traditional in confessing, that is, according to which of the Ten Commandments they break. In contrast to the older manuals they do not suggest penances; the trend was to adjust penances to the penitent rather than to the sin. What they do is to indicate the formal limits of a sin and the difference between 'mortal' and 'venial'; and – crucially for the modern reputation of 'casuistry' in general – the mitigating circumstances which might make permissible a normally forbidden action. It was on this point that there was most room for debate between moral theologians, and eventually three schools of thought arose which were distinguished by their different approaches to the kind of case where the ordinary rules were specially difficult to follow. The 'tutiorists' held that the 'safer', that is stricter, rule should be followed. This in practice meant that they advised people to prefer the less attractive of two alternatives. Such a rule was hardly applicable in the confessional, and it came to be recognized that tutiorism was only appropriate in the spiritual direction of ascetics. Today there is a separate branch of study, called 'ascetic theology', which applies tutiorism to cases. The 'probabilists' held that an action was permissible, from the confessor's point of view, if any respectable authority had ever defended it. This was the school with which the Jesuits came to be identified, not quite fairly, in the seventeenth century. Tortuous arguments to justify the apparently wrongful were necessarily the work of this school, because without the probabilist basic assumption their deviousness would deprive them of all force to persuade. Lastly, the 'probabiliorists' required the confessor or director to balance all the authorities and their arguments, and decide for himself where the weight of conviction lay. This, by and large, was what the systematizers and compilers of compendia tried to do. Many of these systematizers and compilers were Jesuits, and at least in the early days of the Society's fame there were as many probabiliorists as probabilists among them.

This, incidentally, did them no good with their protestant critics. To protestants, *all* papist moral teaching was lax, except of course for when it was inhumanly harsh; in either case, it was hypocritical. I shall have to speak of protestant, and particularly puritan, casuistry later, but I may mention here that the most severe protestant criticisms of catholic casuistry concerned the distinction between 'mortal' and 'venial' and the whole question of telling the truth.

The protestant propagandists, then and for centuries after, were blessed with a simple and scoutmasterlike certainty about the absolute, unconditional obligation to tell the unvarnished truth at all times. It may without undue cynicism be doubted whether they lived up to their own standard, or whether such a standard could ever long survive the actual experience of handling the perplexities of souls in the confessional. To protestants, Catholic casuists who drew distinctions in such a matter were simply demonstrating what protestants had known all along, that the truth was not in them. Yet really it is remarkable how strict the casuists are, how unwilling ever to allow a straight, flat lie whatever the circumstances. It was surely a dread of the lie direct, which their enemies ought to admire, that led them into the labyrinthine complexities of tormented ingenuity in which they sought a way out of the appalling mess which, as we all know, you get into as soon as you adopt truth-telling as your normal practice.

I shall return to this subject, for though it was important it was not the first issue to arise and it did not affect the laity as it did priests. The first moral question Elizabethan catholics had to ask themselves, or ask somebody, was whether and in what circumstances and how far they could comply in the first thing demanded of them: church-going according to the Act of Uniformity. There was an old-established principle, deep embedded in canon law, which forbade *communicatio in sacris* with pagans, heretics or schismatics. There could have been little doubt that the services they were now required to attend were of the forbidden kind, but nobody in England can have been very familiar with the way the rule worked. After the great heresies of the late Roman empire, when it came to be adopted, the rule had applied mainly to Christians in Moslem territory – in which there were as a matter of fact numerous privileged exceptions, such as the Dome of the Rock and the Great Mosque of Damascus where both religions prayed. In England there were no mosques, not even synagogues, and although there was undoubtedly heresy it was a new and startlingly unfamiliar idea that Englishmen could be of two religions. This problem had not really been recognized in Edward's time; it had taken Edward's reign, and Mary's after it, to bring home to most people the nature of the issues in dispute and the necessity of taking some kind of stand. Very likely there were still many who had never heard of *communicatio in sacris*, and oddly enough it looks as if Edmund Plowden was one of them, but if so they of course did not have a moral problem; rather, the missionary priests had a pastoral problem. But did anybody know whether it

73

was permissible to go to church as the law required and just sit in glum silence, absent in spirit and not actually praying with protestants? And what about weddings and funerals?

It is true that answers to such questions were forthcoming from the proper authorities, but it may be doubted whether anybody heard them. F. W. Maitland showed in 1900[1] that some catholic courtiers had sought guidance from Rome – or rather, they had indirectly sought permission to comply with the law – as early as 1562. They had considerably misrepresented the kind of danger they were in, and succeeded in convincing the Spanish Ambassador, who acted as their mouthpiece, that the penalty for recusancy was death; they seem to have been concerned with the duties of a nobleman to attend his sovereign at religious ceremonies – Naaman's problem in the house of Rimmon. The reply was uncompromising; no matter what the danger, there must be no *communicatio in sacris*.[2] This is as good an indication as we need of why the Pope's ruling got so little publicity. The group which requested it were concerned only with their selfish interests and furthermore they had not got the answer they desired; who then was going to spread it around?

In the fairly easy years that followed there were doubtless many priests – it is the common assumption among historians, we should remember that it is not much more – who read the prayer book in public and the mass in private. Such a man, and his clandestine followers, would think of themselves as 'catholics' and be so thought of by protestants. The fact that they were not catholics in the eyes of the catholic church would not trouble them if they did not know it. To bring the wrongness of such compromises home to the would-be catholic was the first and main task of the seminary priests. The lawfulness or not of church-popery was therefore the first moral question that English catholics had to debate among themselves.

The most famous contribution to the debate is Robert Parsons' 'Reasons for refusal', more correctly *A Brief Discours contayning certyne reasons why catholiques refuse to goe to Church*, dedicated by I.H. to the Queenes most excellent maiestie ('I.H.' for Parsons' current pseudonym, John Howlet). In this pamphlet (of 1580) 'Howlet' purports to give the text of a long letter from an unnamed

---

[1] E.H.R. July 1900; *Historical Essays* (Cambridge, 1957), p. 224.

[2] For a single exception, where the case of Naaman was allowed to apply, see the document printed by Mandell Creighton in *English Historical Review* Jan. 1892, p. 81f. It concerned a Catholic lady-in-waiting whom Elizabeth apparently only expected to accompany her as far as the room next to the Chapel. (The date is about 1579, and most of the document deals with the Bull of Excommunication.)

friend, discussing the case of church-going, or rather, the arguments catholics are to use to their protestant friends to show that they have no option in conscience but to refuse. Although the gross flattery of the dedication makes it look as if it really was intended primarily to convince the Queen, Parsons in his memoirs recalled it as a dissuasive addressed to wavering catholics.[1] His arguments, indeed, were not calculated to impress the most sympathetic protestant, as the inferiority of that religion and the invalidity of its sacraments are stressed much more heavily than the scruples of the catholic conscience, while the wrongfulness of outward compliance, which would be the central issue if the tract was really meant for Elizabeth, is assumed without any serious argument at all. Parsons was not, at this stage, interested in the case of Naaman in the House of Rimmon. In a much later work, his *Quaestiones Duae*, he discusses Naaman at length, and specifically in answer to a *catholic* justification of church-popery which (presumably) relied heavily on that example. Remarkably, an anonymous manuscript which fell into the government's hands apparently in 1580 (where it occurs in the State Papers) exactly fills the bill.[2] Endorsed in Burghley's hand, 'A perswasion d[elivere]d to Mr. Sheldon', it makes no reference to earlier stages in a controversy but it does not read like a first shot; it actually answers points made by Parsons in *Quaestiones Duae*. The care and elaboration with which the cogency of Naaman's case is urged make it look as if there lay behind it a first use of Naaman's name and a first refutation on behalf of the Mission. On the other hand I had better admit that it starts out (in the surviving copy, in mid-sentence)

And for so much as yt semethe that this question was never thus moved, nor the case in experience in any age before this tyme, therfore this is nowe made a question, argumentes are sett dowen for Judgment, And these be the reasons to prove that in the case sett dowene ys nether P. nor mortall synn.

(I can only guess at 'P', my guess being 'Paganism'. From other contexts, it cannot very well be 'protestantism'.)

When Naaman the Syrian was cured of leprosy by Elisha, he took it as a proof of the greatness of Elisha's god, and having somehow gathered that this god allowed no competitors, vowed thenceforward to worship no other. He requested, however, one concession. In the King James version, the relevant passage runs:

---

[1] Printed in *Catholic Record Society* vol. 2, p. 178f.
[2] SP 12.144.69 (? December 1580).

In this thing the Lord pardon thy servant, that when my master goeth into the house of Rimmon to worship there, and he leaneth on my hand, and I bow myself in the house of Rimmon: when I bow down myself in the house of Rimmon, the Lord pardon thy servant in this thing.

And he said unto him, Go in peace... [II Kings, 5, 18–19]

In the Vulgate, 'worship' and 'bow down' are the same verb, *adorare*, which favours the permissive side of the debate with an *a fortiori*; Parsons is careful in *Quæstiones Duæ* to draw the distinction, but our anonymous had avoided the trap, and not rested his argument on an ambiguity in translation:

And this is the sense of his peticion, ffor so much as this his entraunce wth his kinge an Idolator, and the conversation of the same place semed to hym a rare and unwonted thinge if not unlawfull, and the rather for y^t the manner of his office abowte the kynge in stowpinge and bowinge dowen to stay the kinge might be Judged some acte of Idolatrye...or for that, if no other, yet at the leaste his servantes which were present at his healinge and had hard hym renounce Idolatrye might by this example take occacon of ruyn ...and beinge perswaded that he ought to avoyde all these yet thinkinge this acte was not so great a fawlt as did cast hym forth of goddes favor: Therfore he made this peticion, that yt might be lawfull for hym wthowt offence to exhibit to the kinge this external service, in the temple of Remnon, he desireth that if herin he committ any offence towardes godd, the same by the prophettes prayers might not be imputed to hym. Then the Prophett to bothe his peticons answered, sayinge, Vade in pace, wch woorde is verbum bene precantis & approbantis, And yt is as muche as if he hadd sayed vade in Justitia, go and procede in this manner of Righteousnes wch thow hast professed...Thus yt is plaine that the peace whiche the prophet speakethe on, is the woorke of righteousnes, and this peace Naaman could never have hadd, yf by this bare entraunce, and beinge amonge other Idolators & service of the kinge he had bene defiled with P. or throwen into mortall synn; And yt is to little purpose that is obiected (*obiec:*) Naaman desired license (*ergo*) withowt license yt was a Synn (*R*) for the argument followeth not, but yt is a good consequent y^t Naaman desired license (*ergo*) he thought yt to be an offence....And yt is plaine that the prophet allowed his doinges, ffor otherwise he wold plainely & directly have sayed, that it was not lawfull...

The author has here foreseen (if indeed he was not warned by previous disputations) most of the objections that Parsons and others were to find to the applicability of this example. He was not confusing the senses of *adorare*; he deals with the point that the prophet did not give explicit permission; and in commenting upon the words 'go in peace' he disposes of the contention that all Elisha was promising was to pray for God's forgiveness for an action that

Naaman knew to be wrong. There remained, but nobody seems to have used the point, the fact that Naaman was a new convert brought up in pagan ways and therefore no close analogy to the situation under debate. As for the idea that this was an absurdly strained and forced way to use Old Testament exegesis, it would have occurred to nobody in that age, catholic, protestant, or betwixt and between.

If you could use the Bible this way, the example to set against Naaman was Eleazar, in Maccabees, who was required by an anti-Semitic ruler to eat pork on pain of death, and when offered an easy way out by sympathetic officials – they would let him eat something else and pretend to believe it was pork – refused for fear of setting a bad example to others. His case was duly cited against Naaman's in *Quæstiones Duæ*.[1] The trouble is – and though our anonymous of 1580 does not mention Eleazar specifically he was onto the point – that this is an instance of heroic virtue, to be commended of course, but not, except to a tutiorist, to be taken as establishing an obligatory rule of conduct.

ob[jection]. Yt is not to be denied that many of the fathfull martirs and confessors in tyme of persecution have utterly refused to come into the churches of P. and temples of Idolators...R. Evenso yt is comendable in them which utterly refused (as many did) to come to theire churches, But this allegacon ex gestis prorum presumpta proveth not against the case before sett dowen for yt semethe no good consequent in every case, Good men and martirs did this, (*ergo*) this not to do, or otherwise to do is P. or mortall synn...[2]

The author of the 'persuasive' was evidently a learned and ingenious casuist, who knew his authorities and could quote strings of them on the lack of obligation to seek martyrdom and on the extent to which normal moral obligations are modified by fear, *metus*.

His line is very competently maintained, and it is genuinely a treatment of a private moral problem. When Parsons came to uphold the opposite view, he was forced again and again to argue from the good of the catholic cause in England, and the propaganda value of constancy, to the duty of the individual catholic. From this point of view, of course, *metus* can be allowed no weight at all. The Anonymous, in admitting it as an argument, certainly had the ponderance of academic opinion on his side and on that point can be called a probabiliorist.

I am setting *Quaestiones Duae* against the 'persuasive' because they seem to match and make a pair despite their disparity in time.

---

[1] Question 1, p. 34 (ed. of 1607).   [2] SP 12.144.69.

It seems reasonable to suppose either that the first part of *Quaestiones Duae* was based on an earlier draft, or that the tract it aimed to answer was based on the 'persuasive'. (The second *Quaestio* need hardly delay us. It answered another anonymous tract which defended hearing protestant sermons and as Parsons himself said this case was covered by the former, although that did not prevent him from urging some more arguments, drawn, as before, from the propaganda needs of the Mission.) At the same time it is necessary to remember that the *Quaestiones* were published in James' reign and that Parsons' contribution to the earlier debate was *Reasons for Refusal*, whose arguments bore almost no relation to those of the 'persuasive'.

Both these were products of the new drive for public repudiation of the Elizabethan settlement inaugurated by the seminary priests and raised to a new pitch of urgency by Persons himself and Campion. The success of this drive helped to provoke the Act of 1581, and the Act of 1581 provoked the *brief advertisement* described in the last chapter.[1] I have already spoken of it as a source of legal argument, but it contained argument about case-divinity as well. After explaining that a catholic was not bound to answer the question, 'do you, or will you go to church?', because it was an improper question in Common Law, the author gives three further reasons

Secondlie because no person is to detecte him selfe of a penall statute esp'ially when the penaltie is so greate, that it importeth the losse of all his goodes and fortunes, and the utter undoinge of him selfe his wife and Children for ever.

Logically he ought to be making a point about 'penal laws' again, but what he really relies on is the 'especially'; the nature of the risk you are running is changed in kind by being so great in degree, it is because the danger of answering amounts to economic ruin that you are not bound to do it. There is no special privilege not to answer questions in the case of 'penal laws' more than other laws, at least to my knowledge, but perhaps the rather trivial status of the law – the fact that the forbidden action, and therefore the one inquired into, is not immoral – allows to the concept of mortal fear more scope than it would otherwise have. Mortal fear is the important issue here. Like many classical casuists, the author will allow it to include the fear of losing most of your possessions; and it will excuse anything less than mortal sin.

The next argument is less classical and more ingenious, and he

[1] SP 12.136.15; above, n. 72.

does use 'penal law'. The law is 'penal', therefore it is not moral, and it is applied in the secular courts therefore the question is asked for a secular reason. The whole context being secular and not religious, the question is secular and not religious – 'and therefore not to be aunswered by profession of faith and religion in this lawlike course of proceadinge havinge noe respecte thereunto' – the normal obligation of confessing the faith when challenged does not apply. The statute, so the author claims, is 'a penall lawe, having no reference to the Catholique Church'. This is a rather startling claim. If I have followed his reasoning correctly, he is contrasting two possible meanings of the question 'do you go to church?' according to the supposed, imputed, intention of the questioner: one of them being something like 'will you burn incense to the official State idol?' (which invites a confession of faith in the manner of the early Christian martyrs, and which you must of course answer truly) and the other being something like 'do you owe the Treasury twenty pounds?', which is the Treasury's own affair to prove if it can.

The fourth argument under this head is still ingenious but quite orthodox, and stems from the duty of not giving scandal, or cause of offence, to your neighbours. (Mind you, the duty of avoiding scandal can cut both ways; at this point we are not taking Eleazar as our model.)

fforthlie because the aunswer therto implieth on every side great danger, and maie yeild matter to the adversarie to exasperate malice ageinst him wch every Catholique if he can choose ought in no wise to minister in respecte of the damnation of the other, althoughe he did knowe his profession to be his owne perfection and glorie.

Although the catholic knows that it is more virtuous to stay away from church than to go, so long as the church is in the hands of heretics, yet in the common opinion, and the one that is bound to be entertained by all heretics, it is more virtuous to go than to stay away. I must not, if I can fairly avoid it, *seem* to confess a moral fault, thereby betraying my unfortunate heretical neighbour into an act of uncharity, and at the same time giving him a dangerously erroneous idea about catholicism.

This aunswere maie geve an occasion to some weake and simple persons in theese synfull deceaved tymes, not only to think that he refuseth indeede to come to godes service at all (wch is most untrue and therfore to maligne him in the profession of his faith) But also maie geve some colour of matter to suggest him to be a godlesse person...and so to be reputed not onlie no christian, but worse then a Jewe gentile turcke pagane or infidell.

(I could of course take special pains to avoid this by explaining why I feel as I do about going to church, but I would be better advised not to. My explanation, right and proper though it might be, would inevitably sound like an attack on the heretical church; this might be considered provocative, and it might lay me open to another legal charge.)

As I mentioned before, this author provides legal arguments but expects them to fail. In his third section he gives instructions, after they have failed, 'howe to aunswere wth most salfetie accordinge to the dutie of a Catholicke'; in effect he coaches the potential victim of persecution in a long and elaborate self-vindication. In this last part of the *Brief advertisement*, as in Parsons' *Reasons for refusal*, there is apparent a certain ambiguity between what an instructed catholic conscience is bound to feel and what makes the most effective demonstration. At this point the catholic, who was advised against it before, should state plainly the grounds in conscience why he cannot obey the law, 'Protestinge wthall, that willinglie he speaketh not, but compulsion by ther aucthoritie and of dutie and due obedience to aunswere ther demaundes', and therefore at this point the author also has to state these grounds of conscience plainly. These are surprising. In the most diffuse part of a diffuse document there is no discussion at all of *communicatio in sacris* or the unity of the Universal Church, no quoting of authorities, apostles, fathers or doctors on the duty of taking part in one kind of service or not taking part in another kind. None of that merited discussion. The line taken is like that taken by 'John Howlet's' friend in *Reasons for refusal*, and, as there, the real purpose is not so much to persuade the heretics or to disarm them as to daunt them by a display of catholic constancy. Like many men who make large claims for the sovereignty of the conscience, the author knows very exactly what ought to be troubling the consciences of other men. In this case, one thing ought to trouble them above all others: the difference between the new English service and the old Latin one. Not particular differences, but the fact that they were different at all, proved that one church or the other must be totally out of God's favour, and His promises did not apply to it. Everything turned on the liturgical question, and liturgically the most crucial consideration was the 'fact' (asserted to be such by both authors) that whereas the Elizabethan prayer book was a new thing devised for one country, the Roman missal was used by the universal church in all ages: the *advertisement* definitely implies that the twelve Apostles used the *Missale Romanum*.

What we have here is evidently not an examination of a problem that posed many men with an agonizing moral choice, with the purpose of helping them to resolve their difficulty. Rather it accepts the moral choice as made, and seeks to school men in their public words and acts so as to extract the maximum propaganda value out of their resistance. As such it strikes a distinctly, if perhaps deceptively, modern note; it reminds us of the careful training offered by modern non-violent protest movements on the techniques and philosophy of passive resistance, sit-ins and the like. This outward resemblance to a modern situation should be a danger signal. The analogy is unlikely to be as close as it looks. In particular, if this document seems to appeal to conscience in a twentieth-century way, it is to that extent untypical of its age. When men of that age took a stand on the point of conscience they did not always show the pride and panache of a sit-in or a draft-card burning. The note struck was rather a deprecatory one: 'Look, I'm sorry, but my silly old conscience is acting up again. You wouldn't want to bring on those terrible guilt feelings I get, would you?' What was claimed for conscience was not that it was right but that a man couldn't act against it without great mental suffering. While no doubt up to a point the difference is simply the one you would expect between our own and a 'deference' society, there is also a certain difference in the meaning of words, as I briefly suggested above.[1] Fortunately we need not spend much time on the history of the word 'conscience', for that work has been done for us by the late C. S. Lewis.[2] It will perhaps be enough here to say that at this time the word retained much more of the sense, 'uncontrollable guilt-feeling', and had taken on less of the sense, 'superego', than in our own day. The man, therefore, who would presume to say in detail what another's conscience ought to stick at was a bold man indeed. (The confessor, who by following the textbook can define the exact point at which an action becomes sinful, is not doing at all the same thing. In that situation it is largely irrelevant whether a man feels guilt about his actions before it has been pointed out to him that they are, by an objective and immutable standard, guilt-worthy.)

Another tract on church-going for catholics lies next to the *brief advertisement* in the State Papers, and like it is misdated to 1580.[3] (The word 'Brownists' occurs in it, as a term of abuse for protestant

---

[1]   Above, p. 38.
[2]   C. S. Lewis, *Studies in Words* (Cambridge, 1960).
[3]   SP 12.136.14 (? January 1580).

sectaries. This word cannot have entered the language before 1581–2.) It does consider the question of personal moral duty in a serious manner, though it contents itself with fairly brisk answer. After the heading, 'Jesus Maria': 'It is a thing most evident and plaine that no catholique Christian can goe to church wthout the daunger of most dampnable scisme...for that the intent of the law is onlie for protestantes service and preaching and not for others' (i.e. we are not to be misled by the specious appearance of virtue in a law that makes people go to church; what is involved is schism, under whatever fancy name or pretence). This is cogent. The argument is rather weakened by a side-swipe at protestant divisions: it is dangerous to go to hear the preaching of an ordinary 'protestant', what we should now call an Anglican, because these people are so utterly unstable and unreliable that the chances are your man is a puritan by now, or will be tomorrow. This suggests, unwisely, that it would be perfectly all right to hear the preaching of a 'protestant' if you could be sure that he was not a puritan – an irrelevant, and politically rash, distinction to draw.

This author does talk about the unity of the church. He speaks of the obligation assumed at baptism, to hold all the articles of the catholic faith. He quotes Augustine (a father whom the protestants admired) on the inevitable fate of the heretic or schismatic, who, 'quantascunque elemosynas fecerit, et si pro Christi nomine etiam sanguinem fuderit nullatenus posse salvari',[1] in which Augustine was actually going further than the universal church was prepared to follow him; it has generally been held, as in the case of the anti-pope St Hippolytus, that martyrdom wipes out schism. More surprisingly he quotes Paul: 'Et si habuero omnem fidem ita ut montes transferam Charitatem autem non habuero, nihil sum'[2] – surprisingly because there are surely neater quotations to be made from that passage; a faith that could move mountains would probably be a sound faith and thus not heretical. To quote Paul on charity, some way or another, was standard form for catholic controversialists in the sixteenth century. Here it is explained that no man can have perfect charity except in the unity of the church. Finally he quotes 'Saint Athanasius', meaning of course the *Quicunque vult*,[3] and out of all these proves

[1] However many alms they may give, and even if they shed their blood for Christ's sake they cannot possibly be saved.
[2] '...and though I have all faith, so that I could remove mountains, and have not charity, I am nothing.' I Corinthians 13. 2–3.
[3] The so-called 'Creed of St. Athanasius' – 'Whosoever would be saved...'

that we must of necessytye fullie and wholie (and not by peces and patches) hold and kepe the chatholique faith...wch ys unpossible to be done yf we go to church praie and comunicate wth heretiques and scismatiques as we must of necescitie wth puritanes anabaptisties familie of love brownistes and the like.

At the last minute he once again drags in the dangerous idea that the protestant church is only wrong because of the religious riff-raff you might find there, and if the Established church would only keep its own house in order it might not be too contaminating for catholics — a damaging admission lurking unseen under a tempting debating point. Otherwise, this, though stiff, is sound casuistry and the catholic who read it might really find that it helped him make up his mind.

The debate on church-going, and on answering the question 'do you go?', continued. If any large number of people attempted to follow the line of protest suggested in the *advertisement*, we unfortunately do not know of them, and I think we should have. Certainly their protest, if made, cut no ice. The statute, as we have indicated already, was administered with difficulty and without much enthusiasm and it was necessary to tighten it up in 1587, but the question continued to be asked by churchwardens or other ecclesiastical officials under the Act of 1559, and the results used to frame indictments under later acts without a qualm. A new discussion of how catholics should answer appeared in 1601: 'Of the lawfull manner of answering to questions of going to Church...'[1] This is much more truly a work of casuistry than the *advertisement* was, and it is particularly interesting since it is concerned with the case of 'equivocation', which greatly agitated the missionary clergy as something that deeply involved themselves. In this tract addressed to the laity there is no such disposition to find excuses for self-exculpatory near-lies as the protestants believed to be typical of all casuists whatsoever and as indeed one does find in many of the standard authorities. To this author at least, truth seems to have claims in its own right, without reference to times and occasions.

First in my Judgm^t. these questions tending to Religion, and to the practice thereof. The answere must be such as may be lawfull in a religious sense. For otherwise the answerer giveth just cause that the demander conceive a sense dishonourable unto God. So: it is not lawfull to say he goeth to Church, because he meaneth a profane going to Pauls: nor that he hath received, because he received his Rents, or a piece of bread at home: or that he hath service: because he hath service of his men, or such like.

[1] SP 12.279.90 (Undated ? 1601). W. R. Trimble, *Catholic Laity*...places this document in a later reign because the phrase 'his majesty' occurs in it; but the majesty referred to is that of God.

2) Secondly if a Man be demanded, whether he doth a Religious action which is by morall estimation of all men in the Country appropriated to the hereticall Religion? it is no way lawfull to say he doth it, or will do it, Such is this question, go you to the Church? receive you the Sacraments? in so much that although one had either heard Masse said indeed in a Church, or been at Masse at Calis: He were bound to express those conditions if he answer that he was at Church: for if other wise, he giveth just occasion ([c]onsidering that there are no publick Churches of catholicks in England) to be understood of going to hereticall Churches.

3) Thirdly if there were indeed use of severall Churches publickly for Catholicks and Hereticks also: then if an heretick asked a Catholick, if he had been at Church: he might answer, yea; though the Heretick should imagin, that he had been at the hereticall Church, for that is the Hereticks folly, to understand him so without any probable cause given by the Catholick.

He goes on to admit a few possible ways out:

it semeth very probable unto me: that a Catholik may say (being asked whether he cometh to the Church) that he doth not. & that he hath service at home... [since the expressions used are not in themselves misleading] neither is it any more dangerous [sc. morally] to answer thus, than if a Protestant should argue a man to be no Papist: because he telleth him that he prayeth unto God whereas the Protestant esteemeth in his conceite, that Papists never pray.

Any resort to evasion must take into account the duties of avoiding scandal and of testifying to the faith. The first matters less if a man is obscure or unknown, and the latter is more incumbent before a public magistrate than a mere churchwarden. Subject to these limitations, a man can try to dodge:

in case there bee no danger of Scandall, nor no certainty of the bond of the affirmative Precept of Confession of Faith: it is always lawfull (which seemeth to be in all Interrogations of Churchwardens or such, who go from house to house proforma & as it were of Custome) to elude the interrogation not by equivocation (which in these cases must not be used) nor by any words, which may seem to promise to go to the Church, or to say we do goe to the Church: but by other indifferent speeches. As think you that I will live like an Atheist? (etc.)

The author actually affirms probabilism:

Finally: Whereas in all morall matters either in common, or in particular (where there is no expresse definition of Faith) there cannot be that certainty, as there is in other Propositions of Speculation: is in sufficient to follow a probable opinion...

but his advice is fairly strict, and I think he should be called a probabiliorist. It will be seen that he draws a distinction between 'equivocation' and the evasion or parrying of a question, and not all answers to questions that are capable of being taken in two senses come under the ban. All the same this is an unusually rigorous insistence on telling the real and unadorned truth.

The main concern of this paper was in dodging the consequences of not going to church. That catholics did not go was apparently taken for granted. There were, however, still some catholics around who wondered whether that was absolutely a closed issue. Parsons' *Quaestiones Duae*, already discussed, was published to answer them in 1607. Although, as I have said, this argument was mainly over familiar ground, it is also the occasion in the whole debate when most use was made of *metus*.

Fear, as such, obviously should not deter one from doing one's moral duty; but certain extremities of fear were recognized by different authorities in different degrees as very considerably mitigating the guilt of sin and sometimes rendering a normally sinful action excusable. 'Mortal' fear, 'rational' fear, and fear 'attacking a brave man' – *in constantem virum cadens* – were all invoked as special kinds of fear; the terms were actually used more or less interchangeably. In the atmosphere of the days after Gunpowder Plot these kinds of fear must have become a pretty familiar experience for catholics, but it seems odd that they could be inspired by the recusancy fines.

Parsons was concerned in particular to refute the contention, advanced by whoever he was answering, that impressive authorities in the field allowed outward compliance with a persecuting religion under the stress of *metus*, when the likely penalty for failing to comply was not much worse than a general kind of public obloquy and some financial loss – the situation, in fact, that the English catholics were in. The names of Azor and of 'Navarrus' (Azpilcueta) were both cited.

The *(Libri) Institutionum Moralium*, the principal work of John Azor, is not known to have been published in 1607 though a Papal privilege was issued for it in 1600. It is clear from Parsons' references that he was a well-known name, and I can only assume that in one way or another the views represented in *Institutionum* had already circulated. On *metus* in general he takes a large view; having explained that 'just' fear, 'grave' fear and so on are the same thing, he extends it far beyond the fear of death:

Quarto Queritur, An metus, quo quis timet amittere omnia bona temporalia,

85

sit iustus? Respondeo, esse...quia patrimonium est necessarium ad vitae conservationem, & communes usus.

Quinto Quaeritur, An si quis timeat amittere maiorem partem bonorum temporalium metus sit iustus? Respondeo, ex communi sententia eorundem utriusque Iursis Interpretum [*sc.* those cited in the previous paragraph] esse: quia est metus gravis periculi & mali.[1]

It is to be observed that he relies for preference on legal authors. He goes on to maintain that fear of loss of reputation, and fear of excommunication, are 'just'. If this last fear is to excuse an act otherwise immoral, he must surely be thinking of the civil rather than the spiritual consequences of excommunication. All this, so far, does indeed make for the comfort of the church-papist, provided that his offence is of the kind that *metus iustus* can excuse. These, according to some, include any act performed in mortal fear of a tyrant ('*non solum mentiri...sed etiam rem habere cum foemina sibi non nupta*'[2]), indeed these would almost certainly absolve the prisoners at the Nuremberg trials, as well as those today who keep a handy machine gun in the fallout shelter. Azor however prefers a stricter view, holding that no fear can justify the committing of a mortal sin, as the death of the body is to be preferred to that of the soul. Thus we come down to the difference between 'mortal' and 'venial', and more particular consideration of the venial. For a specimen, Azor disagrees with Caietan on what Caietan had thought a clear case: the duty of a priest to die rather than omit a minor detail of the ceremonial of the Mass at the bidding of a tyrant. Azor agrees with Azpilcueta that this was a bit hard, and suggests that it depends in what spirit the tyrant gives the order – whether in contempt of the Church or not. Caietan was probably thinking of Germans in the Lutheran states, the two Spaniards could have had Dutchmen and Englishmen in mind; at last the experts were concerned about a problem raised by the Reformation, though only when it touched their own clerical order. The limitations of Azor's human sympathies are pretty narrow; throughout his work he asserts that 'natural' law binds absolutely, and he constantly assumes an identity between natural and Roman law on such matters as succession to property

---

[1] It is asked, Fourth: whether the fear of losing all one's worldly goods is a just fear? I answer, it is...because one's fortune is necessary for preserving life, and common uses.

It is asked, Fifth: whether the fear of losing the greater part of one's worldly goods is a just fear? I answer, it is according to the common judgement of the Interpreters of Canon and Civil Law; because it is the fear of grave danger and evil.

[2] Not only to lie...but to have intercourse with a woman not married to him.

and the legal status of bastards; natural law, the breach of which no terror can excuse, forbids associating with excommunicates or with-holding the Pope's succession-tax on a priest's property. In a country like England, the rule against associating with excommunicates still binds in principle, though one can still do business with one's neigh-bours if they have not been excommunicated by name, and are not *'notorii Clericorum percussores'*.[1] Azor is here following Azpilcueta, to whom he refers. They also agree on what seems to be the crux:

Quarto Quaeritur, An ubi haeretici manifesti sunt, & notorij, sed expressim minime denunciati, aut notorij Clericorum percussores, Liceat Catholicis eorum templa adire, ingredi, & in eis preces fundere, rem divinam, & con-ciones haereticorum audire, ad eorum postea errores confutandos, & haereticam impietatem evertendam. Respondeo ex sententia Navarr'...id esse licitum facere sub triplici conditione. Prima, ne in Catholicorum animis ulla offensio generetur. Secunda, ne ulla sit communicatio ritus, caeremoniae, ac impietatis haereticae. Tertia, ne ullum periculum immineat propriae perfidiae, sub-versionisque, & Catholicae religionis contemptus.[2]

He goes on to differ with Azpilcueta who under certain very stringent conditions would allow the reception of heretical sacraments. This had in any case nothing to do with the problems of English recusants. Had the passage I have just quoted? I doubt it. It looks as if this guarded permission to witness heretical services was meant to apply only to priests, that the casuists were once again overwhelmingly interested in questions that concerned their own order. To whom else could the condition *'ad eorum errores confutandos'* apply? But a priest, girding his loins for controversy, might be licensed to hear a heretic's sermon as he might be licensed to read his books.

I can find only one other conceivably relevant passage in Azpilcueta. Against a typically sweeping judgement by Caietan on those who deny the Faith from fear, he dissents:

Sed huius oppositam sententiam olim pro responso dedimus, interrogati de certis casibus qui cuidam religioso Societatis Jesu apud Saracenos agenti occurrerunt, erga CHRISTIANOS quosdam, qui timore perculsi, et propter

[1] Notorious persecutors of the clergy.

[2] It is asked, Fourth, whether where there are open and notorious heretics, but not con-demned in express words, nor notorious persecutors of the clergy, it is permissible to go to their temples, to enter them, and offer prayers, to hear religious exercises and heretical preaching, for the purpose of later confuting them, and defeating heretical impiety. I reply from the judgement of Navarrus, it is permissible under three conditions. First that no offence be given to Catholic souls. Secondly, that there be no participation in the heretical rite, ceremony and impiety. Thirdly, that there be no danger of one's own backsliding, subversion, or falling into contempt of the Catholic religion.

alias causas, se esse Saracenos finxerunt, & secuti sumus eum qui *Repertorium Inquisitorum* composuit, in verb. Haereticus, col. 24. Quod nunc quoque verius arbitramur, quam quod Caiet. asseruit...Et profecto etiam si hoc nullus assereret, nos eandem sententiam teneremus. Quoniam huiusmodi homo non est vere haereticus, quamvis gravissime peccet...[1]

Here again Azor seems to agree though he does not actually discuss such a case.

'*Etiam si hoc nullus assereret*' are fine bold words, but they do not help much, for Azpilcueta is only saying that the full guilt of heresy or apostasy is not incurred without a real internal repudiation of catholicism. He does not say you can freely behave like a protestant in outward matters. Thus it can be seen that these two authors, who were set up together as champions of the more permissive side, are not very helpful to it, though they had Parsons worried; he not only produced a full-scale refutation, but also claimed that Azor had changed his mind,[2] and repented his earlier laxity on the subject, apparently, of Naaman.

Both these writers were Spanish Jesuits. Azpilcueta's *Manual* was the textbook on casuistry (the only one we know of) at Rheims and Douai (originally written in Spanish, it was available in Latin from 1581). They did not offer much comfort on *communicatio in sacris*, and people who thought that they did can hardly have had a copy handy. I might add that though Azpilcueta's work was called an '*Enchiridion, sive Manuale*', its format belied the name: it was a hefty volume, much too bulky for a Seminary priest to carry about with him. It is perfectly reasonable to suppose that even as late as James' reign the teachings of the approved authorities were not *readily* available to catholics, but by that time anybody who was still a catholic was in some sort of touch with a confessor who had either been trained on Azpilcueta or (if a Jesuit) on him and several others, few of them any milder. Thus it can be said that by the latter end of Elizabeth's reign there was little or no room for argument on the subject of church-going, and argument could hardly any longer be sustained except on some kind of misapprehension, such as faulty memories of a book or document not at hand for consultation.

The young men in the colleges learnt not only what was morally

---

[1] But we once gave the opposite judgement in reply, when we were asked about certain cases that a member of the Society of Jesus encountered when working among Saracens, of some Christians who were driven by fear and other causes to pretend that they were Saracens, and we agree with the compiler of the *Repertorium Inquisitorum*...That now we judge more true than what Cajetan maintained...and even if nobody had said it, we would hold the same opinion. For the man in this case is no true heretic, although he sins seriously...   [2] *Quaetiones Duae*, Question 1, p. 31.

right for their penitents but for themselves. So far as the special problems of the day went, the one that most peculiarly concerned the missionary clergy was the case of truth-telling, or rather (for here casuistry deserves its reputation) how to avoid telling the truth without actually lying. With the single exception of tyrannicide, there was no aspect of catholic casuistry that protestants more eagerly seized on as proving the fundamental wickedness of the Whore of Babylon, and it may as well be admitted that, given the presuppositions normal in that age, on no other side did the casuists lie so open to attack.

The lie direct, indeed, was condemned by all with hardly any reservations. It was precisely for this reason that casuists were driven to elaborate the varieties of the near-lie. Their critics seldom gave them the credit that was their due for insisting, as I think all the accepted authorities did, that the near-lie could only be justified by special circumstances, and was not its own justification by reasons of its technical truth. However, it could be argued that the outright lie in extenuating circumstances was less spiritually dangerous than the intentionally misleading statement, believed by the speaker to be in some important way spiritually superior to a lie.[1]

Two main kinds of misleading statement are involved, though they are not always clearly distinguished: equivocation, and mental reservation (sometimes regarded as a special kind of equivocation). In equivocation the speaker's words if closely examined will prove to be capable of being taken in two senses: the sense in which they are true, and the sense in which he hopes his hearer will take them. This was regarded as fairly respectable; you could resort to it for no better reason than that your interrogator had no right to interrogate you. Mental reservation is much harder to justify, which is doubtless why those who employed it tended to claim that it was a form of equivocation, thus blurring the distinction. In this, the words audibly and expressly spoken amount to one statement, which is untrue, and they cannot be twisted into a true statement, but the speaker 'mentally' adds an understood condition, which would turn it into another, true, statement if it was said aloud. An extreme example would be King Pellinore (in T. H. White's *The Sword in the Stone*): 'Ay said pax non under my breath.'[2]

---

[1] This was the view of the Greek fathers and of many Protestants including Jeremy Taylor in *Ductor Dubitantium*, and I imagine it would be widely held today. The point is discussed by Christopher Devlin, *Life of Robert Southwell*, Appendix C (he defends the traditiona Catholic line).

[2] For those readers who have not read *The Sword in the Stone*: King Pellinore, worsted in single combat, was offered 'pax' and asked for it, mumbling indistinctly in his helmet; then resumed the fight when his opponent was off guard.

To try to turn a false statement into a true one by the addition of an inaudible 'not' would actually be going too far for any casuist I know of, but some widely approved evasions came pretty close. Perhaps the classic case, a sufficiently familiar one, is that of the man whose friend wants a small loan. In the world of the early case-divines few precepts of Christ seem to have caused so much inconvenience as Luke 6.34–5. It was generally conceded that if you were asked, by a known cadger, 'have you any money?' you could legitimately reply 'no', with the mental reservation, 'not for lending to you'. This seems to have been the original occasion of inventing the formula '*Non...ut vobis servisset*', which was to be applied to many and various uses, and was most famously employed by Father Campion when he denied that his name was Campion – that is (mentally understood), he was not Campion 'to serve your purpose'.

This is actually as extreme an example as it is possible to find, but the palm for ingenious outrageousness is generally accorded to Father Ward *alias* Sicklemore, concerning whom the Dean of Durham (W. James) wrote, between amusement and indignation, to Salisbury, the Secretary of State, in February 1606.[1] Ward had made a series of statements on oath which were later disproved by witnesses. In a private interview with the dean he had defended his conduct, presumably in hopes of avoiding a perjury charge.

first he swore he was no priest, that is, saieth he, not *Apollos Preist at Delphos*. Secondly he sware he was never beyond the Seas, its trew saieth he, for he was never beyond the *Indian Seas*.

Thirdly he was never at, or of the Seminaries, *Duplex est seminarium*, *materiale, et spirituale*, he was never of the spirituall Seminarie.

fourthly, he never knew Mr. Hawksworth, verum est, saith he, *scientia scientifica*.

fifthly, he never saw Mr. Hawksworth, *verum est*, saith he, *visione beatifica*

Of these, the fourth, which is at first sight the thinnest of all, could perhaps just be defended as a true equivocation; there are several senses in which you can know a man. The rest are clearly preposterous, but Ward had a sixth point of some importance which unfortunately (to judge at least by the Dean's account) he did not develop. Taxed with 'childish shifts and impostures', he 'said that it was true, that in *foro interiori coram Deo*, these things could not be defended: but in *foro exteriori* before the Magistrate, he could, and doubted not, but that he lawfully might doe it, and defend it.'

[1] SP 14.18.66 (5 February 1606).

Ward must here be relying on a distinction between levels or degrees of right to the truth. All casuists drew such a distinction; the questioner who has a legitimate reason for asking questions and a right to know the truth is not in the same category as a bully or a busybody who wants to know something for an evil or an idle reason. But most would put a magistrate into the first category, and maintain that he had a right to be told the plain truth straight-forwardly. The whole world of equivocation and mental reservation was called into being to deal with the second kind of questioner. This obviously presented a very special problem to clandestine priests. If they did not conceal their identity from the authorities they defeated the purpose to which their lives were dedicated; but if they concealed it, in the face of questioning, they were contravening their own principles, unless they could somehow maintain that theirs was a case not covered by the general rule; and it would certainly seem that Ward was so claiming. (It should perhaps here be remembered that in the Roman legal system, which most casuists had in mind when they spoke of magistrates, *no* question asked by a judge is irrelevant.) It is hard to get out of the trap any way but by asserting that there is no duty of obedience to tyrannical laws, and that the magistrate when enforcing such a law is *pro tempore* not a lawful authority. Such a position, while agreeable to a twentieth-century mind and not wholly beyond a sixteenth-century one, has the disadvantage, from the point of view of a counter-reformation Catholic, of putting a considerable strain on the private judgement. In fact there were massing priests, and the Archpriest Blackwell was one of them, who took the 'tutiorist' view that a priest should declare himself when challenged and take the consequences, and similar principles deterred some regular religious from joining the mission, since it would involve abandoning the Habit. Nothing more clearly contradicts the popular idea that all casuistry is summed up in the theory that the end justifies the means. Had that been an accepted principle, the problem need never have arisen.[1]

The rule that the constituted authorities of Church and State were entitled to a straight answer had another application, which

---

[1] The question of equivocation came up in Court at the trial of Robert Southwell, on which see Christopher Devlin, *Life*...cap. 21 and Appendix C. Also in a case in the Irish court of Castle Chamber in 1613 in the Ellesmere Manuscripts, printed in *Catholic Record Society* vol. 60 (1968), doc. 34. This last gives a very clear explanation of the difference between 'equivocation' proper and 'mental reservation'; it is, however, a pronouncement by a protestant judge, which limits its value. (He claimed that protestants always chose to die rather than equivocate.)

might be called mental reservation in reverse. This was the answer *secundum intentionem remotam*, which allowed a man to tell a technical lie if by so doing he conveyed to the (authorized) enquirer the information he really wanted – which again could be a tough one for the private judgement. The casuists felt so secure in endorsing this principle that some classed it under perjury instead of falsehood; such an answer could safely be made on oath. The classic case may be called the Man from Bologna (though the name of the city might vary).[1] Suppose the town authorities in Rome have heard, incorrectly, that there is a plague in Bologna and have issued instructions to gatekeepers that all travellers must swear that they are not from Bologna before being admitted to the city. A traveller from Bologna, who knows that the plague rumour is untrue, can take the oath with a clear conscience. He should, indeed, avoid the lie direct by either of the usual methods; he can say, or mentally reserve, that he comes from some intermediate point such as Florence. But he is not bound to puzzle the wits of a subordinate officer by quarrelling with the form of the question when he can just as easily tell the man the answer he wants to hear and it makes no real difference anyway. I think it is assumed, where this principle is invoked, that the question is asked by a subordinate with no authority to take into account facts that differ from the official belief. It is clear that on some occasions a different kind of truth was owing to under-officers and to real magistrates; this was implied quite plainly by the author of the *Lawful manner of answering*, who would allow deceptive, though no outright untruthful, replies to the *proforma* interrogatories of mere churchwardens.[2]

The principle of oath-keeping *secundum intentionem* was invoked on at least one occasion by the puritan Thomas Cartwright (who claimed, probably wrongly, that the college statute which he was deprived of his Cambridge fellowship for breaking was never meant to apply to his case),[3] but it was not a popular argument among puritans and naturally it seemed as shabby as any other popish evasion to the conformist mind. It seems to be referred to in a note in the State Papers, *Concerning the Booke of Equivocation these thinges are to be observed*.[4] Although the writer of the note was mainly concerned about the authorship of the anonymous treatise described (he thought it was by Father Gerard and corrected by Father Garnett), he also

---

[1] In Navarrus' *Enchiridion* it occurs in cap. 12. No. 19.
[2] SP 12.279.90. See p. 83, n. 1.
[3] A. F. S. Pearson, *Thomas Cartwright*, p. 66.
[4] SP 14.17.33, 34 (? 12. December 1605).

took the opportunity to point out its moral errors, among them the case just mentioned: '2. that Equivocation is not onely by this booke allowed in cases of relligion, but in cases civill between man and man as by the example of the plague in London &c.', though he was able to produce a better and more pointed instance of the Jesuits' unstraightforward dealing in the title of the book itself: 'ffirst the Auther made this Title, A treatise of Equivocation &c. in steade wherof garnett hath written wth his owne hand A treatise against lyeing and fraudulent dissimulation, Newelie overseen by the Auther, and published for defence of Innocency, and for the instruction of the ignorants.' The treatise, whatever it was called, came out in Elizabeth's reign and the contemporary note is misplaced in the State Papers for 1605 where it stands next to a Jacobean copy. (The later clerk wrote italic and could not read secretary hand; the word 'Auther', in the passage just quoted, appeared in his version as 'Dutch'.) It looks as if the Anglican horror at popish dishonesty, however genuine or artificial it may have been, was mounting through Elizabeth's reign to an early Stuart crescendo of propagandistic venom. It is worth remembering that up to this time the conformist wing of the established church had not begun to develop a casuistry of its own. Significantly, it began to do so after the establishment had been seriously threatened by the puritan revolution, and the most stolid work of Anglican 'case-divinity' ever to be written – Jeremy Taylor's *Ductor Dubitantium*, published in 1660 – was written when Anglicanism was proscribed and, at least in theory, subject to persecution. In times of adversity real thought had to be given to the moral issues which had seemed crystal-clear in the days of prosperity.

The puritans, as we shall see, ran into such problems earlier than the conforming protestants did, and developed their own casuistry earlier. Here the great name is William Perkins, and mention of Perkins brings me to the name of the only Roman casuist – so it would seem – that he was familiar with. This was John Vermeulen or Molanus, a Belgian, whose *Theologiae practicae compendium*[1] is cited, if only to hold it up for derision, in Perkins' *A Reformed Catholike*, published in 1598. In his earlier *Discourse of Conscience* (1596) he denounced Roman casuists in general and not by name, implying that he had read several; their arrogance, 'wil yet more fully appeare to any man, if we read Popish bookes of *practical* or *Case-divinitie*, in which the common manner is, to binde conscience

---

[1] Joannes Molanus, *Theologiae practicae compendium, per conclusiones in quinque tractatus digestum* (Cologne, 1590).

where God looseth it, and to loose where be bindes'[1] – a charge too
vague to pin down to any passage in any author, but two years later
Molanus is the only one he ever cites, and the phrase 'practical
divinity' echoes Molanus' title (it was not a particularly common
name for casuistry). In his major work on the subject, *The Whole
Treatise of Cases of Conscience* of 1608, Perkins gives no indication
of having consulted papistical precursors at all. (In the *Reformed
Catholike* he had to, because the plan of the work required him to
show the exact points of difference between himself and them.) To
all seeming, therefore, Perkins' information about catholic casuistry
is derived from this one source.

Thus, on the subject of equivocation Perkins is content to instance
Molanus and nobody else as an example of the notorious untruthfulness of papists. Everybody knew

> that in their doctrine they maintain periurie: because they teach with one
> consent, that a Papist examined may answer doubtfully against the direct
> intention of the examiner: framing an other meaning unto himself in the
> ambiguitie of his words. As for example, when a man is asked, whether he
> saide or heard Masse in such a place: though he did; they affirme, he may
> say, No; and sweare unto it: because he was not there, to reveale it to the
> examiner: whereas in the very lawe of nature, he that takes an oath, should
> sweare according to the intention of him that hath power to minister an
> oath: and that in truth, iustice, iudgement.[2]

Molanus in fact recognizes three cases of permissible swearing against
the exact truth:

> primum quando est violenta & iniusta petitio; ut, si iudex petat a reo
> iuramentum super crimen occultum, aut si maritus cogat iurare uxorem
> quod non commiserit occulte adulterium. Deinde licet aliquando contra
> propinquam interrogantis intentionem iurare aeqivoce. Ut, si puteris ex
> civitate pestifera venire, & scias ibi pestem non esse, sed contra finem iurare
> non licet. Ac postremum quando aliquis importune ac familiariter interrogat
> quod ad eum non pertinet: ut, ei dicat, Iura me an is de me male locutus sit.[3]

Molanus proceeds to quote Augustine, and Perkins to borrow the

---

1 William Perkins, *Discourse of Conscience*, p. 52.
2 William Perkins, *Reformed Catholike* (Cambridge, 1598), p. 346f.
3 Molanus, *Compendium* proposition 5 (pp. 86–7): 'First, when the demand is violent and
   unjust; as, if a judge demands an oath concerning an undiscovered crime, or if a husband
   makes his wife swear that she has not committed adultery in secret. Further, it is lawful
   to swear equivocally against the immediate intention of the person asking. As, if you are
   thought to have come from a plague-stricken city, and you know there is no plague
   there, but not against his real purpose. And lastly when anyone pesters you for an answer
   on what does not concern him; for instance, 'Swear whether so-and-so speaks ill of me.'

same quotation, so presumably he read the whole passage; his reference is only to the second of the cases above, which is the only one where the interrogator can be supposed to have a right to the truth. The intention of 'him that hath power to minister an oath' was not in question in the other cases.

Perkins appears to be using Molanus in something like desperation, because it really is very difficult to find Roman casuists who authorize the picturesque and ingenious evasions all protestants were brought up to expect from them. Anyone who has tried to pin down what 'equivocation' really involved should feel some sympathy for his predicament.

After equivocation — after it in conspicuousness, possibly before it in intrinsic horror — the aspect of catholic casuistry that made it most detestable to good protestants was the fact — well known — that it justified against rebellion lawful authorities, and even allowed catholics in the cause of catholicism to murder princes. This above all showed the 'Macchiavellianism' of the Jesuits; this was where you ended up, if you started believing that the End justifies the Means. Was the accusation a fair one?

Although violent death was nothing new, the sixteenth century seems to have witnessed either a real increase in the incidence of political assassination or at least an increase in popular interest in the subject. And when you consider the comparative lack of modern refinements — of all the major victims, only William the Silent was shot with a gun — there really does seem to have been an increased expectation of sudden death for public figures. As to the interest in the subject there can be no doubt, and the impression somehow came to be quite firmly fixed in the protestant mind that political murder was a characteristically popish device, and specially congenial to those new-fangled super-papists, the Jesuits. No amount of official disclaimer has ever sufficed to convince the really staunch protestant that Roman confessors cannot give absolution in advance, and therefore cannot use their sacramental authority to legitimize a crime which they have assisted in planning. This, on the whole, was the line that the accusation against the Jesuits, of complicity in the death of princes, usually took; but it might be urged as an alternative that they shared with the protestant left, with the Anabaptists and (to Anglicans) with the Calvinists the odium of teaching the duty, or permissibility, of tyrannicide.

The sixteenth-century debate about tyrannicide was conducted mainly on a level of political theory rather than theology, and mainly in France. No English discussion of the right of the subject to resist oppression reached the intellectual level of Hotman's *Francogallia* or the *Vindiciae contra tyrannos*, nor do these seem to have influenced English readers to any significant extent.[1] Yet the issue was a sufficiently live one in the days of the Throckmorton and Babington plots and the Bond of Association. Tyrannicide was an open question, however, only to those who could not afford to avow their opinion. To loyal subjects and members of the reformed church in England, to lift impious hands against the Lord's Anointed was, almost literally, the worst sin imaginable; as the prince's authority partook both of the divine and the paternal such an action offended against the first and fourth as well as the fifth commandment, and was viewed with peculiar horror in several places of the Old Testament, quite apart from the newfound enthusiasm for the civil state and for patriotism which all but the radical protestants then shared. As for the English catholics, if they did not quite think of Elizabeth as a nursing mother in Israel they were only the more concerned to claim that their loyalty was as sincere as that of any reformer, and that catholicism was, if anything, a better friend to secular government than its pretended zealots on the protestant side.

This point had been argued, for instance by one 'G.T.', whom Walter Travers undertook to answer in 1583. I must confess that I know of G.T.'s work only through Travers' refutation of it in *An Answere to a Supplicatorie Epistle, of G.T. for the pretended Catholiques: written to the right Honorable Lords of her Maiesties privy Councell*.[2] From this it appears that he had claimed for his religion that it caused kingdoms to flourish (Travers asked in refutation, what about the Assyrian and Persian empires?), and that it encouraged law-abiding in various specific ways: because Roman Catholics cannot have absolution for theft without restitution, because vows to God put men in the habit of keeping promises, because fasting saves food and clerical celibacy prevents over-population, because that religion forbids undesirable practices such as rack-renting and divorce, and teaches obedience to magistrates. Most crucially, it may be thought, of all, 'this Author chargeth us that *Calvin* saieth: *No law of man can bind the conscience*. Whereof (saith he) *it must needes followe that the obedience wee yeeld, is onely for pollicie and*

---

[1] What influence there was is described by H. J. Salmon, *The French Wars of Religion in English Political Thought*. On the Catholic side, the most interesting contributions concerned the Succession question, and dealt with resistance only incidentally; see T. H. Clancy, *The Papist Pampleteers*, esp. cap. 3.

[2] London, 1583.

feare.'[1] This raises a more central question, about the nature of conscientious obligation, than I can conveniently go into here; but be it noted that on the narrow point of 'policy', G.T. was prepared to claim that his religion was more politic. For the purpose of keeping people in their proper places, and securing quiet obedience to the laws, it was useful to make a distinction between mortal and venial sins, and to teach the measured and balanced pains of purgatory rather than the protestants' stark alternatives of Heaven and Hell. 'Because if al be mortall, who will strive against sinne: whereas admittying all not to be mortall, though a man be carried into a veniall sinne, yet would he strive to refraine from mortall, consideryng it bringeth damnation.'[2] (Travers is content to reply, 'This is to reason like an Atheist.') It cannot be said that G.T. has made a very formidable case for the superior civil utility of the roman religion, but Travers in refuting him goes beyond this, and lays stress not only on the notorious propensity of the papacy in all ages to encourage rebellion but also on the readiness of its agents to resort to murder:

In Spaine and Italie the cheefe seates of ye bloudy inquisition, besides many which were openly murdered: poysons, strangling in prisons, drowning in rivers, and sondrie other secret executions which came not to so open knowledge of the world (according to the depth & most suttle practises of Satan), are reasonably thought to have destroyed many more then have been consumed by the light fyers of England.[3]

This, of course, is the language of wartime propaganda. English protestants believed, or were willing to believe, that papists felt no moral revulsion from rebellion and murder when these served the purposes of their religion (purposes in themselves, of course, essentially nefarious). What did the catholics believe about the attitude proper to those of their faith on these points, in the new circumstances of a state at odds with catholicism – and not just in the quite old and familiar circumstances of a state at odds with the Pope?

G.T. believed that catholics were better subjects; his reasons were not very cogent, nor very catholic, for his main point was that catholicism disposed men to be law-abiding, and therefore even a non-catholic legislator ought to favour it. He was not urging upon catholics the duty of submission. Was anybody? It seems to me entirely reasonable for the Elizabethan Privy Council to fear that the priests of the Mission were laying little stress on any such doctrine. Some catholics certainly thought that their religion could be fitly

[1] *Ibid.* p. 234.   [2] *Ibid.* p. 248.   [3] *Ibid.* p. 40.

served by the overthrow and even the death of their sovereign, though many others did not. If the Pope could be said to have given any guidance by *Regnans in Excelsis* he had suggested that it was the duty of the English catholics to rebel, and the *explicatio* issued by his successor did not go much further towards an endorsement of civil obedience than a bare assurance that the individual catholic, for the moment, was not personally obliged to depose Elizabeth but could wait for a convenient time. We know as a matter of fact that most of them did not stir hand or foot in the matter. Is it possible to say what, in theory and on their own principles, they ought to have done?

The missionaries would not find very much help in Azpilcueta. He includes the duty owing to kings under the fourth commandment, and his only mention of tyrants by that name indicates that subjects of such a ruler are entitled to regulate their attitude toward him by a purely prudential standard:

[still on the subject of duty of honoring parents] nec etiam est talis ea quam subditus alicuius tyranni qui dominium & iurisdictionem alicuius status usurpavit, eidem dat, petans iustitiae administrationem aut beneficium, seu gratiam aliquam honestam.[1]

Co-operation with a tyrannous regime in the conduct of normal governmental responsibilities is perfectly proper, but such a regime has no supernatural claim to allegiance. Following Caietan,[2] Azpilcueta talks as if only usurping rulers were tyrants. From the contemporary catholic point of view this of course applies to Elizabeth I after the publication of *Regnans in Excelsis* though not (in England) to James.[3] Azpilcueta condemns the deliberate seeking of martyrdom; he says nothing about rebellion, or even about the papal power of deposition, and his section on murder does not make a special case of tyrannicide. If this really was the sole authority in moral theology on which the seminarians had to rely, they can have got very little comfort from it but insofar as it had anything to say it would encourage civil obedience rather than the reverse.

It is convenient to bring in the slightly later Azor as a comparison, though it is essential to bear in mind that he represents the best and

---

1 Navarrus, *Enchiridion* cap. 14. No. 31: 'This (obedience as of duty) is not the same as what a subject offers to a tyrant who has usurped the government, when he seeks (from the tyrant) the enforcement of law, or some legitimate benefit.'

2 Whom he quotes, *passim*.

3 James could be regarded as a usurper in Scotland until his mother's death in 1587; thereafter he had a good claim to both kingdoms, though not an undeniable one; Robert Parsons, in his *Conference about the next succession to the Crown of England* (1595) lists half-a-dozen candidates and leaves James out.

most judicious strain in late sixteenth-century Jesuit casuistry but was not available to be consulted in the 1580s. By the time he came to publish, the issue was too evidently topical (in France especially) to be ignored. Azor is explicit on the Pope's right to depose, and its frequent exercise in the past. On the right of an oppressed people to rebel (which he clearly does not confine to the case of a usurped government) there are nevertheless distinctions to be drawn:

(Nono) quaeritur, An populo, qui nullum alium praeter Regem superiorem habet, ius & potestas sit diiciendi Regem e regno?...Respondeo: Si sermo sit de Regnis, quae sunt apud Ethnicos, posse Regnum totius populi concursu Regibus abrogare, non quidem pro libidine, vel arbitrio populi, sed iustis in causis...[1]

He further limits this right in a manner which seems impossibly narrow today but was not uncommon in the sixteenth-century debate, and could be matched among protestants.

Nomine vero populi intelliguntur Senatores, vel procuratores civitatum, & regni proceres, & Nobiles. Constat enim populus, ut minimum, ordine, & statu nobilium, & plebeiorum, sive popularium...
Si autem sermo sit de Christianorum Regibus, non videtur populus id iuris, & potestatis habere absolute, vel inscio Pontifice Romano.[2]

More immediately to the point:

(Decimo) quaeritur, An privato homini liceat occidere gladio, veneno, proditione, insidiis, aliove quovis modo, Regem tyrannice dominantem?

He quotes several examples in favour, and notes that many authors distinguish according to the tyrant's title, holding that the case is different with one who is not the rightful ruler.

Haec sententia quamvis tot Auctorum testimonio comprobetur, mihi tamen dubia est,[3]

Reasoning that there can be no righteous execution without

---

[1] (*Libri*) *Institutionum Moralium* Pt. 2, Bk 11, cap. 5: 'It is asked, Ninth, whether a people, who have no other ruler than the King, have the right to depose the King from his kingdom?...I reply: if we are speaking of pagan kingdoms, kings may be deprived of their authority by the general act of the people, yet not however out of whim or caprice but for just causes...'

[2] *Ibid*. 'By the word "people" is to be understood councillors, governors, leading men and nobles. For a people is composed, at the least, of a noble and a common estate...But if we are speaking of Christian kings, the people do not seem to have this power absolutely, or without the consent of the Roman Pontiff.'

[3] *Ibid*. 'It is asked, Tenth, whether a private man may kill a king who rules tyrannically, by sword, poison, treason, sedition or otherwise?...This judgement appears doubtful to me although approved by so many authors.'

4-2

judgement, no judgement without public authority. On this he claims to be in line with Augustine and Aquinas. Relying again on Augustine, and on Ambrose, he cites the case of the Christian troops of Julian the Apostate who (allegedly) obeyed him when they were poetically ordered, '*producite aciem pro defensione Reipublicae*',[1] but refused when ordered to massacre Christians or worship idols.

Quare dicendum est: si mandata Principis, alioqui tyranni, sint aequa, & iusta, parendum est.[2]

Anglicans were to give essentially the same advice in the even more immediately awkward circumstances of the interregnum.[3]

We do not, of course, know what the Fathers of the Society said in the confessional (either as confessors or as penitents), and there is no means of absolutely gainsaying the frequent accusations, or insinuations, by their enemies that they used it as a convenience in plotting political crimes. It would seem, though, that the persistent protestant propaganda story about Jesuits who licensed their penitents to murder princes had very little basis in fact, or at least, in any facts that the propagandists could conceivably know about. (Let alone that Jesuits were a small minority among the missionary priests.)

What of Molanus, who as we have seen was the sole Roman source of the sole controversialist on the puritan side who could claim to be an expert on case-divinity? As might be expected from a Belgian writing in the 1580s, he regards diversity of religion as the worst catastrophe that can happen to a state, and he explicitly discusses heretical misgovernment rather than misgovernment in general. It is the duty of churchmen to put princes in mind of their responsibility towards true religion, and that God has given them the sword in order to cut off heretics, schismatics and the like. If indeed they themselves should offend,

...& potestate sua ad Evangelii persecutionem abutantur, privata authoritate occidi nequeunt: possunt tamen a proceribus & populo a regni administratione removeri.
Si vero subditi hac in re officio suo non consulunt, sed ipsi etiam, eadem peste infecti, veritatis hostes foveant, atque Ecclesiam Dei oppugnant, a potestate eligendi regem iustissime excludi possunt.
Imo Pontificis erit, reges, in Christianam religionem pertinaciter delinquentes,

---

1 'Advance your steel for the defence of the Republic.'
2 'For it should be said that if the commands of rulers, even if they are tyrants, are just and right, they are to be obeyed.'
3 Jeremy Taylor, in *Ductor Dubitantium* (1660), was to argue that any government was better than none, and therefore the provisional republican government was to be obeyed.

a regno per sententiam deponere, & subditos a iuramento fidelitatis absolvere: & ne illis fidelitatem observent omnibus modis prohibere.
Poterit etiam aliorum fidelium principum operam implorare, ut tam impij Reges a sui regni gubernaculis repellantur.[1]

While there is nothing in all this that was not perfectly orthodox in the Middle Ages, the last two clauses especially look as if Molanus had England specifically in mind — and that he thought little of the relaxation of the duty to withhold obedience contained in the *Explicatio*. Indeed it is rather surprising that Perkins does not trouble to denounce Molanus over this point. If he was generally regarded as a central and representative casuist the passage just quoted gives excellent corroboration for the idea that casuists as a class are seditious, and that they encouraged English papists to give aid and comfort to their country's enemies. But he still does not approve of tyrannicide, or even of executing the Pope's sentence by private men.[2]

The science of casuistry, virtually a creation of the late sixteenth century, continued to flourish and to produce a mass of literature, largely repetitive, in catholic countries in the seventeenth. In catholic countries, casuists continued to discuss the case of *communicatio in sacris* as it affected catholics in protestant countries. In England it would appear that the main lines of catholic opinion on this and similar subjects were fixed by the early years of James I and hardly

---

[1] Molanus, *Compendium* tractatus 2., cap. 2 (p. 76): '. . . and abuse their power by persecuting the Gospel, they may not be killed by private authority; but they may be removed from office by nobles and people. If indeed the subjects do not perform their duty in this matter, but themselves, infected by the same disease, become enemies to the truth, and attack the church of God, they may rightly be denied the power of choosing a king. Rather, it is for the Pope to depose kings who persistently offend the Christian religion from their kingdoms, and to absolve subjects from their allegiance; and to forbid them by all means to obey them. He may also call on other, faithful rulers, to drive such wicked kings from their dominions.'

[2] If the right of tyrannicide was asserted by any casuist in these years, it was by Francisco Suarez, S.J., in *Defensio Fidei Catholica et Apostolicae adversus Anglicanae sectae errores* (1613). This was not a work of casuistry, but a polemic contribution to the debate on the Oath of Allegiance; it was specifically answering James I's attack on Bellarmine. It does however draw on casuistic thought, and on authors such as Azor. While he deprecates the idea of private vengeance against a tyrant, and draws a familiar distinction between the usurper and the merely bad legitimate ruler (who, however, becomes a usurper the minute the Pope deposes him), his qualifications still leave a very wide discretion to the enraged citizens (Suarez, Bk. 6, cap. 4). Indeed, I cannot find the qualification that Fr T. H. Clancy mentions (*Papist Pamphleteers*, pp. 103–4), that the sentence could only be carried out by the designated heir. I read Suarez to say (para. 17) that the Pope's sentence must be waited for, whether the Pope designates an heir or not; but the execution of the sentence may be left up to anybody. And Suarez seems to offer a complete liberty of resisting a bad ruler short of killing him. (The case of tyrannicide is also discussed in the documents printed by Mandell Creighton in *E.H.R.* Jan. 1892 mentioned above, note 2, p. 74.)

changed until the great thaw of the nineteenth century – indeed, on *communicatio in sacris* itself the thaw is a phenomenon of our own day, and not an English but a world-wide one. The English catholic of moderate and peaceable disposition, who was amenable to the moral teachings of his own church and knew what they were, was definitely discouraged from seeking any kind of private compromise with the persecuting State. He was not definitely encouraged to seek any positive alternative. His clearest course was to endure and suffer.

7
Solutions

A Catholic might have the luck to avoid any confrontation. This was a matter of luck, it was not open to choice. If fortune did not serve him, his remaining options ranged from martyrdom through political subversion to flight, to religious resignation under adversity, and finally to surrender.

Martyrdom is the most extreme of options. It was not offered to catholic laymen for the mere fact of being catholic laymen. Normally it was easy, and morally permissible, for a layman to avoid the kinds of conduct that would put him in its danger. There can have been no guarantee of this; as long as hot persecution lasted there was always the chance that the man who wanted only to live in quietness and obscurity would be faced with a situation in which he either had to become an accomplice in technical treason or shamefully betray the cause of his religion. What could you do if a hunted priest came to your door, with nowhere else to go? It was no answer to say that he should not have come. For the sake of the mission it was the priest's business to stay alive and at work until the moment came when he could only serve his church by a faithful witness unto death; and since these were the only terms on which catholicism could survive in England, helping it to survive on these terms was the plain duty of every catholic. But a priest would be a madman to rely, except in the last extremity of need, on anyone whose commitment or resolution he was not sure of. On the whole we may assume that every lay martyr was brought to the gallows by some positive act against the laws that went beyond his bare religious duty and was essentially voluntary.

Martyrdom *was* offered to priests of the English Mission for the bare fact of being priests of the mission after 1571 and even more after 1585, though it was not always or consistently offered. The priests of course accepted this danger when they were ordained; it was always open to the moderate man not to become a priest. Some priests were bolder than others, some were more political than others, and some differed from others, conscientiously, on where the true line of duty lay. I will not elaborate on this for two reasons: people who willingly, knowingly and ahead of time committed themselves to the possibility of martyrdom are not my present concern, and the story of the divisions among the priests – the quarrels in the college at Rome, the Wisbech Stirs, the Archpriest Controversy, the false hopes held out by Burghley to those who would oppose the Jesuits – make a tale that has often been told.[1]

All options less extreme than martyrdom can be called moderate options by comparison. Rebellion is less extreme than martyrdom, but more extreme than anything else. Flight is less extreme again. Perhaps we should here include fruitless plotting, that did not actually result in treasonable acts, though that is hardly a real option; it is more in the nature of mental solace for those who were taking one of the other courses. The last option that the catholic church could allow was simply to stay and suffer. For those who would have liked to be good catholics, if they could, but were forced by the pusillanimity of their nature to be bad catholics, there remained one rare possibility – to spy for the government on your fellow-catholics, uncovering or pretending to uncover their political plots, and thereby purchase for yourself safety in this world at some likely cost in the next; and one very common possibility – to comply outwardly with the minimal requirements of the law, and be a 'church-papist'.

Rebellion as a course of action was evidently very unattractive. Considered as a course of action it includes serious rioting and serious plotting, since these involve an essentially similar personal decision, a recourse to violence. In England in the reigns of Elizabeth I and James I there was one full-scale armed insurrection inspired by catholicism, the rising of the Northern Earls in 1569; there were also a number of plots – the Ridolfi, Throckmorton and Babington plots in favour of Mary, Queen of Scots are the obvious ones – which depended for their success on either a sudden, unplanned rising by the catholics or on total inactivity by the protestants. Even without the suspicion that the Babington Plot, in particular, was helped along by *agents provocateurs*, there is an amateur air about this kind of scheming. Then, in 1605, comes Gunpowder Plot whose leaders

---

1 See e.g. Patrick McGrath, *Papists and Puritans under Elizabeth I*; Philip Caraman, *The Years of Siege*; Philip Hughes, *Rome and the Counter-Reformation*; D. Mathew, *The Celtic Peoples and Renaissance Europe* (rather sentimental); P. Renold (ed.), *The Wisbech Stirs, 1595–1598*, publ. *Catholic Record Society* vol. 51 (1958); Gladys Jenkins, 'The Arch-priest Controversy and the Printers, 1601–1603' in *The Library*, 5th series, vol. 2 (1948).

undoubtedly meant business. Apart from these there were a few odd riots;[1] what constitutes a riot is a matter of definition, and we do not know how many there were, just as we do not know how many abortive plots there were. We can say that with the possible exception of 1569, which was a special case arising out of the throwback feudalism and perennial unrest of the Border, the catholic community were never prepared to take the field at the bidding of the Pope, the King of Spain or any native conspirators. Lack of organization would explain this, but there is no reason to doubt that the majority of catholics were, as they so often protested they were, loyal to the Crown in civil matters. Certainly the catholic underground was overwhelmingly non-violent, from whatever cause. The teaching of the church, on the subject of armed resistance, was conflicting and always furnished the peaceloving individual with an escape route. The priests, who were bound to have ambivalent feelings about the State if they were not absolutely the King of Spain's men, tended as a matter of policy or conviction to stress the non-political character of the faith and of their own mission. Their example was likely to be followed by all but the natural hotheads, not because English catholics were particularly 'clericalist' but because the priests were the hard-liners, they were constantly pointing out the high and rocky path to salvation to those who were reluctant to tread it, and this made their argument the more persuasive when they defended a course of inaction.

The unreadiness of the catholics for a resort to violence can be illustrated by the way Gunpowder Plot went to pieces. This was an extreme case, not a typical one. The conspirators were desperate and resolute men; they knew they were going to cause bloodshed, they saw no alternative and they had counted the cost. If anybody could be depended on to carry the thing through they could. Even now we cannot be quite certain what went wrong. It seems clear, however, that the Privy Council knew about the plot and was just letting it simmer; and it seems most likely that some of the plotters knew, or strongly suspected, that the Privy Council knew. The plot was sabotaged from within, not by double agents or turncoats, but by genuine conspirators who had become sure that it was going to fail. The leak to Lord Mounteagle was contrived in order to scare Catesby and the inner ring into dropping the whole thing and flying before it was too late. In the event the counter-plot was too late; the leaders tried to go through with the original plan, and the consequences

[1] Roland Mathias, *Whitsun Riot*.

were catastrophic, for themselves and for catholicism in England. Nothing the catholics did in the Armada years fed so straight into the hands of their enemies. Anti-catholic paranoia was already closely associated with English patriotism; it was nourished, for the next two hundred years, on memories of the Fifth of November.[1]

The catholic underground was politically quiescent, most of the time. When it resorted to violence or to outright, conscious sedition it did so ineffectively and with interior misgivings that almost guaranteed unsuccess. All the same, it was permeated with an atmosphere of conspiracy. In the war years, both its friends and its enemies expected it to furnish a fifth column.

With hindsight it is easy to see the entire reign of Elizabeth I as dominated by the single issue of the problem of national security posed by militant catholicism at home and abroad. It is once again necessary to bear in mind that the issue hardly existed for the first ten years of the reign, while in the last ten, and in the reign of James, the issue while still there had to compete with several others for public attention. However, this might be true for the ordinary citizen without being true for the kind of citizen we are chiefly concerned with, namely the would-be loyal and would-be peaceful catholic. His life could be affected by the militancy of other catholics at any time and in two distinct ways: as a member of the same grapevine society he might acquire guilty knowledge of plots or of seditious rumours, and he might be placed in a moral dilemma by efforts to recruit him for the cause; and simply as a catholic at all his position in a hostile society was affected by the way in which his coreligionists behaved or were believed to be behaving. As soon as the government was frightened enough to embark on real repression – and it made no difference to the essential situation whether this fright was rational or not – a new temptation was born – the urge to demonstrate one's own loyalty and reliability at the expense of the embarrassing radicals who got your community such an unfairly bad name.

I call this a temptation because it obviously was one. I do not mean to imply that those who took this course were necessarily wrong. Undoubtedly there were among the catholics political hotheads whose schemes deserved little sympathy and no support, and there was no good reason why men who sincerely deplored the excesses of those who planned rebellion or spied for a foreign invader should not say so, and make their own contrary stance conspicuous

---

[1] See Joel Hustfield, 'Gunpowder Plot and the politics of dissent', in *Early Stuart Studies*, ed. H. S. Reinmuth.

and unmistakable. After the rebellion of the Northern Earls, th social leaders of the recusants mostly made protestations of their personal loyalty to the Crown whose genuineness there is no reason to doubt. At the same time, from the purely private point of view it must have made a man uneasy to denounce, and claim credit for denouncing, intrigues which might be very silly and which he might not wish to touch with a barge-pole, but which he would be almost bound to give thanks for if by any chance they should happen to succeed.

This however might not apply to all catholic intrigues. It would be possible for a perfectly sincere catholic to feel that religion had been restored at too high a price if the Armada, or Gunpowder Plot, had restored it. On the strictly religious issues posed by the Act of Uniformity and its supporting legislation against recusants, the Seminary Priests and the Fathers of the Society were apparently able to achieve a very impressive measure of unanimity among the catholics as a whole, and those 'church-papists' who continued to compromise did so from frailty and at the peril of their souls. No such solidarity, no such clarity, was achieved on the proper political attitude of catholics. This was a point on which priest differed from priest. It was a point on which final certainty about a catholic's duty was not attainable then, and has not been attained since.

Burghley, Walsingham and other security-conscious Elizabethans not unnaturally saw every papist as a potential Spanish agent as soon as it was clear that Spain rather than France was the ideological enemy. Burghley's own statement of the Government's position is unattractive[1] but it seems unnecessary to suppose, with some historians, that he was wholly hypocritical and was merely using the accusation of political disloyalty as a pretext for religious persecution.[2] This would imply an odd set of priorities in Elizabeth's chief minister. There is still a 'Spanish Party' among catholic historians of this period; it is a little unfair, as it would have been a little unfair in the 1580s, to identify this with the Jesuit party.

Obviously the kind of catholic I am concerned with would not have been a supporter of the 'Spanish Party' of that day. He is not much likelier to have been active in the 'Scotch Party', but that faction if any would have commanded the sympathy of moderates.

[1] *The Execution of Justice in England*, ed. Robert Kingdom (New York, 1965).
[2] This assumption runs right through, for instance, Fr Leo Hicks, *An Elizabethan Problem*. But another assumption which also runs through Fr Hicks' work is that any alleged catholic who was not working in the interests of the King of Spain cannot have been a sincere catholic.

Would a moderate ever actually work *against* any body of catholic conspirators? Could he, with any pretence of catholic conscience, spy on such conspirators for the government?

I think he could, and on occasion did, but the circumstances had to be rather special and no one, probably, would go about to create occasions – no one, that is, but the natural informer, the professional fisher in troubled waters, whose religion might happen coincidentally to be catholic and to furnish him with useful introductions. In a world of intrigue, at least if there is any money in it, double agents of course flourish. What I am interested in at this point is the honest man who finds himself involved in the fringes of a conspiracy or an intelligence network with whose purposes he does not agree although he might quite reasonably have been expected to. When the whole English catholic church was an 'underground', this kind of thing was bound to happen all the time. It was perhaps likeliest in the émigré societies in and around the continental seminaries but of course there were instances in England as well. Gunpowder Plot furnished two famous ones: Father Gerard, who did not tell, and Lord Mounteagle and his friends, who did. This was the only specific case that aroused contemporary discussion of the duty to tell, or not to tell. Unfortunately this discussion was wholly absorbed in protestant–catholic polemic and produced nothing of much value for resolving the individual, psychological tensions that must have faced the involuntary accomplice and potential misprisioner of treason.

Turncoats and double agents, however, are marginal to any discussion of moderate men. They are men in the middle, men who are trying to get away with a personal compromise, but they are not moderates, not eschewers of violence; they are immoderate men who are also unstable, men who have chosen violence and cannot go through with it, hotheads with cold feet. Moreover they are outside our reach because, more even than the common run of humanity, they keep their motives to themselves.

Flight for religion's sake – emigration to catholic asylums overseas – was imputed by Bishop Corbet to the fairies.[1] Hardly anybody else seems to have done it. Jane Dormer, Duchess of Feria, made a fortunate marriage in Mary's reign and was able, as a very wealthy

---

[1] In *Farewell, rewards and fairies*:
> But now, alas, they all are dead,
> Or gone beyond the seas,
> Or further for religion fled;
> Or else they take their ease.

expatriate in Spain, to befriend wandering Englishmen.[1] Others, whose motives were more political, were on the King of Spain's pension list. Others could starve. In sixteenth-century Europe there was no established pattern, no normal opportunities, of migration between states, no empty lands where settlers of alien birth were automatically welcome. King Philip's generosity to persecuted catholics was great, but it did not extend to letting them colonize his empire and there seems to have been no suggestion at all along these lines. The new-discovered countries, vast as they were, were jealously monopolized by their discoverers. This was resented by those who wanted to trade with them, but the desire to go and build cities in the wilderness was as yet unborn. We live in an age, and I live in a country, where emigration is one of the most obvious solutions to human discontents. In the sixteenth century it was still rare, and still usually thought of as a private calamity. Governments could try to move their own populations about, more or less successfully, and so the King of Spain moved some Castillians to New Spain; rulers of England, including Philip II during his brief marriage to Mary Tudor, attempted to plant Ireland. Thriving towns could use resident aliens, might even naturalize them, and might have a special welcome for the religious refugee. Inside the Holy Roman Empire there was a great deal of migration of that kind. The process did a lot to alter the ethnic character of Amsterdam and Geneva, and something to alter the ethnic character of London and Norwich. For whatever cause, it seems to have been an opportunity mainly for protestants.

The English catholics who did seek and find a refuge overseas, this early, were most typically those with a religious vocation. Apart from the Jesuits and, a little later, Benedictines engaged in the mission, no form of regular religious life could be practised on English soil, and the claustral and contemplative lives could not be practised there at all. Thus, from this age down to the French revolution, the odd Englishman who wanted to be a cloistered monk and the much commoner Englishwoman who wanted to be any kind of nun, had to go to the continent of Europe in order to satisfy that ambition. In Belgium and France, around Douai, there grew up predominantly English houses, and there was a nunnery in Lisbon. One element of English catholicism, the mystical tradition that dates back to the fourteenth century, was kept alive, and could be kept alive, only in these places of refuge. The monastic profession is a kind of flight,

[1] A. J. Loomie, *The Spanish Elizabethans* cap. 4.

a seeking asylum, even when the world that the novice is leaving behind is a sympathetic one. Monastic writers do not hesitate to use the language of retreat from danger, of escape, of exodus from Egyptian or Babylonian bondage to the Promised Land. They can draw on exactly the same Biblical imagery that is popular with colonizing sects. The parallel, however, is more psychological than material. Men or women who needed to live in the Thebaid for their spiritual health and comfort would have to leave home, whether catholics were persecuted at home or not. Catholics who lacked this extra motive for exile do not seem to have gone into exile.

This became particularly clear when the chance of settling overseas did open up. The great colonizing effort of the seventeenth century opened new horizons, socially as well as geographically, and for the first time a man might choose a country to live in as he might choose a career. In new-founded commonwealths overseas he could have a much wider choice of career, and if he was bold enough he might even choose a social rank and station. Religion could be a factor in the choice, we need not put it any higher. In 1632 George Calvert, first Lord Baltimore, obtained the grant of Maryland from Charles I and planned to make it a colony of refuge for his fellow-catholics. Unlike most Lords Proprietor, Calvert had spent some time in America and had given serious study to problems of colonization; of all Englishmen who planned plantations in that age he was perhaps the best equipped with practical knowledge. He died the same year but his two sons worked hard and well to put his ideas into effect. Maryland suffered fewer initial hardships than most plantations and went on to prosper, but it was never predominantly a catholic colony. From the start, most settlers were protestants. The intention of the Calverts to maintain complete equality between all forms of christianity (since they could not quite establish catholicism in a province of England) was defeated by an Anglican majority in the assembly before the end of the century. However we are to explain it, English catholics in general were very unwilling, and less willing than English puritans, to leave home for religion.

They mostly stayed home and suffered for religion. I have said something about the official teaching of that religion, here it would be germane to say something about its *ethos*. John Bossy has suggested[1] that the reduced circumstances of the catholic community had compensations, social and emotional, at least for the squire class who came to enjoy a new kind of patronage and domestic power,

[1] John Bossy, 'The Character of Elizabethan Catholicism', in *Past and Present* 21 (1962).

He also argues that this patronal influence availed to moderate the policies of the missionary clergy. Bossy's argument certainly helps to explain how the catholic laity found their lot endurable at all. I think we need also to take into account the flavour of late-medieval piety which continued in the 'old religion' and in what little of the 'counter-reformation' England ever experienced. This, as I see it, was indrawn and individualistic, and tended to give a very central rôle to penitential contemplation of the passion and sufferings of Christ. Such a piety has an obvious relevance to a church 'under the Cross', and I think this background helps to explain the missionary priests. If I say no more about it here it is partly from a sense of my own lack of equipment to discuss such subjects and partly because the line of explanation, whether it will serve or not, is not needed to explain the attitude of those who wanted to stay out of trouble.

A good catholic could extract some religious comfort from his situation. He could profit by his hardships, 'offer them up' in the language of modern catholicism or (as a protestant might put it) hope to escape some time in purgatory for them. There were bad catholics as well. The last, most universally despised of all solutions was that of the 'church-papist', the papist at heart who outwardly conformed. Such a man was a lost soul in the eyes of the recusant body, and he earned himself little credit with the protestants either. A church-papist, said John Earle in his *Microcosmographie* of 1628 (the most famous description)

is one that parts his religion betwixt his conscience and his purse...Once a month he presents himself at the church, to keep off the church-warden, and brings in his body to save his bail. He kneels with the congregation, but prays by himself, and asks God forgiveness for coming thither...He would make a bad martyr and good traveller...and in Constantinople would be circumcised with a reservation.

Earle's work is a *jeu d'esprit* in the genre of Theophrastian character. He is much more concerned to make an effective phrase than to analyse a social phenomenon. His own religious standpoint was that of a mild and tolerant conformist with hopes of promotion – handsomely realized; he became tutor to the young prince Charles, and eventually a bishop. He stuck to his Anglican principles in the interregnum, and did not become a persecutor later. His more or less good-humoured contempt for the church-papist was the attitude of a reasonably honest and upright man, and no doubt it was typical of many such. The *Microcosmographie* was a successful work.

Presumably to many individuals their own case did not seem so clear-cut as it did to Earle or the seminary priests. Church-popery, or conformity with reservations, was the obvious recourse of the half-convinced. It was what the laws officially encouraged. What looked like church-popery to outsiders may sometimes have been in reality the same kind of throwback Henricianism that Queen Elizabeth practised in the Chapel Royal to the scandal of reforming bishops. We get a stray glimpse of this, or so it would seem, when two parishioners of Easton in Hampshire excuse themselves for not communicating, in 1586, because the minister did not use wafer cakes as the Queen's injunctions laid down; in 1593 somebody else in the same village was making the same excuse, and a man and his wife and servant at Meon Stoke and no less than nineteen people at Houghton in the same county.[1] In the same sets of *detecta* come the excuse that a man is out of charity with his neighbour, and there-fore in no fit state to communicate – a standard church-papist ploy according to Earle, who was writing after the act of 1606 that im-posed a fine for non-communicating – and more detailed objections to the irreverence or, possibly, puritanism of the parson; at Durley in 1586 eleven parishioners objected apparently because the minister followed the prayer book of 1552, and offered to communicate with another minister. Here nothing that you could call 'popery' is in question, but these cases seem to differ from each other in nuances merely.

The church-papist was obeying the law, and from Rome's point of view he was an apostate. He should have worried the priests of the mission more than he worried the government, and in general this seems to have been the case. There are a scatter of references to church-popery in the state papers and related documents, but they are few and mostly refer to the suspect husband of a recusant wife or master of a recusant servant. From the diocese of Winchester again, in 1580, the bishop wrote to Walsingham:

touching ye last letters we receaved of y^r Ho. concerning an order howe suche women are to be dealt w^thall as are relapsed in this Diocesse, whose Husbandes come to Church...we have called before us many of ye Hus-bandes...and hope we shall doe some goode therein: But at the beginning they thowght it something strainge, that they shall be punished for theyre wyves fawltes[2]

which continued to be a problem. Parliament was unwilling to tackle it in 1593, and, as J. E. Neale has shown, some quite devious

---

1 Winchester Consistory Court Books 59 and 64.
2 SP 12.144.36 (22 November 1580).

manoeuvring to get an appropriate law on the books did not succeed in binding a clear liability on the husbands of recusant wives.[1] They were, of course, liable in the ordinary way for their wives' civil debts and were dunned for the twelvepenny fine. Earle represented this as the typical situation: 'His wife is more zealous and therefore more costly, and he bates her in tires what she stands him in religion'[2] – he deducts the fines he incurs on her behalf from her dress allowance. The non-conforming members of his household might be expensive to the church-papist, and they could very easily draw down unwelcome attention on his head. Without them as a complicating factor in his life, there was really no way to tell him from his good protestant neighbours. In another generation there might be no way at all. The logical consequence of a long continued course of church-popery was to turn the man concerned from a bad catholic to a bad protestant. This may seem an unimpressive result for the State's best endeavours, but it was the only result they were likely to accomplish.

[1] Neale, *Elizabeth I and her Parliaments* vol. 2, Pt. 4, cap. 4 *passim*. The act of 1606 however (3 Jas. I, cap. 5) did exclude the husbands of recusant wives from public office.

[2] Earle, *Microcosmographie*, character of 'A church papist'.

Part 2 – The Puritans

8

The nature of the quarrel

The situation of the Elizabethan puritan was of course fundamentally different from that of the papist. The differences may be worth describing but need no elaboration. The puritans, we may be sure, were a much smaller minority to start with, a more specialized section of the nation; and instead of standing firm by the old ways, they stood for ways newer than the new.

In 1559 all the population, many of them for most of their lives, had been exposed to some form of catholic teaching – certainly in most cases very elementary, but at least catholic rather than protestant – and almost all had taken part in some form of catholic rites. By contrast, hardly any of the ordinary laity had any experience at all of a protestantism more extreme than that of the Edwardian prayer-books. Moreover this remained the case throughout this and the next reign. 'Puritanism', in this the earliest period of its history, was overwhelmingly a movement of clergy – including in that term, as the middle ages would have included them, aspirants to orders who were never canonically ordained. The desire of the faithful to enjoy the consolations of the puritan religion without interference from a less faithful State was only theoretically a factor in the problem, which was much more importantly a problem of the clerical classes.

Even these were not in a situation remotely like that of the missionaries from Douai, though in some ways it might bear comparison with that of the deprived Marian clergy. The minister, or would-be minister, who shared the aspirations of the more high-flying protestants could not with a clear conscience do exactly what the Act of Uniformity required him to do, but if he could get a parish he had a fair chance of doing more or less what he wanted so far as it rested in him; at the same time he was definitely in the danger of the law if his superiors ever bothered to find out, and the little compliances with uniformity that might be necessary or prudent if he was to keep his place unmolested all constituted fallings away from the strict principles of his party.

The 'puritans' or 'precisians' may in a sense be said to go back to Bishop Hooper under Edward VI or the followers of Knox at Frankfurt and Geneva. Both names, apparently with exactly the same connotation, enter the language together in the early 1560s and it is only sensible to assign the same date to the emergence of a self-conscious movement. There may have been, already this early, fundamental differences of theology or of world-view between those who could be called by these names and those whom it is natural for us to call 'anglicans', but the differences were more latent than apparent at the time.[1] Conformists equally with puritans were engaged in the unfinished task of making the country protestant. To both, Rome was still the enemy chiefly to be feared. In the circumstances it was reasonable for conformists, and almost inevitable for puritans, to feel that the puritan party was merely the more extreme and radical wing of the same movement. Puritans could believe that they were moving faster than other people in what was, nevertheless, everybody's direction; they could thus feel optimistically that the future was theirs, and self-righteously that the one thing that marked them out from other reformers was their own superior dedication and zeal. Such a view was extremely flattering and for that reason tempting, to all on the puritan side except the most ideologically minded; it also had its appeal to 'men of goodwill' among the conformists, who liked to believe that the reformation movement was united on fundamentals and who indeed were accustomed to assert this, hotly, against the contrary accusations of the catholics. It is easy to see how it went against the grain for Jewel or Grindal, or even much later for Thomas Fuller,[2] to admit that the two groups differed on matters which were crucial to both. If the leading figures of the puritan side were not similarly restrained by an eirenic spirit, they also denied that any question of principle divided them; in their eyes the conformists were men without principle.

It was thus always possible in the formative age of the movement for its supporters to feel that they were more loyal to the true purposes of the Anglican establishment of religion than were those who abided

---

1 For opposite views of this question, see C. H. and K. George, *The Protestant Mind of the English Reformation*, and John New, *Anglican and Puritan*. Both these seem to me to overstate their case.

2 Thomas Fuller, *Church History of Britain*, and the same author's *Worthies* which consistently treats leading puritans sympathetically though Fuller himself must be reckoned as Anglican.

by its rules, and this in Elizabeth's reign continued to be the keynote of pretty well all puritan polemic. This provided them with a logically sound reason for doing what they pleased, and disregarding the Act of Uniformity, as long as they could get away with it, but it still left them with a problem or two. How far could a godly preacher go in complying with the demands of the State and the Ecclesiastical authorities, bishop, archdeacon or Queen's commissioner (granted that none of these ought properly to exist) rather than imperil or absolutely lose the chance of godly preaching? And how far was it legitimate to talk and behave as if a half-reformed church in which a few of the godly were able to do good, more or less by stealth, was a genuine reformed body with the enormous authority over the individual Christian and even over the whole society he lived in which Geneva standards laid down as the minimum that a true reformer should be content with?[1]

Puritanism, as the word was commonly understood in Elizabeth's time, could imply what it means now: a certain attitude to the world and its pleasures, which a man might perhaps put into practice in his private life without requiring any other man's permission or co-operation, and even with some plausible claim to be meeting officially approved norms better than his neighbours. So far the isolated precisian had no problem. But the name also implied, and more importantly from the point of view of the truly dedicated, a programme for the church, and for the whole society conceived as a reformed Christian commonwealth in a 'covenant' relation to God. It is with puritans in this sense that we are concerned.

The puritan religion no more than the catholic could exist as a cult for individuals, without the church; indeed, the full practice of puritanism required the active co-operation of a like-minded, and ultimately subservient, state to a degree that was not true of catholicism. Puritan and papist however needed the church in quite different ways. The private catholic needed to be linked by the priesthood, the ordinary channels of the sacraments, to the universal body and

---

[1] Those who would accept Zurich standards can be traced, occasionally, in the *Zurich Letters*. Thomas Lever wrote to Bullinger, protesting about the enforcement of clerical dress, in 1560 (*Zurich Letters* I, p. 84), and there was a long correspondence on this subject in 1566–7 (I, pp. 134, 148, 151, 153, 157, 168, 176, 345, 347), in which John Sampson and Laurence Humphrey, from Oxford, urged the utter unlawfulness of the prescribed dress, but Bullinger (and Peter Martyr) agreed with Jewel and Grindal that the issue was a trivial one. Clearly they did not positively favour the cap and surplice; the 'puritans' (this is just about the moment when the word came into use) were confronting, not High-Church ritualists but, what Dr Harry Porter would call 'Establishment Liberals'.

specially to its earthly head, the Pope. The puritan, on the other hand, needed to be in fellowship with a local congregation which was adequately exposed to the Word of God through biblical preaching, and among whom a godly spiritual discipline, which ought ideally to be mutual, was publicly exercised. This last detail was the great and crying lack in the anglican settlement as puritans saw it. Whereas a man need not wholly lack instruction and edification who could read his own Bible, moral discipline in all its steps from brotherly admonition to excommunication was by its nature a communal act, and could not be very effective without the backing of the civil police power. To the ordinary lay sympathizer with the good old cause it may well be that the absence of sermons in a conformist parish was a more severe grievance than the absence (or comparative desuetude) of public penance, but to the true zealots of the movement this was the rock of offence, and so long as those in authority continued unregenerate it was a fault for which there was no remedy. The various half-measures and semi-secret private arrangements whereby the godly might seek to patch and palliate the deficiencies of the 1559 settlement were useless in this case, or very nearly so. The utmost that was occasionally achieved – in Northamptonshire, in Bury St Edmunds or the Channel Isles – was the co-operation of lay magistrates in enforcing a rigorist code of morals, and while this was gratifying to the gospellers in a general way it still was not 'godly discipline' administered in and by the Church. On this matter England throughout our period lacked one of the 'notes' of a truly reformed church, and the puritan problem was how to reconcile himself to the fact of that lack.

(It could be argued that another 'note' was lacking too – that is, that although the Gospel was freely preached – in some places – the sacraments were not 'sincerely' performed. This was disputed among puritans, and the English church was usually reckoned to possess this note, if not in an ideal degree, at least adequately. Two factors made this judgement easier to come to. Where puritan ministers performed them in puritan congregations they could often afford to ignore those requirements of the Anglican liturgy which they disliked – the cross in baptism could be omitted, the communicants could be allowed to sit. Moreover, despite the very prominent place occupied by the sacraments in early Protestant controversy, the puritan school tended to reduce their place in church life; less emphasis was placed even on baptism than the Anglicans gave it, and the communion was looked on almost as an optional extra – certainly as something that a church could live quite healthily without, for years if need be. This attitude was translated into actual practice in Scotland. English puritans, like their counterparts on the Continent, if they were content with quarterly communions were not content with less as a standard to aim at. A communion was, however, and in the puritan tradition has always remained, a special, exceptional occasion and thus the easier to do without.[1] We can see this already in the 'troubles at Frankfurt', whose anonymous chronicler – usually supposed to be William Whittingham[2] – describes the alterations the proto-puritan cell of exiles decided to make in the 'service', and adds as an afterthought that they also made decisions, unstated, about the celebration of the sacraments. (Incidentally, 'excommunication' as the puritan party understood the term, had no particular connexion with communication in the Eucharist. The excommunicate were of course to be barred from the Eucharist, but not from it specially, and not they alone.)

If a preacher came to live in a place where puritanism was unknown, it was plainly his duty to make it known, and to make friends for the godly party even if he had no hope of bringing in the godly discipline. The predicament of the solitary puritan layman whose lot was cast in a place where the church remained unreformed, or reformed only by Anglicans, was naturally one of more deprivation, though the famous Mr Richard Greenham of Dry Drayton could see possibilities of spiritual advantage, or consolation, in it.

To one asking him why it came to pas, y^t hee found himself better affected in a barren place wher the word was not preached, then wher the means were purely and plentifully used, hee said it was the corruption of our nature, to bee most dul in most plentiful means. But to come nearer hee sayed first this may come, because having the means, more abundantly in publique places, wee remit our private exercises, wh^{ch} before wee used wth great stryfe, and continuance generally [sic, for 'secondly'?], wee do not so much reverence, and greedily receiv the means, being often as when they be but seldome...Sixtly because it may be a man was or thought

---

[1] The extremely elaborate preparations considered necessary, examining the life of all church members and so on, reinforced this tendency throughout the Calvinist world.

[2] E. Arber in his 1908 edition of *The Troubles at Frankfort* (sic) accepts the tradition of Whittingham's authorship. For other suggestions see Patrick Collinson, 'The Authorship of *A Brieff Discours off the Troubles begonne at Franckford*', in *Journal of Ecclesiastical History* 9 (1958), (nominating Thomas Wood) and Martin Simpson, 'Of the Troubles Begun at Frankfurt, A.D. 1554', in *Reformation and Revolution*, ed. Duncan Shaw (nominating John Field; Simpson also puts forward a reinterpretation of the tract as a whole and the circumstances that produced it, involving a new theory about what happened at Frankfurt. We now no longer know what happened).

himself the best in an whole town, and seing nothing in others, but corruptions pleased and provoked himself the more, in good things, but being among many good men, wee thinck our weldoing is not so praiseworthy, or wee trust so securely to ye goodness of ye place. Seventhly a man may like himself better when hee is instructing others, and more impatient of silence to hear others.... Lastly a man may thinck this [*sc.*, the change from solitary godliness to the company of other puritans] is the sorest temptation, because it is the last, even as a man shal thinck the last sicknes the sorest, because hee feeleth the present evil, though hee had more greevous sicknes before, but they are forgotten. The last remedy then against this dulnes, is a careful and continual use of private and publick exercises.[1]

In the ordinary way, 'public exercises' and the company and example of the godly were a part of the puritan way of life, without which it could be led only subject to severe handicaps. Early puritanism was not a creed of spiritual individualism. Thus, although the reformed divines were full of particular criticisms of the way the papists had misused the confessional, and they might on occasion – like Greenham, just quoted[2] – use the phrase 'auricular confession' in a pejorative sense, they nevertheless approved and encouraged the use of the confessional. If Greenham is any indication,[3] they assumed rather too readily that a good party man was qualified by his theological studies to be a director of souls, and it was some time before anything like the systematic study of case-divinity was attempted by anybody on the puritan side. As with catholics, any public discussion on how puritans were supposed to act in adverse circumstances was apt to be overlaid by dubiously relevant considerations of party advantage.

The puritans, however, were more like a party than the catholics, and less like an underground church. The main body of puritans in our period were consciously working within the national church to transform it, as a leaven in the lump; respectable puritans united in denouncing the breakaways of the sectarian Left as schismatics. Thus every mainstream puritan, from the first emergence of the Brownists in the 1580s down to at least the Civil War, regarded himself as a moderate, relative to the sectaries, even though it was still natural for him to regard himself as a principled radical, relative to the conformists – those pale and half-hearted revisionists who could find

---

[1] John Rylands Library (Manchester), English MS 524. f. 48v – (I am indebted to Prof. Patrick Collinson for my references to this MS).
[2] *Ibid.* f. 6v.
[3] But Greenham may have been untypical. His position was something of an anomaly; he had been the mentor of Robert Browne while still a parish minister (he moved to a lectureship later).

it in their conscience to accept high promotion in the establishment and persecute their more dedicated brethren. The church of England has had a whole succession of such parties; this was the first. Only hostile catholic observers, like Nicholas Sander then or Fr Francis Clark now,[1] asserted for propagandistic purposes that puritans and non-puritans within the Anglican fold taught two different religions.

If sectaries are left out of account, and for my purpose they easily can be, puritans were Church-of-England men with a difference. Clearly this applies to the man of puritanizing sympathies who only wanted a quiet life. His quiet life would be led, theoretically at least – theoretically, even in Massachusetts – inside the bosom of the national establishment though he might not agree with all of its rules. The laws which were intended to make every English subject an English churchman were no problem to the ordinary puritan.

Puritans did not like the Act of Uniformity, because they thought they could improve on the prayer book; they did not object to the clauses about church-going (except marginally, to the requirement of going on saints' days). They had not yet discovered any offence to their principles in the Act of Supremacy. The later statutes for enforcing conformity in religion were directed either against popish recusants or against sectaries. The law that bore hard on the puritan party, the source of nearly every grievance, was not statute but ecclesiastical law.[2]

This fact helped in more than one way to determine the political direction the movement took. Puritanism was opposed to the existing system of church courts anyway, because they were not framed on the Geneva model or because they were not framed on the model of the primitive church. (They were not aware of any difference between these two.) On top of this, the church courts were the worst enemies of godly non-conforming ministers. These two facts in combination helped to make ecclesiastical polity – the source of legitimate authority in the church and the way it should be exercised – the central issue which it plainly was from the *Admonition to the Parliament* of 1572 onwards; it was more central in English Calvinism than it ever became in the Calvinism of the Continent, or even than it was in Scots Calvinism by as early as 1572. And in singling out the ecclesiastical courts and the canon lawyers as their chief enemies,

[1] See Fr Francis Clark, S.J., *Eucharistic Sacrifice and the Reformation*, cap. 1.
[2] This fact indicated a possible direction of future research. So far little work has been done on court records from this point of view apart from Ronald Marchant's pioneering study of the Archdiocese of York; but see the unpublished Ph.D. thesis of my student, Ogbu U. Kalu, 'The Jacobean Church and Essex Puritans', Toronto 1973.

the puritans were drawn to the common lawyers as their natural allies. Incongruous as it may sound, and flat contrary to their stated principles, the main body of English Calvinists down to the time of the Westminster Assembly in 1643 were always making common cause politically with secularizers and erastians, and apparently without misgivings.[1]

The church courts still had large powers of interference in the lives of laymen, and it was for this reason chiefly that the common lawyers viewed them with dark distrust. The puritans, strange bed-fellows of the Inns-of-Court men, had no quarrel with that power of interference in itself, had the courts only been better, purer courts. If the discipline had only been properly godly, the laity could not have had too much of it. But the party was a clerical party to start with, and the Elizabethan puritan who fell foul of the ecclesiastical jurisdiction usually did so because he was an ecclesiastical person, a member, in medieval terms, of the spiritual estate. This status carried with it civil privileges which supporters of the new ideas did not approve of and obligations within the spiritual estate which they found very hampering and irritating. Their objections ranged all the way down to such an idiotically small matter as the proper street dress of the clergy and up to such a crux as the question whether a bishop, simply as bishop, was entitled to canonical obedience from his fellow-presbyters. The dress question was actually the first to arise, and was an echo of troubles that had occurred in the reign of Edward VI. When the words 'puritan' and 'precisian' came into use in the mid 1560s, with a sense approximate to 'nit-picker' and with the adjective 'peevish' in tow, they referred to a group of ministers who were making a big issue out of the obligation to wear a surplice in church and a cassock and square cap out of it. They had not yet made a stand on any other issue.

The rhetoric of this protest, like most puritan rhetoric of protest, concentrated on the fact that the offending garments had been the uniform of the old church and were therefore contaminated with popery. The bishops, with Luther, claimed that this was not ad-missible as a principle: *abusus non tollit usum*. The lines thus drawn were taken up again and again, though on most other contentious issues the puritans had graver arguments and naturally preferred to use them. On the dress question it was hard to deny what the bishops

---

1 The Westminster Confession, though accepted by all Scots Presbyterians until the 1790s, originally offended the Scots on account of the authority it allowed to the godly (secular) magistrate.

contended, that black and white, or round and square, were things indifferent in themselves, *adiaphora*.

Behind the rhetoric we may sense another objection, though it was not made explicit in the 'vestiarian controversy'. What the puritan ministers wanted to wear, instead of a surplice, was a black 'Geneva' gown of academic cut; and instead of a square cap a round one. This would have assimilated their appearance to that of other professional men such as lawyers (out of court) and physicians. (Indeed I had better say that it actually did assimilate the appearance of many of them, for this was the first widespread act of civil disobedience by puritans.) The square cap was academic as well as clerical – it is the ancestor of the modern mortar board – but it was not worn by laymen outside the universities. The surplice of course was designed for religious occasions only, originally for choir offices and later, by the Tudor age, used indiscriminately for all services. You did not need to be ordained to wear one, but if you were ordained you could be made to, and that was the point. The puritan clergy were clericalists in their own way but they had no love for the idea of a separate spiritual estate – the separation that used to be symbolized by the tonsure. They wished to de-emphasize (not to abolish) the sacrament, or 'sacramental', or mystery, of ordination – something which they were as yet still dependent on the bishops for, something which they shared with every ignorant 'Sir John Lack-latin'[1] and every malignant conservative Massing-priest from popish times – and emphasize, instead, their character as learned preachers of the Word. Logically they might just as well have stressed another kind of alternative qualification, namely a 'call' from the people they were to preach to, and in the later history of the puritan tradition this qualification for the ministry bulks very large indeed. It was even quite prominent in theoretical discussions in the Elizabethan age. But there was no obvious way of making the minister's costume symbolize his 'call', and there was the further difficulty that hardly any of the new preachers could plausibly claim that they had been 'called' by a congregation in any sense of the term. On the other hand, many could claim to be learned. They had no objection to a costume, such as the ordinary professional man's long gown, which implied both a learned avocation and gentlemanly rank but did not imply any mysterious or priestly dignity.

If this interpretation of the vestiarian controversy is correct then

---

[1] 'Sir John Lack-latin' was the standard nickname of an uneducated clergyman throughout the sixteenth century, until the honorific 'Sir' for clergy dropped out of use.

the point at issue was less trivial than it might seem, and the thinking on the puritan side less woolly, but the demonstration can be criticized as a demonstration because it did not make itself clear. It had one merit as a demonstration: it won support. Many clergy did not want to wear the old order of dress; many sympathized with them; the bishops did not want to use severity in such a matter, and when they did they drew down hostility upon themselves.[1] There is moreover the detail that every minister who decided to join his brethren in protesting about dress, by the fact of that protest, adopted a visible badge of his party. In those ways the row over clerical costume deserves to be regarded as a 'movement-building action'. It had its usefulness in an age that had not yet discovered the monster petition or the street march. Both of these were adopted, and perhaps invented, by the puritan movement in its later phases.[2]

The surplice question lingered on and was unresolved in our period although outward conformity was generally enforced by the end of it. Its last echoes were heard in the 1840s,[3] just before it paled into insignificance beside the Victorian ritual controversy, which was much more thought-out and theologically serious. On the cap question the puritans more or less won, in the sense that the practice they favoured became so general that it could not be stopped; in the early seventeenth century English clergy of every ecclesiastical stripe could be found wearing the round cap; the square cap, like other High-church ornaments – the cope, for instance – tended to be worn in the Laudian age only by senior clergy and thus to become a badge of rank.

The vestiarian question was still the issue uppermost in the public mind when the *Admonition to the Parliament* was published in 1572. The *Admonition* did a good deal to change this and give priority to the question of ecclesiastical polity, though it still complained about the surplice. A passage inserted in the second edition makes the change of emphasis explicit. 'Neither is the controversie betwixt

---

1 This becomes clear from the harking back to the vestiarian question by all parties in the 'Admonition' controversy. Unfortunately we do not know the numbers involved, and in the nature of the case we can never know how many conformed against their will after an unofficial warning from Bishop or Archdeacon. On balance I think it right to regard the vestiarian question as trivial because Bishops, Admonitioners and nearly everybody at the time said it was. Exceptions were Sampson and Humphrey (above, n. 1, p. 119).

2 They were specially common tactics of the Levellers, who though a secular movement grew out of a radical puritan milieu; see H. N. Brailsford, *The Levellers and the English Revolution* (ed. Christopher Hill, Stanford, 1961).

3 Owen Chadwick, *The Victorian Church*, Pt. 1, p. 215f.

them and us as they wold beare the world in hand, as for a cap, a tippet, or a surplesse, but for great matters concerning a true ministerie and regiment of the churche, according to the word.'[1] The *Admonition* despite the disadvantage of being anonymous did something to give leadership to the party and pull it together, to set guidelines. It was the first manifesto of puritanism (as W. H. Frere called it), the first important and widely-read document to refer to puritans (under that name) as 'us'. It led directly to the Admonition Controversy between Thomas Cartwright and John Whitgift,[2] in which early puritanism found its classic expression and Anglican anti-puritanism its earliest expression. 'Martin Marprelate' took up cudgels in the same affair, and Hooker in the *Laws of Ecclesiastical Polity* was still consciously answering Cartwright.[3] Every corruption of the old church, or of the establishment, which puritans as a body objected to (not counting the points that sectaries divided about) was given an airing in this debate, and its main thrust was where the main thrust of the movement was to be – for a generation – on the contrast between the Presbyterian system with its godly, yet loving and charitable, discipline on the one hand, and the old rigid authoritarianism of the prelates and the canon law courts on the other. It is a pity that the two sides did not find better champions – both Cartwright and Whitgift were intolerably narrow-minded, and their debate was conducted with little courtesy for each other and no consideration for the reader – but their partisanship does at least throw the differences between their positions into strong relief. We get a kind of new light on the vestiarian controversy itself when Whitgift taunts Cartwright about the fairweather sympathizers who adopt the party badges out of fashion:

I might improve your wearing of a turkey gown and a hat, bycause that kind of apparel being a token of such persons, as mislike the gowne and the square cap, and pretende preciseness above the rest, is notwithstanding commonly worne of such as in other places than in London, both weare and like the other, and be precise neither in lyfe nor doctrine.[4]

Whitgift is even more revealing on what the word 'puritan' conveyed in 1572 – which was not very different from what it conveys four hundred years later:

[1] W. H. Frere and C. E. Douglas (eds), *Puritan Manifestoes*, p. 36. n. 3.
[2] D. J. McGinn, *The Admonition Controversy* (New Brunswick, N.Y., 1949). This deals only with the interchanges between Cartwright and Whitgift.
[3] Hence the marginal references to 'T.C.'.
[4] J. Whitgift, *Defence of the Answer*, p. 731.

but in deede the conditions and qualities of the Phariseys doo moste aptely agree wyth the authours of these libelles and theyr adherentes: for the Phariseyes didde all that they did, to be seene of men, and sought the commendation of the common people...and so doo they: The Phariseys when they fasted, disfygured theyr faces: and these walkyng in the streates, hang downe their heades, looke austerely, and in companie sighe muche, and seldome or never laugh.[1]

Cartwright was stung by this, and took the description to himself, complaining that Whitgift had called 'us' Pharisees. Whitgift had gone on

Some of them meeting their olde acquayntance, beeyng godlie Preachers, have not onely refused to salute them, but spitte in theyr faces, wishyng the plague of God to lyghte upon them, and saying that they were damned, and that God had taken his spirite from them, and all this bycause they did weare a cap.[2]

This Cartwright refused to believe, and did not try to defend. Cartwright was concerned to turn the wrath of his own side onto worthier objects of hatred than mere wearers of the official dress. It is hard to say how far he succeeded.

Cartwright's most impassioned eloquence was called forth by the severity of the bishops and their officers in enforcing the *minutiae* of outworn rules and regulations on their brethren. Whitgift retorted that the real persecutors were the puritans themselves, and that they were crying before they were hurt. He took the opportunity of reviving two ancient anecdotes, a story about a wife who beat her husband and cried out to make the neighbours believe that she was being beaten, and one about a thief who avoided discovery by shouting 'Stay the thief!' Cartwright was offended by this levity:

Sed etiam quodam in loco facetus esse voluisti, Deus bone, quam te illud non decet. Heere M. doctor was disposed to make hym selfe and hys reader mery, but it is wyth the bagpipe or countrey mirth, not wyth the Harpe or Lute, whych the learned were wont to handle. For he hath packed up together the olde tale of the curst wyfe, and of the theefe that toke away the priestes purse, very familiar and homely geare: It might peradventure make M. doctor hoppe about the house, but the learned and the wyse can not daunce by thys instrument[3]

This quarrel was duly pursued through the *Defence of the Answer*

1 J. Whitgift, *Answer to the Admonition* Appendix, 'A brief ansere to certayn Pamphlets', Nn. iii, verso – iv. Harry Porter, *Puritanism in Tudor England*, pp. 3–4, quotes other portions of the passage.
2 J. Whitgift *loc. cit.*; Thomas Cartwright, *Reply to an Answer*, p. 177.
3 Thomas Cartwright, *Reply to an Answer*, p. 156.

128

and the *Second Reply*, though there was little to say after Whitgift's marginal comment: 'But what divinitie call you this? alacke poore spite at the bagpipe.'[1]

This acid interchange gives the flavour of the whole argument pretty well, and casts a light on the relationship of Cartwright and Whitgift. It is guesswork that it conveys the atmosphere of the wider party strife. On the subject of persecution, which of them was right? Reluctantly, I think one would have to say that at this point Cartwright had more to complain of.

If an ecclesiastical subject of a bishop did not observe the various laws he was supposed to observe, and if he was found out and disregarded all warnings, he could lose his licence to preach, if he had one, or to officiate as a curate; he could be suspended from all sacred functions; and ultimately he could be excommunicated and perhaps might have to spend some time in the bishop's prison before being admitted to penance. More importantly, if he was beneficed the next sanction after suspension was deprivation of the benefice, and suspension itself involved the burden of paying a substitute to perform the duties which the suspended clergyman was forbidden to perform. All this was slow and difficult because it had to go through the 'due process' of the ecclesiastical courts, which I have described already.[2] It existed as a possible threat hanging over the puritan's head. If it happened, it was a grievance. From the bishops' point of view it was excessively difficult to make it happen as often as it ought. The bishops therefore tried to use their general canonical authority to make the system work, thereby creating new grievances.

In particular, the bishops acting concertedly as a body had adopted the policy of requiring all clergy, or in practice all clergy suspected of puritan principles, to subscribe a declaration that there was nothing in the Book of Common Prayer 'repugnant in itself to the word of God', and that the subscriber would himself use the book and observe the orders of the church. This was the situation when the *Admonition* came out in 1572, and it was one incidental purpose both of the *Admonition* and of Cartwright in the ensuing controversy to show that something in the prayer-book *was* repugnant to the word of God; or at least that an honest and god-fearing man could reasonably find it impossible to say in conscience that nothing was. The bishops may have hoped that they were choosing the least objectionable language in their power. What they actually achieved was to instigate a search of the prayer-book for details to object to.

---

[1] Whitgift, *Defence of the Answer*, p. 707.   [2] Above, pp. 18, 19.

Naturally the puritans could come up with several; at this point perhaps one detail can serve for all. The clearest possible case where the prayer-book was repugnant to the word of God was where the prayer-book misquoted the Bible. In the proper gospels for two Sundays – second after Easter and twentieth after Trinity – a phrase was inserted at the beginning, 'Christ (or Jesus), said to his disciples'. In the first case (John, 10.14) the whole phrase is an interpolation, in the second (Matthew, 22.1) it is an adaptation, but in both cases the last audience named was the Pharisees, therefore the teaching in question was *not* addressed to the disciples. As biblical exegesis this does not deserve much attention; as a response to a challenge to find something un-biblical in the Anglican liturgy it was the best anybody could do, and it went on cropping up until the Hampton Court Conference,[1] after which the point was actually conceded and in later editions the offending words were dropped.

Many, however, who were unable to point to specific contradictions between the two books, were unable in conscience to subscribe in the form the bishops wanted. By refusal if they were beneficed they risked suspension and deprivation, or if they were only ordinands they lost all chance of proceeding to orders. They are surely entitled to respect.[2] The demand for subscription, carrying consequences on refusal that were likely to be dire and immediate, was a much tougher test than the surplice business had been. Unfortunately it is not possible to be sure what considerations decided them to refuse, not because they did not offer reasons but because they offered too many.

The *Admonition* leapt to the defence of those who refused to subscribe; appended to the main text of all editions was 'A view of Popishe abuses yet remaining in the Englishe Church, for which Godly Ministers have refused to subscribe'; I may note in passing that if the authors by that time had been able to say 'godly ministers have been deprived', they would undoubtedly have done so. It can be doubted whether the Admonitioners really spoke for the ministers concerned, because some of the arguments they lend them have singularly little to do with the matter. Under the first article, which was the one stating that the prayer-book contained nothing repugnant to the word of God, they gave a long, wandering and rhetorical attack on the book itself or on the way in which its ceremonies were

[1] BM. Add. 38492 f. 44.
[2] The demand for subscription was formalized by Whitgift as Archbishop in his 'Three Articles' (not to be confused with his doctrinal 'Lambeth Articles'). The three are essentially the same as the earlier set.

conducted, in thirteen sections by their own count, some of it valuable historical evidence on other points but quite unhelpful on why ministers could not subscribe that article. From section Fourteen on they lose sight of the prayer-book, on the excuse that the ordinal was part of it, and talk about the manifold abuses of the bishops: '19. What shoulde we speake of the Archbishops court, sith all men knowe it...' What, indeed, since it is not mentioned anywhere in the prayer-book?[1] '20. And as for the comissaries court, that is but a pettie little stinking ditche, that floweth oute of that former great puddle...'[2] and so on. These digressions, including the one just quoted, are not unimportant; the abuses named were real grievances, and very possibly real abuses, though they had nothing to do with the article of subscription.

The second article required the subscriber to agree that the orders, about ceremonies and so on, 'appointed by publique authoritie' (such as the Queen's Injunctions or Parker's Advertisements) ought to be obeyed. The third concerned the Thirty-nine Articles. The Ad-monitioners left them almost alone, no doubt having exhausted them-selves. In the later controversy, the articles of subscription came up again. Whitgift in the 'Answer' of course needed to answer the Admonitioners on this subject. Thus, the *Admonition* had objected to the word 'repugnant', 'Wherin they deceive them selves, standing so much uppon this woorde repugnant, as thoughe nothing were repugnant, or against the word of God, but that which is expressely forbidden by plain commaundement...'[3] which is what the phras-eology chosen by the bishops does in fact imply. To this, Whitgift comments plaintively and justifiably, 'But you do not...let us understande, what you thinke this worde (repugnant) doth signifie.'[4] The *Admonition* pointed to the rubric after the Nicene Creed in the Communion. 'After the Crede, if there be no sermon, shal follow one of the homelies already set forth, or hereafter to be set forth by commune aucthoritie' (text of 1552, unchanged). How could the godly minister be sure, when he subscribed, that public authority at some subsequent date might not set forth a homily which contained something contrary to the word of God? Whitgift at first was content to say that nobody was under any obligation to read a given homily. Cartwright thought the point a more serious one: 'it is not meete, nay, it is merely unlawfull, to subscribe to a blancke',[5] which reduced Whitgift to, 'If you be disposed to quarrell,

---

[1] Frere and Douglas, *Puritan Manifestoes*, p. 32.   [2] *Ibid.* p. 33.
[3] *Ibid.* p. 21.   [4] Whitgift, *Answer to the Admonition*, p. 156.
[5] Cartwright *quoted* Whitgift, *Defence of the Answer*, p. 716.

it is an easie matter to picke out occasions, but your suspicion is without cause, and I thinke a modest protestation in that poynt would not be refused.'[1] The subscriber could say at the time that he did not mean his subscription to extend to cover unwritten homilies, and if he was polite about it the bishop would probably not mind. This was probably true, though by descending to such a common-sense level Whitgift was breaking the rules of the controversy game.

As these examples may serve to show, the argument about subscription was largely about words.[2] This was fair enough, since the whole concept of subscription to articles is one that ascribes all power and virtue to verbal formulae. If the puritans hunted the letter more sedulously than their opponents, they were under attack and it was their opponents who had powers of coercion. Whitgift's plea for favourable construction is hardly fair in the circumstances.

In the realm of words, however, Whitgift was right in supposing that the puritans might win concessions. In one or two matters of detail they eventually did.[3] The case is otherwise with actions. For controversial purposes a godly preacher might pretend to mind terribly about the gospel for the twentieth Sunday after Trinity. He probably did mind terribly about having to wear a surplice; about having to make the sign of the cross in baptism; about using the ring in the marriage ceremony; about the fact that his people were supposed to receive the Communion kneeling instead of sitting. These, and others like them (but these were the most often mentioned) were the points on which the sincere puritan was most likely to be driven by conscience to an overt act of defiance. It would not always be a very risky act. Subscription to the articles was a much greater threat to a minister's livelihood, and it is in the context of subscription to the articles that a puritan could be most easily accused – either by a right-wing conformist or by a left-wing sectary – of conforming outwardly and against his conscience from base mercenary motives. Whitgift had used that accusation:

If your doings proceede in dede from a good conscience, then leave that living and place, which bindeth you to those things that be against your conscience, for why shold you strive with the disquietnesse both of your

---

[1] Whitgift *loc. cit.*

[2] In this, no doubt, the argument was merely concealing a deeper antipathy to the book as a whole, and possibly in some cases (though it is early days for this) to the whole idea of a set liturgy. At this stage, however, and in the context of subscription, the avowed objections were to details and even to tiny details.

[3] At Hampton Court; notably the exclusion from the Prayer Book of older references to lay baptism.

selves and others, to kepe that living which by lawe you cannot, excepte you offende against your consciences? what honestie is there, to sweare to statutes and lawes, and when you have so done contrarie to your oth to break them, and yet still to remain under them, and enioy that place which requireth obedience and subiection to them?[1]

Cartwright was himself blameless in the matter since he was never beneficed and probably never ordained, but he had to reply: 'What conscience is there that bindeth a man to departe from hys living in that place where he lyketh not of all the orders whych are there used? Is it not enough to abstaine from them...when as the reformation is not in hys power?'[2] which is coming very close to the real issue of conscience which faced puritan ministers and which continues to face minority clergy in highly-structured churches. In the Anglican church, in the nineteenth century especially, both sides of the argument became drearily familiar. Unfortunately Cartwright almost immediately lost the thread (how he ever got the reputation for being an effective disputant I cannot imagine), but he did suggest that it is a minister's duty to stay where he can do good, rather than simply leave the field open for the corrupt party – a good point and an interesting parallel with the catholic seminary priests, who had to run the moral risk of 'equivocation' and deception if they wanted to stay at large and at work.

Tougher puritans refused subscription. If they already had a parish this might or might not mean that they eventually lost it, after the cumbersome ecclesiastical machinery had had time to get rolling. (They could not be deprived for refusal by itself, but refusal implied an intention of not observing the law, and drew attention to whatever they were doing.) In any case they took that risk. If they had not already got a parish, refusal could stop their career right there. Milder puritans did not refuse. Some who subscribed were persuaded by Cartwright's logic or the motions of their own hearts that a higher duty bade them disregard what they had subscribed. They wore their Geneva gown at the public prayers, they omitted the sign of the cross, they taught their people not to kneel. I find it hard to imagine what they did about the ring in matrimony, but if they could arrange matters there would be no ring.

At this point of course the canon law courts came into it; those unreformed, unspiritual, unbrotherly courts which were such a blot on the English reformation. Also those slow and inefficient courts,

---

[1] Whitgift, *Answer to the Admonition*, p. 147.
[2] Cartwright, *Reply to an Answer*, p. 156.

which I have already described. The puritan objections to them included objections of substance, not wholly inspired by partisan feeling – excommunication and absolution dealt out by a lay judge on purely bureaucratic criteria *were* a crying disgrace. But the ineffectiveness of the antiquated system was something that the typical ordinary puritan would have to be glad about. In the hopes of giving him less cause for gladness, authority resorted to two expedients above others. A new court – High Commission – was superimposed on the old structure with the particular task of forcing puritans to conform, and bishops, archdeacons and all took to strengthening their own hands by freer and more frequent use of an old canon-law device, the oath *ex officio mero*.

High Commission was authorized by the Act of Supremacy, 1559, Clause 8:

And that your Highness...shall have full power and authority, by virtue of this act, by letters patent under the great seal of England to assign, name and authorize...such persons or person...to exercise, use, occupy and execute under your Highness, your Heirs and successors, all manner of jurisdictions, privileges and preeminences in any wise touching or concerning any spiritual or ecclesiastical jurisdiction within these your realms[1]

The Act of Uniformity of the same year spoke of the Queen acting 'with the advice of her commissioners appointed and authorized under the great seal of England for causes ecclesiastical'[2] and therefore presumed the existence of such a body of commissioners (they were not given any title in the earlier act). This all looks 'erastian' enough to annoy anybody who got his ideas from Geneva, but actually the main body of puritans were reluctant to quarrel either with the Royal Supremacy (as they understood it) or with Parliament. However, the 1559 acts did not describe or necessitate a new court of law. As long as Parker was Archbishop of Canterbury Elizabeth used him to give effect to her will and to incur any necessary odium for so doing. It was in Archbishop Grindal's time, and because of his unreadiness to crack down on puritans, that High Commission arose in the form that made it hateful. Its first major task was to put down 'prophesyings' when Grindal refused to do so and was suspended from his metropolitical jurisdiction in consequence. (The Commission in those years also had to do everything, of a non-sacramental nature, that an Archbishop of Canterbury normally has to do. In an ordinary vacancy this would have fallen to the Bishop of London as Dean of the

[1] 1 Eliz. I, cap. 1; here quoted from G. R. Elton, ed. *Tudor Constitution*, doc. 184.
[2] 1 Eliz. I, cap. 2; Elton, *Tudor Constitution*, doc. 195.

Province, but as this was Aylmer, one of the commissioners, it made little difference.) From the 1570s the High Commission was a court whose powers overrode all other ecclesiastical courts. There were local high commissions for the North, the Counties Palatine and elsewhere,[1] but the London one could override these as well. Its most prominent members were bishops; those who became most famous in the rôle were Whitgift, Bancroft and Laud. In this period, when a puritan attacks the bishops of England, as distinct from attacking the institution of episcopacy itself, and as distinct from attacking any individual bishop, as like as not he is attacking them for being active on the Commission rather than for falling down on their pastoral duties or lording it in Parliament. All of these were good reasons for punning on 'bishop' and 'bite-sheep'; an ageing quip by this time, it was also a favourite among the seminarians of Douai.

In puritan polemic 'the bishops' were the enemy within the gates, the betrayers of the Reformation, the source of all bad policy in religious matters and the engines of oppression. In this last capacity they were most effective when they were commissioners. Polemicists did not distinguish; in early years, at least, the High Commission was not often singled out, by name, for special dispraise. It was more convenient to castigate 'the bishops' as the authors of everything that was wrong with the Church including the High Commission itself, rather than call in question the authority of a body that was clearly based on the Royal Supremacy. If, in the end, it proved easier to abolish the High Commission than either the bishops or the royal supremacy, this is certainly in part because the court had aroused the ire of secular lawyers who were not particularly wedded to the cause of godliness, but who resented and feared the High Commission for much the same reasons that they came to resent and fear Star Chamber. As much as anything else the unpopularity of the court, outside the puritan faction, and therefore the likeliest source of public sympathy for the faction itself in its sufferings under the court, was to be explained not by what it did but how it did it, by arbitrary procedure and above all else by the oath *ex officio mero*.

The bishops, and the ordinary canon-law courts, used such an oath on occasion. Following the judicial tradition, ultimately Roman, which prevailed on the Continent and in university faculties of law, the canon law courts accepted a duty to establish the truth, and to

---

[1] Oddly enough we do not yet know how many there were; local commissions issued for many counties or dioceses, but may have been merely temporary. The point is discussed by Manning, *Religion and Society in Elizabethan Sussex*, p. 30, n. 1.

interrogate witnesses to that end, rather than rely as the Common Law did on the presentation of two views of the facts by the opposing parties, each producing his own evidence and seeking to impugn that of his adversary. Technically, the method whereby the canon-law, or civil-law, judge sought to discover the facts was known as the 'inquisitorial process', which makes it sound more sinister to our ears than is altogether fair. When a judge interrogated a witness, he might (he did not always) require the witness to swear an oath; and anybody could be called on to give evidence on the mere ground that he knew something about it, a category that naturally included the accused. A judge could require the truth, on oath, from someone whom he suspected of a crime, when he, the judge, was conducting the case on behalf of the court, by virtue of his office – hence *ex officio* – as distinct from the times when a case was conducted by a private person, or rather by his proctor on his private behalf ('instance').

The practice of tendering such an oath was well established in the church courts, in England as in every country of Western Christendom. There were supposed to be certain limitations on it, but in practice these were up to the discretion of the judge, and were no protection. A similar practice obtained in Star Chamber, presumably on the strength of the statute '*Pro Camera Stellata*'.[1] Apart from tradition, and authoritarian Roman common sense with its indifference to the individual, it would be possible to defend the use of the oath in church courts on religious, pastoral grounds. If you were prepared to ignore totally the gulf between theory and practice, you could argue that the whole object of ecclesiastical jurisprudence was not to find and punish culprits but to diagnose, and cure, spiritual ills which endangered the sinner's soul. (The argument had been available for torture and for burning at the stake; in the sixteenth century it was coming to seem old-fashioned, and as a matter of fact it was seldom relied on by the High Commission.) The objections to the oath were basically an appeal to the contrary tradition of the Common Law and to the supposed principles – humanitarian or libertarian – which lay behind it. The actual, historical, origins of the Common Law and its curious procedures were then understood by nobody, and to professional defenders of that tradition they were becoming in this age a very vexed question indeed.[2] Religious writers who

---

[1] See Elton, *Tudor Constitution*, p. 159f and doc. 78.
[2] J. G. A. Pocock, *The Ancient Constitution and the Feudal Law* (Cambridge, 1957), *passim*.

wanted to denounce the *ex officio* oath were content, on the whole, to talk in vague terms about the immemorial liberties of Englishmen and the abstract unkindness of asking anyone to accuse himself.

Incidentally, it would be accurate enough but not entirely fair to add that Calvinist church courts, where they existed, showed no hesitation in demanding self-incrimination, and it would be hard to imagine how anyone expected to enforce the 'godly discipline' without it. It must be realized that the canon-law courts which the English puritans encountered and objected to, especially including High Commission, were courts of a thoroughly ordinary, professional kind employing their own equivalents of tipstaves, serjeants and attorneys, collecting fees and fines and relying on the methods of secular coercion; their judges might be laymen, and in any case were chosen for the same qualities as lay judges, for their technical learning and not for any particular holiness of life, pastoral zeal or spiritual insight. It was impossible to regard the work of such bodies as the remedial treatment of sick souls, and the official use of language suggesting that this was their function could only strike a normally serious minded person as a ghastly travesty. None of this was the case with kirk sessions; however ignorant, arrogant, bigoted or plain brutal they might be, they remained, and remain, essentially spiritual bodies bent on a pastoral task.

The oath *ex officio* was not a strong point in the Anglican church's ideological armour. But it was a very important shot in its locker. It had the inestimable merit, from the authoritarian point of view, of eliminating all the preliminary steps normally necessary to prepare any kind of case against anyone for anything. If you merely had been given to understand that a certain minister was suspected by somebody of unreliability unspecified, you could oblige the man himself to fill in all the details. You could then proceed to discipline him according to his own admissions. The method evidently worked. There is no body of puritan casuistry justifying equivocation or mental reservation in such cases. Indeed it would have been hard for them to develop such means of evasion after the round and uncompromising way in which they had condemned the same devices on the part of the papists. It would seem however that the resort to an oath was crucial. The preciser sort of brethren might perhaps sometimes be found putting ingenious constructions on a form of subscription or a merely secular undertaking, but the puritan conscience, borne down by the weight of the Third Commandment, could in no wise trifle with the sacredness of an oath.

They were accordingly very unwilling to take one. In the logic of their position they might have quoted the text, 'Swear not at all; but let your yea be yea, and your nay nay',[1] except that this would have made them look like the Anabaptists, whom everybody condemned. In common with all the respectable reformation, the Calvinist school allowed oaths when required by the lawful magistrate. The puritan's best hope, therefore, was to make it appear that the authority under which an incriminating oath was required was in some way not lawful.

In party polemic, the whole argument against bishops, as popish usurpers, as unbiblical, unapostolic or even unpatriotic could be dragged in here.[2] In tighter corners, tighter arguments were needed. As mentioned above, it was distinctly unwise to question the lawfulness of the High Commission itself; the objection had to be to the procedure. This was getting outside the sphere of competence of the ordinary godly preacher, and it fell to the common lawyers to take up the cudgels. (This some were ready enough to do, not necessarily from puritan sympathies but from antipathy to Canon Law.) The godly preacher was still left with the problem of deciding whether to take the oath when it came to the point, and of facing the consequences. There can be no doubt that the oath was felt as a very severe grievance; it could leave the individual puritan alone and powerless in face of an accuser who was also his judge. It was not simply an issue invented to make the best of a party's case and to win sympathy, but it had considerable potential that way as well.

In discussing the whole question of the puritans' quarrel with authority in the English church of their day, it is necessary to remember that they had positive aims. They did not merely want to be left alone, but to change other people. This means that any moderates the party might contain had two separate sets of problems: how to do or leave undone what their consciences required of them to do or to leave undone with as little trouble or danger as possible, and how to put into effect as much of their programme as they could manage. The two might conceivably lead a man's conscience contrary ways. If a minister wanted to give puritanism a chance in his parish he had to contrive to keep the parish; it did no good to get himself deprived or imprisoned in no matter how excellent a cause. We have seen Cartwright make this point against Whitgift, and tactically it is a very strong one. A true party man with a revolution to accomplish

---

[1] Matthew 5. 34, 37; James 5. 12.
[2] Thus, these are all mixed together by authors like 'Martin Marprelate'.

would have to be very moderate indeed, very lukewarm in the cause, if he was mainly concerned about a decent personal chance of staying out of hot water. He also had to consider, and so must we, what the chances were of working inside the system to achieve the aims of the party. Only when it became clear how far this could be done would it be clear at what point the system had to be finally rejected and openly defied.

9
Half a loaf

The party of the sincere gospel could feel, in 1559, that it had secured the single thing most immediately necessary – the liberty, more or less, of gospel preaching – and that the rest of a godly reformation might be expected to follow, even though some rags of popery were suffered for the time out of respect for old-fashioned feelings. Some even then, must have thought that this respect was more tender than it needed to be, and amounted to indulging ignorant superstition or mere idle ceremoniousness – candlesticks and copes in the Chapel Royal and similar mummery intended, so the godly imagined, only as a discreet camouflage, for suspicious foreign eyes, of ultimately Calvinian intentions. Men who had seen in exile the face of a church fully and sincerely reformed could not witness Elizabeth's early temporizing without pain, but they were borne up by the hope that their embarrassment and the Queen's perilous flirting with forbidden idolatries would not last long. This trust and this hope were shared not only by those who could later be aligned clearly on the puritan side, but by returned exiles in high places like Jewel or Sandys.

There was thus to start with no reason why puritans should trouble the ambiguous religious peace of the 1560s. At the same time, they would not be true to their mission as reformers if they took no steps to prepare for the fuller and more systematic reformation that the country, they charitably supposed, was being gently educated up to by the cautious policy of the Queen. If opportunity offered, it was clearly a minister's duty to introduce his people to as much of the true life of the reformed church as he could contrive, in ceremonies and in discipline as well as in preaching and teaching.

In times of absolute persecution, such as Mary's reign had been, the true Christians could legitimately separate from the worship maintained by the State and form their own secret conventicles, the true church 'under the Cross', and these of course they would be free to run in any fashion that seemed good to them within the limits of the possible. In Mary's reign some courageous souls had formed such a church in London, as well as the churches formed in Frankfurt and elsewhere by the exiles (though it was the destiny of these latter to have the more profound effect on puritanism, doubtless because they were public and their doings became matters of record). No protestant would suggest that the members of such a group were less respectable than their conforming neighbours, though in an obvious sense they were more radical. They were not, even in Mary's reign, a revolutionary cell, and when a better day dawned they thankfully accepted it. A secret and separating conventicle formed in such circumstances was a very special case. Its members differed from those protestants who avoided in any way contravening the law only in their greater dedication to the common cause; they could claim to stand, in the esteem of other protestants, somewhere between the martyrs and the exiles.

The case was quite different, everybody or nearly everybody agreed, under a Mother in Israel such as Elizabeth. Separation from the body, even on the plausible ground of seeking a more apostolic standard of doctrine, life and worship was an act of schism when the body itself was, however inadequately, a product of reformation. Thus the Elizabethan puritan was bound to condemn the odd groups of zealots which occasionally arose – even before Brown and Barrow – and set up purified *ecclesiolae* of their own in conscious condemnation of the prevaricating and half-reformed Establishment. Puritans could be scathing about the defects of the Establishment precisely because it was their mission to remedy these defects, which implied, ultimately, loyalty to the Establishment. Their language (though it may not always have sounded that way) was the language of charitable admonition, at the utmost that of righteous rebuke to erring brethren, not of war propaganda.

Separation from the body was schism and no part of the 'platform'; but the life of the body did not everywhere and always involve all the imperfections that gave pain to a precisian, and it was sometimes possible to contrive a good deal of the outward face of a church sincerely reformed on the Continental plan, without separation. In the whole province of York, for instance, there was official support for 'Prophesyings' and official connivance at departures from the ceremonial standards of the second year of King Edward VI.[1] The surviving

---

[1] Parker's *Advertisements* did not apply to the Northern province, and Grindal and Sandys as Archbishops supported prophesyings. High Commission only attempted to put an end to this under James I. For the North-West, see R. C. Richardson, *Puritanism in North-West England*.

medieval corruptions of the half-reformed church might themselves prove a convenience. In odd privileged pockets, extra-parochial or extra-diocesan 'peculiars', donative cures or other special cases where for any reason the ordinary course of ecclesiastical discipline did not hold sway, puritans who would never have allowed such anomalies to exist if they had had the ordering of the church could sometimes take advantage of them.[1] Thus, the Inns of Court enjoyed such an immunity, and Walter Travers was enabled to carry out his liturgical experiments by reason of it. But such occasional positions of favour could hardly do more than whet a puritan appetite for better things. In themselves they were of little account. It is significant that Travers is famous for his public controversy with Hooker and his alliance with Cartwright while his liturgical innovations (rather good ones from a twentieth-century point of view) are as forgotten as his long years of honoured and useful activity in Ireland.[2]

From the point of view of the good party man, who hoped one day to see the party triumph, and in the meantime wanted to be reassured that the Church of England did genuinely belong in the reformed camp, the most hopeful exceptions to the general rule must have been those few places where a concatenation of unusual circumstances allowed a local establishment on 'platform' lines to be set up, in vivid contrast to the Establishment proper, but neither disowning nor disowned by it. This happy state of affairs could be seen in English congregations abroad, most notably at Antwerp (and later Middelburg), in foreign congregations in England, in the Channel Isles, in Northamptonshire where for a brief period extraordinary co-operation between Bishop, magistrates and godly preachers a reformation worthy of the Rhineland if not of Switzerland seemed an accomplished fact, and in Bury St Edmunds where something less far-reaching on the same lines was attempted, and proved just as sore a trial to the authorities when they tried to suppress it. All these differed in detail, but had it in common that they allowed people who quite correctly regarded themselves as members of the Church of England and not dissenters from it to practise something very like a 'Presbyterian' or at any rate a 'Genevan' church order in the reign of Elizabeth I and with the backing, in some sense, of her authority.

[1] An outstanding example was the parish of the Minories in London, described by Gareth Owen in two articles (presenting nearly the same facts): '"The Liberty of the Minories", – a study in Elizabethan religious radicalism', in *East London Papers* 8 (1965), and 'A Nursery of Elizabethan Nonconformity, 1567–72', in *Journal of Ecclesiastical History* 17 (1966).

[2] S. J. Knox, *Walter Travers: paragon of Elizabethan Puritanism*.

Of course the puritans who could take advantage of these exceptions in order to live the kind of church life they preferred without disobeying the law were a small minority, even a handful. I am suggesting that they functioned rather as morale-builders than as refuges, and as such they were more useful to revolutionaries than to moderates, but most useful of all to moderate revolutionaries. The success of the one country – Russia, Cuba, or wherever – where the revolution has really and truly occurred, may be an inspiration to the dedicated to go on fighting, but it is also a comfort to the peace-loving well-wisher, who can hope that the world will ultimately be won by the sheer moral force of such an example. It would I think be these people rather than the true militants who suffered the greatest agony of soul when, eventually, either Elizabeth or James suppressed every one of the puritan oases I have mentioned.

(By the time the last of them was suppressed – the Channel Isles – such exceptions were being argued as a precedent for Virginia, and not long afterwards the greatest and most lasting of Anglican Genevas was founded in New England. I cannot afford to pursue that part of the story too far, but will pause here to say that quite a number of people who were active in promoting puritan colonies had no intention of colonizing them, and the example of Massachusetts as a shop-window exhibit of what puritanism could accomplish was valued, down to the nineteenth century, by many in England who were content not to enjoy its blessings in their own persons.)

The case of the English church in Antwerp is particularly interesting because its founders seem to have used a certain amount of conscious, if pious, duplicity in setting it up on the 'reformed' model. It was not a foreign-language congregation of the local protestant church, like the later Scotch church in Rotterdam or the contemporary Dutch church in London; strictly it was a chaplaincy of the Company of Merchant Adventurers (which is why it moved to Middelburg when their staple moved) and was established under diplomatic auspices. Its status was thus something like that of the first English churches in India, or the present-day English churches in Paris and Rome. There was no obvious reason why its discipline and ceremonies should differ, any more than these differ, from the church in the Mother country. Moreover it does not appear that the Merchant Adventurers themselves were anxious it should. It does appear that Elizabeth's ambassador in the Low Countries, an intimate in puritan circles, conducted the initial negotiations in such a way that the new church was required, as a condition of its existence, to conform to the orders of the local

THE PURITANS

protestants.[1] In this instance it is clear beyond doubt that a condition
ostensibly imposed by the local authorities for their own reasons was
actually suggested to them by the same Englishmen who were soliciting
the favour conditionally granted, and it is also clear beyond serious
doubt that they could have had the favour without the condition. The
arrangements were eventually confirmed by a catholic governor.
Undoubtedly the ambassador was acting in the interests of a puritan
faction, and not taking his own government into his full confidence.
The episode is reminiscent of the first round of the 'Troubles at
Frankfurt';[2] there, the English were allowed a church of their own
provided they conformed to the orders of the French congregation,
which had only just arrived and from England at that, and there was no
obvious reason why one refugee congregation should thus be erected
over another. The English took this as authority to be as protestant as
the Frenchmen, but did not feel obliged actually to consult them.
When other Englishmen, arriving later, protested and demanded the
use of their own customs, the magistrates immediately permitted this;
it was plainly something they had never been asked for before.[3] It looks
as if what historians have called the 'Knoxian' party at Frankfurt had
attempted the manoeuvre of getting their own way by persuading the
local authorites to impose it on them under a misapprehension. Again,
when William Whittingham (who was certainly one of the moving
spirits at Frankfurt) became chaplain to the English forces at the siege
of Le Havre in 1562, he followed the practices of the local (i.e. the
Huguenot) church in his ministrations, putting his own rather large
interpretations upon them. (The Huguenots, who might approve of his
sermons, would not approve of his un-clerical behaviour in personally
bearing arms.) The plea that the Antwerp church was obliged to
follow the customs of local protestants on the insistence of the Government was peculiarly impudent when that government was not protestant, and even if we did not know for certain that this was the case
(which we do) we might have suspected that this insistence was
manufactured.

What the sincere party achieved by this devious machination was
not a lot. The Antwerp church was headed by two successive ministers,
Walter Travers and Thomas Cartwright, who were not episcopally
ordained and could not have ministered legally in England.[4] Both men

1 A. F. S. Pearson, *Thomas Cartwright*, pp. 170–5.
2 Arber, ed., *Troubles at Frankfort*, pp. 23–4.
3 Further on this see Martin Simpson, article cited above, n. 2, p. 121.
4 Pearson, *Thomas Cartwright*, p. 334. Travers was ordained 'presbyterally' specially to accept
this post, by ministers of the Dutch reformed church; a reasonable procedure given the

were chosen primarily to be preachers of the Word, and seem to have considered that they had no other duties that mattered very much. If discipline was maintained at all it was presumably maintained by the Merchant Adventurers under whatever kind of extra-territorial juris-diction their company was permitted to exercise on Netherlands soil. As for the Prayer Book, naturally Travers and Cartwright did not use it, but eventually an officer of the company, who cannot possibly have been a party to the original curious arrangement, demanded to know why an allegedly English church did not employ the English form of service, and its use was actually enforced; an underling read the prayers while Cartwright remained silent and uncontaminated, later emerging to preach – a compromise that was resorted to by puritan parsons in many English parishes, and which, in time, the High Commission would duly attempt to suppress. After this compromise had been adopted, in fact, the Antwerp church enjoyed no privilege of purer polity and worship than could be enjoyed by any market town with a puritan lecturer, except that of course as long as Cartwright remained with them they had the benefit of his reputation.[1]

The *Ecclesia Anglantuerpiana* (Cartwright's name for it) was the best known and most nearly official of the English congregations abroad; indeed at this period the only other one to attain a regular existence was that of Geneva which was the asylum of admitted extremists and cannot concern us. Turning to the foreign congregations in England we can observe that though they enjoyed a reasonable amount of favour from Elizabeth's government and were suffered to write their own liturgies and govern themselves through their elected elders in the proper reformed fashion they were not the privileged institutions they had been in the days of King Edward.[2] There were, for the time being, fewer of them; the French weavers did not return to Glastonbury and almost the only congregation outside London was the one at Norwich. There were indeed French-language congregations at Rye and else-where in the Cinque Ports, and in Southampton, from early in Elizabeth's reign; but for different reasons they were peculiar. The church at Rye was a daughter foundation and subsidiary of the prot-estant church in Dieppe and did not become organizationally distinct

view of church polity held by Travers and the Dutch ministers alike. It cannot have been known at the time whether this would be recognized in England or not. When Travers was succeeded by Cartwright it is not clear what happened, but reading between the lines of his own far from straightforward account he was never ordained at all.
[1] But cf. BM Add. 28571 f. 169.
[2] F. A. Norwood, 'The Strangers' "Model Churches" in Sixteenth-century England', in *Reformation Studies*, ed. F. H. Littell (deals only with Edward's reign).

from it, though for some time after the Massacre of St Bartholemew it is likely that the Rye church rather than the Dieppe one was the headquarters. Other churches in the same locality, of which some evidence survives at Winchelsea and Sandwich, were presumably dependent offshoots of Rye, too tiny to function on their own and only made possible by its proximity, like cottage meetings in a Wesleyan circuit. Whether refugees or resident traders, these Frenchmen were clearly not regarded as a special case within the national church. Those at Southampton, on the other hand, were undoubtedly within the national church, and the only question was whether they were a special case. Although the majority of the membership were, probably, refugee Frenchmen and Walloons, the church was supposed to serve Channel Islanders also and was unequivocally under the jurisdiction of the Bishop of Winchester. According to later Huguenot tradition, services in this church followed the French Reformed rite until the eighteenth century by tacit allowance of the bishops.[1] In London there were French, Dutch and Italian churches, but the office of a central 'superintendent' once held by John à Lasco, was not revived. The refugee congregations were harmless, they might prove to be of some slight propaganda value and their presence established England – not an unmixed blessing – as the protector of oppressed protestants of all nations. But they were not, as they seem to have been at their first founding, living and working models of what a protestant community should be, erected for the edification of the country at large; pilot schemes for eventual imitations. At least, they were no longer so regarded by those who now occupied the seats of power. They were still a distinct improvement on the ordinary London parish church from the point of view of zealous reformers, for after all they did have elders and they did not have the Book of Common Prayer. Presumably they did not have surplices. They constituted the most encouraging sign, of anything legal and visible that went on in the metropolis, that England was bound on a course that would ultimately secure her full and godly reformation. To a puritan, the foreign congregations were experiments that *had* to succeed. Apart from that they were rather outside his ken. He could not belong to them. He was unlikely anyway to be edified by a sermon in Dutch, but neither was he free to experience the blessings of godly discipline by the 'signory' or 'consistory' in their fellowship.

At least, this was the case for most people. There were exceptions. The Italian protestant community in London was neither as large

[1] F. De Schickler, *Les Eglises du Réfuge en Angleterre*, vol. 1, cap. 7.

146

nor as ideologically sound as the French and Dutch, and could not run its church without a certain amount of outside help which might take remarkable forms. Thus, when after adopting the church order of the London French church (of 1561) they proceeded to set up a court of elders – which they only got around to in 1570 – of the six elders four were called (more or less) 'Michaele Blount', 'Gulielmo Vvintropio', 'Bartolomeo Uvarners', and 'Pietro Vuanduall'. (The last name occurs later as 'Vandwalle'.)[1] It is apparent that the election was not acceptable to some of the congregation, and this importation of English names was doubtless both an effect and a cause of division. Certainly, after the election had been reported to the general monthly meeting of the Strangers' Churches the support of that body was sought and obtained for the imposition of a sincerity test on the membership, in the form of a subscription to the statement of faith and church order: 'domandando a ciascheduno di sottoscriversi alla confessione che habbiamo nel fine del nostro catechismo, et ancora la procedura da noi tenuta nell' elettione de seniori e di diaconi.'[2] It is clear from the whole episode that members of this church thought themselves free to resign from it, and considerable efforts were undertaken to dissuade them. The membership was wide enough to include, besides the rather un-Italian names already noticed, one Bechman or Bichman, a Martin Wandersanden and a Paolo Typoots, besides a Farias and a Molinas who look, if anything, Spanish. It hardly seems credible that an Englishman who happened to like their style of churchmanship was equally free to join, but there are those unmistakably English elders. Presumably they could speak Italian.

The device of requiring everybody to bind themselves by subscription to accept the discipline of the congregation is a give-away. It clearly reveals both that that discipline was irksome to many members and not working smoothly, and also that the church could not count on the backing of the godly magistrate as in the true Genevan system – and even up to a point in the ordinary English parochial system – it could. Exactly the same device was resorted to at Middelburg, long after Cartwright's departure, when similar divisions rent the church; by then it was much more the church of an expatriate colony and much less that of the Merchant Adventurers, or things would hardly have been suffered to come to this pass. The Adventurers, indeed, were clearly hostile to this attempt to introduce godly discipline into their chapel.

[1] BM Add. 48096 (Yelverton MS 105) contains the minute book.
[2] Requiring everyone to subscribe the confession which we have at the end of our catechism, and also the procedure followed by us in the election of elders and deacons.

A form of subscription drawn up at Middelburg by Francis Johnson and pressed by him on the English residents was opposed by the local representative of the Merchant Adventurers in 1591. This latter, Thomas Ferrers, sent home a copy of the offending document with notes. Perhaps its most remarkable passage ran:

Wee doe acknowledge, that God in his ordinarie meanes for the bringinge us unto and keepinge us in this fayth of Christe, and an holie Obedience thereof, hath sett in his Churche teachinge and ruling Elders, Deacons, and Helpers: And that this his Ordinance is to continue unto the ende of the worlde aswell under Christian princes, as under heathen Magistrates.

Wee doe willinglie ioyne together to live as the Churche of Christe, watchinge one over another, and submittinge our selves unto them, to whom the Lorde Jesus committed the oversight of his Churche, guidinge and censuringe us accordinge to the rule of the worde of God.[1]

Johnson had given it as his opinion that anyone who signed would no longer be morally free to join any other church, in England or else-where, unless it was one in which this form of discipline was established.

Johnson was not in any useful sense a compromiser with the Elizabethan establishment. So far as lay in him, he had unchurched it. He was, however, taking advantage of an ambiguous situation in the expatriate church which was also available to those in Middelburg – and to those later in Massachusetts – who wished to practise the full puritan system while still considering themselves members of the Church of England.

The most fully official of all these half-way houses was the Eliza-bethan church in the Channel Isles. It had the advantages, for a time, of approval by the authorities of church and state; it was untroubled by any bishop; and it enjoyed the services of good Huguenot ministers and of Thomas Cartwright. It must sorrowfully be confessed on the other hand that considered as a demonstration of what the discipline could do to reform the morals of a community and set up the rule of earthly saints in godliness and mutual charity it was something less than a shining success. It was always bedevilled by weaknesses which arose from the same root causes as those which made the local reformation take a different turn from that in England. The islands were not a part of England, but were held by the Crown as the last vestiges of the Duchy of Normandy; they formed part of no English diocese but belonged, technically, to that of Coutances. (They had been transferred to Winchester by one of the anti-popes of the Great Schism, and returned to Coutances when the schism was healed.

[1] BM Add. 28571 f. 169.

Eventually they were again assigned to Winchester, but the bishop of that see was content to leave them alone until the time of Lancelot Andrews.) Episcopal authority had naturally been weak in the years when it had to be exercised across a permanently hostile frontier, and had been represented, after a fashion, by two 'deans of peculiar', one for Jersey and one for Guernsey and the rest. These were local parsons, dependent on an ordinary parish living. The ecclesiastical structure in some ways paralleled the civil; for purposes of day-to-day government the islands formed a couple of petty republics except insofar as they were dominated by the military.

The inhabitants traditionally lived by piracy, and were unpromising soil for the sincerity of the Gospel, though not more unpromising, it might be maintained, than the Scots or Genevans. Their small society was a natural breeding ground for feuds and intense personal rivalries. These were not much helped by the fact that the leading citizens all tended to alternate with each other in public office with responsibilities for law-enforcement, and in this age the office of Elder was added to those of bailiff, constable and the like.

To the English government the question of religion was bound up with security, and the neighbourhood of strongly papist Brittany was a matter of the highest concern. The royal governors had a special interest in promoting the cause of protestantism; added to which it so happened that the governors in this period were personally inclined to puritanism. We can see this mixture of religious and military concerns in a report of Sir Amyas Paulet from Guernsey in 1559. His news is all of secret contacts between papists and the mainland. 'Whearof yt maye lyke the righte honnorable the lordes and others of the quenes ma^tes Counsaill to consyder for that the lawes of this realme in soche cases as aforsaid extende not to the said Isles but as the same maye be signefied by commissyon from the Quenes highnes.'[1]

Guernsey had recently witnessed the single most revolting episode of the Marian persecution, when the bailiff set out to burn a pregnant woman and ended by burning her newborn child as well. This is doubtless to be seen in the light of the family feuds already mentioned, but all in all it would seem that whoever had to protestantize Guernsey had an uphill task. The government in England had the Book of Common Prayer translated into French, but the real work fell to the two garrison commanders and such ministers and elders as could be found.

Something of the resulting atmosphere can be seen in an altercation

[1] SP 15.9.53/I (n.d. ? January 1560).

between the consistory and a leading citizen, Louis DeVic (various spellings), which came to a head in 1582 when one of the consistory's supporters passed on some of the accusations against DeVic to Walsingham.[1] He was accused of assault, of insulting ministers and troubling the church, and incidentally fornication (with his maidservant), but nothing which obviously concerned the Secretary of State. The charges, though numerous, were all rumours reported by ministers; no lay witnesses could be found, nobody at all knew who had informed Walsingham, and one minister 'n'a veu en luy que toute pieté bonne vie & religion'[2] – from all which it looks as if DeVic was a powerful man as well as an irascible one. (He minimized one assault charge but admitted another.) His main line of defence was a counter-attack on the consistory, whom he accused on several grounds of disloyalty to the Anglican establishment:

And for conclusion youre humble suppliant...mainteineth that the sayd Monanges Baudouin, and other the Ministers have preached factiouslie and sediciouslie: for they preach:
1.) Againste the Supreame Royall prerogative of the Quenes Matie the aucthoritie of the most honorable Councell, and against the Civill Magistrate
[.   .   .   .   ]
3.) They are whollye bent againste the orders and the Ecclesiasticall Pollicie, the kinde of Government, used and allowed in the Realme of England...[3]

Even the unfortunate matter of his assault on M. Quytheville stemmed from *odium theologicum*; he had told the consistory:

if they wolde acknowledge the Bishoppe of Winchester to be superintendant over them, in Ecclesiasticall causes, and dismisse certaine of his knowen enemies then in presence, wch he refused to be his judges, and the wch for their parciallitie and defectes in the administracon of Justice were put outt of theire offices of Jurattes...[4]

he would answer to the articles against him. Baudouin and others, however, 'full freighted with superfluous Ire', had sent Quytheville to Alderney to inquire into the affair of the maidservant and report back to the consistory, 'and using more vehement wordes and arrogant terms, wth other circumstances then the aucthoritie of his Office could permitt; [DeVic] rewarded him with a couffe.'[5] To the accusation that they had departed from the English form of ecclesiastical government and of worship the ministers replied that they had acted through-

---

[1] SP 15.27a. 111/I (5 September 1582).
[2] *Ibid.* He had seen nothing in him but all piety, good life and religion.
[3] SP 15.27a. 112 (? September 1582).   [4] *Ibid.*   [5] *Ibid.*

out on the orders of the governor, though at one point they admit a little more:

They never took upon them to doe or Change any thing in the Churche touching service w^{th}out order or leave of the Governor wth the consent of the Antients and Deacons of the Churche. And therefore, de Wic doethe them great wrong to charge them perticulerly manifesting the ill will he beareth to his Minister, and to Beauvars his brother-in-law.[1]

In Jersey, one Philip Maret was alleged to have been denied the sacraments because he preferred the English liturgy and church government to that locally obtaining, but the same man had earlier been suspected of popery, conceivably on the same facts.[2] It was of course easy for a kirk session in such a community to set up a petty tyranny, because any government in such a community is likely to become tyrannous. Not only was all justice likely to be swayed by local and private considerations, but so was the islanders' judgement on larger issues. Thus, for one thing, we should be careful how we deduce episcopalianism or its opposite from the efforts of the islanders to have government by the deans restored. There were those who urged this restoration, long before it actually took place under James I. When that happened it was greeted with puritan fury, in England, but it had been urged by people in the islands who would clearly regard themselves as friends of a thorough-going reformation. Thomas Olivier, a minister of Jersey, wrote in this sense; it is clear that he thought the decanal authority was essential as a counterweight to the authority assumed without law by military governors, and though he was sufficiently aware of the history of the last half century to know that church matters in England were ordered otherwise than at home, he saw no reason why a more authoritarian polity should upset existing island customs; he expected elders and a consistory to continue, and hoped that the King would allow a few sensible departures from the prayer book – exactly the kind of 'moderate' concession the English puritans were always pressing for, after so many disappointments.[3]

Of all these quasi-legal presbyterian experiments the most hopeful, in its day, must have seemed that in Northamptonshire, in 1570–2.[4] If we doubt, with Mr Collinson, whether the scheme ever got off the drawing board,[5] it evidently enjoyed an impressive – to all appearances

---

[1] SP 15.27a. 113/I (? September 1582).
[2] SP 15.41.43 (1 July 1617); cf. SP 15.40.15 (? 1611).
[3] SP 15.41.70 (20 February 1618).
[4] Complete text in Claire Cross, *The Royal Supremacy*...doc. 45, p. 213 (spelling modernized).
[5] Patrick Collinson, *The Elizabethan Puritan Movement*, p. 141.

an unbeatable – list of patrons: the bishop of the diocese, the quarter sessions of the county, the mayor and corporation of Northampton, and, somewhere in the background, the Earl of Leicester. The moving spirit, Percival Wiburn, was apparently invited in to reform the county rather as Knox was called to Scotland or Bugenhagen to Denmark, to a legislative position *sui generis* and standing outside either the existing ecclesiastical order or the one he was to bring in. The acquiescence of the bishop is perhaps the most remarkable feature of a by no means ordinary state of affairs. The diocese of Peterborough exactly corresponded to the county, it was a much more convenient size and shape than most English dioceses and would have been an ideal theatre for a zealous bishop to carry out his own reforming experiments had he been that way minded. As it was, however, the bishop consented with no surviving signs of reluctance to a new order of church government which in effect replaced his authority by that of a godly consistory of preachers, magistrates and aldermen. It furnishes only a partial explanation when we observe that the order adopted in June 1571, which is the most complete account of the experiments, refers almost solely to the town of Northampton.[1]

The order employs the present tense, and in its title the perfect, describing its own provisions as 'established and set up'. This kind of language, in which the desiderated state of affairs is described as if it actually existed, sounds strange to English ears, at least to English ears accustomed to Acts of Parliament, but it is used for drafting legislation in many countries, and is probably common enough in the rules of private clubs. Certainly it cannot be taken as establishing the otherwise unproven point whether Wiburn's system of church order was ever in fact a working reality. Against the likelihood of this we may note the phrase 'such penalty as shall be appointed' and the assumption that every parish minister is a preacher. On the other hand the description of the minister's exercise – the equivalent of a 'prophesying' – is introduced by the words: 'There is on every other satterdaye and nowe every satterdaie...', which could even mean that the ideal plan is relaxing the severity of the custom already in use.[2]

As for the content of this reformation, one thing that stands out is the lack of animus against the prayer book. The public services of the church are taken from 'the Queen's Book', as it is consistently called, and though there may be omissions there is no indication of any substantial revision. The organ is suppressed, and there are several refer-

---

1 SP 12.78.38 (5 June 1571).
2 Cf. moreover: 'There is hereafter to take place ordered... (para. 17).

ences to the singing of psalms by the people, but organs in parish churches were rare in any case, and Anglicans sometimes fail to realize that the metric psalms (before and after sermon) were regularly sung in this period and were authorized by the Queen's injunctions.

A sermon was to be provided in the principal church every Sunday, and the service times in other churches were to be adjusted so that the parishioners could go to the central sermon if none was preached in their own church. In service time the population were forbidden to sit or walk idly in the streets; this presumably refers to the time of the sermon just mentioned, for in the time of service in their parish churches they were of course supposed to be there. The following is worth quoting particularly for the spirit of compromise in its language: '(6) The youth at thende of eveninge prayer every sondaie & holydaye before all the elder people are examyned in A porcon of Calvyns Cathechisme wch by the reader is expounded unto them & holdeth an hower.'[1] Here we have holy days, which can only be saints' days, equated with Sundays, and catechism instead of sermon in the evening, both Anglicanisms detested by many. We have a reference which sounds as if it recognized the authority of a class of 'elders' but really doesn't. In fact we have standard Anglican practice of this date, but on the other hand we have, quite barefacedly, Calvin's catechism. The communion arrangements, though specially detailed, are again not at all out of line with rubrics and injunctions. There were to be four occasions a year, all carefully led up to with announcements and exhortations on four successive Sundays. Parson and churchwardens were to visit every family in the parish, collecting names and examining potential communicants; so far so good, but there is a departure in the procedure, in which we may see either an attempt to set up the consistory or simply the effect of the fact that the Northampton reformation was being carried out with municipal support:

amonge whome yf any discorde be founde the parties are brought before the maio^r & his bretherne [i.e. aldermen] beinge assisted wth the preacher, & other gentillmen before whome there ys reconsylement made, orelles Correcon & puttinge the partie from the Comunyon wch will not dwell in Charitie.[2]

Non-communicants were similarly to be reported to the mayor,

who wth the mynister examyneth the matteir, & useth meanes of perswasion to induce them to their duties.[3]

We should probably read a half-confession of helplessness, rather than anything sinister, into those 'means of persuasion'. No reformer,

---

[1] *Ibid.*   [2] *Ibid.* para. 8.   [3] *Ibid.* para. 9.

puritan or Anglican, ever found any such means that really worked. The active co-operation of the civil head of the community in inducing people to accept against their wills what they were theoretically supposed to regard as an inestimable privilege was unedifying but welcome. We may recall Mr Spectator's complaisance in recording that Sir Roger de Coverley took attendance in church, and could make his own example effective because he was the landlord of the whole parish.[1] On the communion day there were to be two celebrations in every parish, an early one for servants and a later for the more leisured, so that none should have to stay away for lack of opportunity. This was a sensible arrangement if it was reasonable to expect the minister (as, in fact, the rules required) to preach two sermons, each of an hour, on one morning. Each service was expected to take three hours all told. There were no serious tinkerings with the liturgy; the one admitted departure was that instead of everybody coming forward into the chancel at the invitation they were supposed to stay in their pews until the actual communion of the people, and then come up by groups in turn. This was shortly to become, and remain, standard Anglican practice; there is nothing puritan about it and the reason for adopting it was apparently a merely practical one. Nothing is said about whether the people knelt, sat or stood to receive.

We may pass over the exercise, which was no way remarkable (except for one detail: it was divided into an earlier public expounding of scripture, with laity present, and a later private conference for ministers alone); as already noted, it was to be fortnightly. Another regular assembly was more revolutionary in its conception:

There is also a wekely Assembly every thursdaye after the lecture by the maio[r] and his bretherne assisted with the preacher mynister (*sic*, in the singular) & other gentlemen appointed to them by the Bisshopp for the correction of discorde made in the towne as for notorious blasphemy, whoredome, drunkenes, raylinge agaynst religyon or the preachers thereof, skowldes, rybauldes & such lyke w[ch] faultes are eche thursdaye presented unto them in writinge by certein sworne men appointed for that cervice in eche parrisshe, so [by] the bisshopes aucthoritie & the mayo[r] ioyned together beinge assisted wth certein other gentillmen in Comyssion of peace yll lyeff is corrected, Goddes gloary sett fourthe and the people brought in good obedience.[2]

Of all the public orders for the church of Northampton this last, for all its talk about the bishop's authority, is the most Genevan in spirit and intention and the most objectionable from the point of view of the Elizabethan hierarchy. It was also the one most calculated to

[1] *The Spectator*, No. 112.   [2] SP 12.78.38. para. 13.

make the reformation unpopular, apart perhaps from the rules 'fencing the table' at the communion. It was definitely an attempt to bring in puritanism in the vernacular sense, to impose moral rigorism on the common people. As such it was hardly revolutionary; the reform of manners was the kind of thing that all respectable people agreed to be necessary, and just this kind of reform of manners was what magistrates and mayors did all the time. You could not very well object to the proposition that drunkards and scolds should be put in the stocks, though Wiburn may have got a reputation for encouraging excessive severity. But the use of the regular machinery for social coercion was one thing, and erecting what was in all but name a new court and claiming to be doing so for religious reasons was quite another, and not the sort of thing a government can afford to tolerate. The only wonder, and it says a good deal for the extent of devolution and local initiative in the English government of the day, is that the central authorities took sharp action.

The order concluded with very detailed regulations for the regular exercise of ministers of the town and county. Neither in the arrangements proposed nor in their quite astonishing meticulousness ('. . . the first speaker shall fully fynisshe whatsoever he hath to say w'thin the space of three quarters of one hower. . .')[1] are these regulations unusual for their time and context, but in one respect the devisers can be called audacious; they appoint a form of subscription, presumably to be imposed on all ministers, though this is not stated. It amounts to a comprehensive confession of puritan faith, and since its declared intention was 'to cutt of all occasions of quarelinge, and sclaunderous reportes, of o[r] dissentinge amonge o[r] selves, in matters of faith and religion to the woundinge and hurte of the symple',[2] it would hardly have served its turn if any refused to sign it; though it is not clear where Wiburn and his friends proposed to look for the power to enforce it on any clergy who were unwilling – and unwilling some of them may well have been. Having declared that the canonical scriptures of the old and new testaments 'contayne in them selves perfect, and sufficient doctrine aswell for the trade of all mens lyves as also for their fayth', the declaration goes on to impugn the authority

not of the pope of Rome onelye who is verye Anthicrist and therefore to be detested of all Christians, but of the Churche also of councelles, fathers or other whosoever either man or Aungelles. Then wee condemne (as a Tyran'ous yoke wherew[th] poor soules have bene oppressed) whatsoever men have

---

[1] *Ibid*. 'The order of the exercise. . . para. 5.
[2] *Ibid*. Preamble to 'The Confession'.

sett upp of their owne invencons to make ar^cles of o^r faith, or to binde mans conscience to their Lawes and statutes. . . [1]

What, *all* articles? we might well wonder; or how, after this sweeping claim for the purely individual and unconditioned interpretation of scripture, the subscribers are to preserve the basic tenets of their party, let alone demonstrate to the world that they do not dissent among themselves in matters of faith and religion. But there was a very simple way out of this difficulty; having set up scripture as the only guide, and condemned all inventions of men, the authors were careful to indicate which beliefs fell into which class. Thus, human inventions included

the doctrine of the supremacie of the sea of Rome, purgatorye, the Masse, transubstantiation, the corporall presence of Christes bodie in the sacrament, adoration thereof, manes merites, freewill, iustifycacon by woorkes, prayenge in an unknowen tongue, to saintes departed for the deade, uppon beades, extollinge of Images, pardons pilgrimages, auriculer confession, takinge from the laie people the Cupp in the admynistracion of the sacrament, prohibition of marriage distinction of meates apparell, and daies. . . [2]

In condemning all these they were not, of course, seriously at odds with their more conventionally Anglican neighbours, but there is a certain difference to be observed between rejecting a possibly corrupt custom, such as 'praying in an unknown tongue', and denouncing a doctrine, such as 'freewill', in such terms as to imply that the opposite doctrine is a simple truth of scripture. Incidentally, the Thirty-nine Articles had been passed through the Canterbury convocation eight years before; did the general condemnation of articles and statutes extend to these? It would almost seem so; for besides the fact that the act of convocation was, surely, a human invention, one would gather from the form of subscription that Northamptonshire had never previously been reformed, but languished until that time under popery – a system described in the confession as 'A dyvelisshe confusion established as it were in despite of God and to the mockerye and reproche of all Christian religion.' [3]

The rest of Wiburn's order can be accepted as an effort to produce an essentially puritan church order while keeping within the limits of what the Queen and bishops allowed, or at least incorporating enough of the prayer book and rubrics to preserve the face of the Anglican settlement. The bishop's authority was formally acknowledged, and it was made as easy as possible for him to accept the remarkable doings in

[1] *Ibid.* 'The Confession'.   [2] *Ibid.*   [3] *Ibid.*

his diocese. They probably could not have been tolerated for long by any ecclesiastical government that meant to see its orders obeyed, but the plans do seem to have been drawn up in what could pass for a conciliatory spirit. But the confession of faith was a piece of sheer insolence. Very likely this was completely unconscious. It was the product of an unguarded moment when the underlying spiritual arrogance of the godly party showed through. The fact was revealed that the 'half-reformed' church of England might just as well not have existed at all for all the attention the sincere brethren were prepared to pay it. Clearly, the puritans were the church in Northamptonshire, and the alternative religion of the county was that of Antichrist, the Pope; Henry VIII might never have set up a bishopric in Peterborough.

Such an attitude was not altogether at variance with the facts. If we can identify Lancashire as the most catholic part of England and East Anglia as the most puritan, a case can be made for Northamptonshire as the region where the two extremes most nearly divided the field. It was the county of the prince of recusants, Sir Thomas Tresham. Throughout our period, recusancy among its gentry, and puritanism among its ministers, flourished publicly for all the government could do to stop it. Under Snape, the successor to Wiburn's mantle, the county was a centre of the 'classical Movement', of which we get a vivid picture in 1590, in a paper of articles delated against Snape

(12) Item, he declared in these, or the lyke wordes: How say you (sayd he) if we devise a waye, whereby to shake of all the Anti-christian yoke and government of the Bishopps: and will ioyntlie together erect the discipline and government all in one day? But peradventure it will not be yet this yeare and this halfe.

[. . . . .]

(15) Item, that the discipline of the Church is of an absolute necessitie to the Church; and that the Churche oughte of necessitie to be governed by Pastors, Doctors, Elders, Deacons and Widowes;...

(16) That here one, and there one, picked out of the profane and common multitude, and put aparte to serve the Lorde: maketh the Churche of god; and not the generall multitude...

(17) That as nothinge maketh a separacon betwene man and wife, but whoredom: so whatsoever beinge devised by the brayne of man, & is brought into the Churche to be used in the outwarde worshippe and service of god (seeme it never so good and godlye, never so holie) it is spirituall whoredome; out of the second Commandement.[1]

[1] BM Lansdowne 64. No. 16. While Item 15 is the orthodox Calvinist opinion, much of this sounds like 'non-separating congregationalism'.

The last detail is reminiscent of the Northampton confession or 1571, with its ingenious use of the concept 'human invention'. It would seem, however, to go further, for if the reference to separation between man and wife means anything at all it means that in the case envisaged – the introduction into the services of the church of things devised by the brain of man – separation from the church was lawful. And did any puritan doubt that this was the case with the Church of England?

If the puritan movement in Northamptonshire in the 1590s was fertile ground for this kind of language we may say that Wiburn, shortlived as his experiment was, did not labour in vain. The source of the last quotations certainly regarded the county as a puritan hotbed, and Snape's evident desire not to tarry for the magistrate was shared by many of his country neighbours. The atmosphere of the region remained one in which the sincere party could feel at home; at any rate it was one in which they made recruits. It is impossible to say whether this made life easier for the mild puritan. It must have done, up to a point, for it always makes life easier to live among people who share our views. But Northamptonshire was not Lancashire. It was not a remote, poor and semi-barbarous corner of the kingdom, but the heart of the fat Midlands and the kind of place where courtiers built summer residences and entertained the Queen. It was much too central to be ignored. The strength of puritanism, and catholicism, in the region is attested by a wealth of evidence, but it does not mean that the puritan or the catholic life could be lived there in quietness. It must have been the home of a quite unusual degree of domestic bitterness and tension in religious matters. It is true, however, that those inhabitants who yearned to hear Mass or a good Genevan sermon can never have long lacked for an opportunity.

Northampton was a notorious puritan centre, the 'chief fountain of that humour',[1] as a Jacobean writer called it. Bury St Edmunds was if anything more notorious still. Here again, though nothing so elaborate as Wiburn's scheme for Northampton was ever projected, we find a combination of complaisance by the bishops and active participation by puritan magistrates in the task of godly reformation, and eventually, after the quasi-official reformation had been repressed, we hear of treasonous talk in private meetings and conventicles. This was to be the district most intimately associated with Bancroft's activities as a detective.[2] Long before that day its open puritanism had given rise to altercations and forced the government to intervene.

[1] SP 14.12.96 (26 February 1605).
[2] Collinson, *Elizabethan Puritan Movement*, p. 188.

East Anglia was the most puritan part of England; the most populous, the most economically advanced, and the closest in touch with the
Low Countries. It contained Cambridge, the academic home of the
movement, and apart from the little, Cambridge-dominated see of Ely
it was divided episcopally between London and Norwich, which was
second only to London in size, commercial importance and cosmo-
politan contacts. Bury was a town of secondary rank but it was in
easy reach of these places, and of Stourbridge Fair, which the early
presbyterian movement used as a cover for conferences. It was no
great journey to the district of the Dedham Classis. It is probably
unnecessary to add that it was dominated, physically, by the shell of a
spectacularly ruined monastic church in order to indicate reasons why
it should have been a place where the party of thoroughgoing reformation was particularly active.

Bishop Parkhurst of Norwich greeted the first signs of this spirit
benignantly. In 1573 he was requested by a group of local clergy and
laity to authorize a public exercise or 'prophesying', and responded not,
like other bishops at this time, with a set of regulations designed to keep
the new and experimental institution under control, but with a commission to three named clergy to order it as they pleased. Mr Collinson
has pointed out the sweeping nature of the powers conferred.[1] The
three were in effect given power to discipline the clergy, with a promise
that the bishop's commissary would back them up,

And whatsoever shall seme unto yow the forsaid persons to ordre and decree
for the better execucon of the premysses i do by theis presentes promyse to
ratefye confirme and allowe (being not ageynst the Lawes of the Realme
[*inserted*]) not doubting that of your wisdomes and godlye zeale yow will
forsee that all your doinges may holy tende to the advancement of the glory
of god . . .[2]

Many bishops thought that 'prophesyings' were a good thing, but it
would be hard to match this confidence in other people's discretions
to order them aright.

Parkhurst in this instrument was promising to give rather a lot of
support to reformers in his diocese, but he was only contemplating the
extension of a new kind of discipline over the clergy. Real puritanism
of course needed more than that; a note of a church sincerely reformed
was that discipline was publicly administered in it to the people as a
whole. Not that Parkhurst would necessarily have tried to prevent this
development in Bury also had it been proposed at this time. Indeed,

[1] Collinson, *Elizabethan Puritan Movement*, p. 183.
[2] Cambridge University Library MS Ee. 11.34 (114. f. 106).

later that year (November) he wrote in reply to a letter from the bailiffs of Great Yarmouth, commending in no uncertain language their intention of reforming the morals of the town.

Concerning your l'res I do give you that auct'ie I may to punishe synne and I cannot but comend your honest, and godly intent hearin. All that I, and you, with all my officers, can do, is to little (synne doth so much abound) and punishment therof is so slack. Yf I may perceive any defalte in my officers being therof by you advertised, I will se it amended[1]

Parkhurst ought to have been a bishop after the puritans' own hearts, if such a thing could be. Perhaps it could not. On one occasion, certainly, he preached a sermon in which he defended the wearing of surplices, and inspired a reply more in sorrow than in anger from his lower clergy:

Beloved father in the lorde Jhesus so longe as you walk sincerelye in this trueth and contynewe in the same we beyng somewhat agreved with your late sermon are moved in conscience to utter some parte therof desyering your wisdome not to be offended because we use not the name of Lorde which willinglye we woulde have done if god did approve it by his holye worde...[2]

It would seem that on the whole, and at the cost of a good deal of indulgence of irregularities on Parkhurst's part, his relations with the puritans of his difficult diocese were good. The next ten years saw a change of bishop and a deterioration.

The bishop of the day had warmly commended the bailiffs of Yarmouth for their anxiety to punish sin, and had promised them the full co-operation of his officers (though he had ventured to ask them not to interfere with the regular jurisdiction of his commissary). It seems possible that he was not consulted about the moral reformation of Bury, which lacked a municipal corporation and was accordingly governed by the neighbouring justices of the peace. Four of these drew up a code of laws for the town in 1579. Its general tenor is well conveyed by the second clause:

Whosoever shalbe knowen or voyced commonlie to be a Papiste or manteyner of Poperie or anie other heresie, he is to be punished according to the statute, and further bounde with suerties for his good behaviour, or els to remaine in prisone till he hathe satisfied this order.[3]

The reference to 'the statute' is typical, and recurs throughout the document. It could be supposed to protect the justices against any

[1] *Ibid.* 175, f. 141.   [2] *Ibid.* 18, f. 15.   [3] BM Lansdowne 27. No. 70, para. 2.

charge that they were taking it upon them to make new laws, but in fact that is precisely what they were doing. There was, of course, no statute that punished a man for being 'commonly voiced' to be a papist, or a murderer if it comes to that; and as for heresy, how were these lay magistrates to judge it? In a similar vein they threaten the (non-existent) penalty of 'the Statute' against any who 'shall refuse to communicate in the prayers of the churche or sermons to be par-takers of the Lordes table so often as by the order of this churche is appointed',[1] where it is not perfectly obvious whether 'this church' refers to the Church of England or to St Mary's, Bury. But they did not always feel it necessary to invoke a statute; blasphemers and common swearers were to spend three days in the stocks on bread and water, and boys above the age of ten — and thus outside the Acts for coming to church, which applied to those over sixteen — who were 'evil occupied or idle' in sermon time, were to be whipped by father or schoolmaster in the presence of the constable, the whipper being also fined a shilling for his neglect. Scolds, brawlers and contentious persons were (if male) to spend a day and night in the stocks on bread and water, and (if female) to be ducked 'in the common river' on market day. Female fornicators were to have their hair cut off, and fornicators of both sexes were to be tied to the whipping-post on Sunday for a day and a night, and the next market day to be whipped, 'receavinge thirtie strypes well layed on till the blood come'. Drunkards and 'ribalds' got two days and nights in the stocks on bread and water. All other offenders were punished 'according to the statute', whatever that might mean, varied with binding over, the jail being used for those who could not find sureties. Offences so punished ranged from being publicly reputed a witch, enchanter or soothsayer (carefully distinguished from being proved one) to 'keeping evil rule in his house or drinking at unseasonable or unlawful times', and also, not unnaturally, for being 'a rayler, depraver or Contemner of the Magistrates or preachers'.[2]

Of course such punishments for these petty offences were by no means unusual. The justices refer to the parish as already possessing stocks, whipping-post, and 'Cockqueanes stoole', and no doubt most populous parishes did. Nor would most respectable people see any-thing but commendable zeal in the magistrate who made frequent use of them. The Bury ordinances however were symptomatic of a desire on the part of their authors to make men godly as well as merely well-behaved. They trenched on matters that properly belonged to the

---

[1] *Ibid.* para. 4. [2] *Ibid.* esp. paras. 7, 13.

ecclesiastical courts, and in the end they attracted the resentful attention of the ecclesiastical authorities.

The four justices of the peace who signed the orders were Robert Jermine, John Heigham or Higham, Thomas Andrews and R. Ashfielde. Ashfielde seems to be a minor character and Andrews changed sides. Jermine and Heigham were to get into serious trouble with the judges of assize for taking too much upon them, and eventually were excluded from the commission of the peace.

As for Andrews' change of sides, it had already begun when he signed the orders of February 1578–9; for in the previous December he had taken depositions in the anti-puritan interest from prisoners in the jail. One of these, a clergyman called John Gyll (presumably a debtor) had attempted to read prayers out of the book on a holy day, but was interrupted by a fellow-prisoner, John Coppyn, who

rebuked this sayed deponent for sayinge the sayde common prayour, and called this deponent dumme dogge, sayinge further that whosoever keapeth any sayntes daye appoynted by the sayde booke of common prayour, is an Idolatrer – And then also further syde that the Quene (meanynge her ma^tie that nowe is) was sworne to keape goddes lawe, and she is periured.[1]

There were several witnesses to this piece of impudence. It is not apparent whether anything came of it, but Andrews' part in the affair may help to explain, what his colleagues bitterly resented, that his name was never linked to theirs in subsequent complaints against the over-zealous magistracy of Suffolk.

The new bishop, Edmund Freke, complained to Burghley in 1581 about the length to which puritanism had been allowed to go in Bury. He placed the blame on the preacher, Handson, who was 'in very dede the only man y^t bloweth the coals, whereof this fier is kyndled',[2] and he also warned against the danger of tolerating a man like Robert Browne, who was then forming a private conventicle in the town, but a large part of his objective was to support his commissary, Dr Day, against the magistrates who (so the bishop complained) were obstructing him in the discharge of his office. Here it might be as well to point out that magistrates could conceivably obstruct episcopal commissaries on anti-clerical or libertine grounds. We are fortunate in this instance to have the evidence that enables us to say that the collision between the two authorities arose out of puritan hostility to the hierarchy, or at least that such a hostility existed and might exacerbate a normal piece of official jealousy between rival jurisdictions.

[1] BM Lansdowne 27.28, f. 53.   [2] BM Lansdowne 33, 13, f. 26.

What had happened was that Dr Day had tried to empanel jurors or 'questmen' to assist him by presenting offenders against the moral and ecclesiastical law – a law of which he believed himself to be the local embodiment. Higham, Jermine and another J.P. called Badby had sent for him, forbidden him to proceed, and called him opprobrious names, such as 'jack', 'knave', and 'tosspot'. They had threatened him with prison, and bound him to good behaviour, all, apparently, on the theory that by empanelling jurors he was exceeding the powers of his office which was not technically that of a magistrate. It may be recalled that even Bishop Parkhurst, in his congratulatory letter to the bailiffs of Yarmouth, had had some qualms about the authority of his commissary. Jermine and his colleagues had taken a high theocratic line in which they could hardly brook any rivals. In the upshot, as Mr Collinson shows,[1] the Privy Council favoured the magistrates while the judges of assize opposed them, in each case taking a line that was consistent with their attitude on other occasions if it was flatly inconsistent each with other. The difficulties of knowing which earthly governor to please, in Elizabethan England, may sometimes have made it easier to seek to please only God.

Such, no doubt, had been Sir Robert Jermine's intention. He was eventually to try to enlist Walsingham's support, after he and Higham, Ashfield, and Badby had been required to answer two sets of articles (the first, at least, drawn up for the bishop) on their doings in Bury, and had been removed from the commission of the peace. Their impenitent replies to the articles survive.[2]

In the first set (the bishop's), the first three articles were denied. These attempted to establish a connexion between the puritan justices and the objectionable Coppyn, mentioned above, and his jailbird friends. The next article concerned the bishop's efforts to introduce a conforming minister to St James' parish, and the justices' efforts to prevent him. For a long time before that, said Freke, there was no service in that parish but 'Geneva psalms and sermons'. The accused took exception to this language:

...we cannot but mervayle at the butt of these articulers that they durst offer unto your L. a Butt of Geneva Psalmes & Sermons. the Psalmes were Davids...the necessity of sermones your L. knoweth. Suerly we cannot but lament that any pretending religion and obedienc to her Matie should be so farr caryed as to utter such unchristian speches...[3]

[1] Collinson, *Elizabethan Puritan Movement*, pp. 204–5.
[2] BM Egerton 1693 f. 91f. (and cf. BM Lansdowne 37. 28, f. 59; this last MS does not contain the original articles).
[3] *Ibid*. Reply to the 4th article.

but what it all amounts to is that the article is plainly true; they did try to treat the bishop's appointee, Wood, first as a puritan minister on probation, 'preaching for a call', and later, on the ground that the congregation had not confirmed his calling, Badby in particular had treated him as an intruder (whereupon Freke and the turncoat Andrews had had Badby indicted for disturbing the peace).

Fifthly, the justices at their ordinary meetings had handled ecclesiastical causes; which by their own admission was true, though they claimed that they had the bishop's permission, and if this was in Parkhurst's time I suppose they well may have had. The remaining articles dealt directly or indirectly with the altercation between the justices and Dr Day. While allowing that high words may have passed, nobody would admit, or could remember, the actual words 'knave', or 'tosspot' (somebody unnamed had called him 'Jack'). Day himself was as insulting as anybody. Their fullest answer was to the tenth article, that they had tried to prevent Day from swearing in questmen and forbidden those sworn to observe their oaths. From a very long explanation it appears that this, in fact, is what they did; the only justification offered being that they had warned Day not to swear his questmen, he had seemed to agree, and then he had gone ahead and sworn them after all. Furthermore he had used intemperate language. They also in substance admitted the truth of the next article, that they had tried to have the law on a preacher, a Mr Phillips, who had denounced non-conformity from the pulpit. While the answer laid more stress on the language used and less on the doctrine it also relied on the fact that Phillips was 'brother' (I suppose brother-in-law) to Day, and therefore contemptible.

These answers could scarcely hope to satisfy anybody who was not thoroughly on the magistrates' side to start with. (They not unnaturally supposed that Burghley, Walsingham and the Privy Council were.) Thus, while the content of the replies was hardly satisfactory from the point of view of a defence lawyer, the tone was one of high self-righteousness, and the document concluded by demanding a public censure of the bishop, to whom personal malice or worse motives were imputed throughout.

It was not enough. The same four were called upon to answer another and longer set of articles.[1] These concerned either attempts by the justices to circumvent the bishop's authority particularly in the placing of ministers, or assumptions by them of powers of ecclesiastical jurisdiction. Once again, the overall impression of the answers is that

[1] BM Egerton 1693, f. 96f.

whether or not it was a specially terrible thing to do, Jermine and his friends had done what they were accused of or something very like it. Sometimes the difference between a grossly improper invasion of the bishop's sphere and a perfectly ordinary and sensible exercise of the normal responsibility of a leading citizen might depend entirely on how you looked at it. Jermine certainly did urge the inhabitants to accept as minister for a vacant church whoever Dr Still or Mr Knewstub should advise. Since Still and Knewstub were prominent in the puritan movement this was highly partisan advice, but was it more than Jermine was entitled to say? Had he backed it up by suggesting from the Bench that the bishop's views on the matter should be disregarded? And did this happen before or after the bishop attempted to institute Mr Rowland? Jermine's own account would seem to show that his activities had been those of a disinterested bystander and that nothing had been further from his thoughts than any wish to override the bishop in his proper office. In such a case the disavowal however insincere it may have been would be as good as a victory for the bishop and might have been accepted. But the justices went beyond what could be ignored or explained away when they heard cases that manifestly belonged to the bishop's court, and this without a shadow of a doubt they had done. They could justify themselves only by taking a high moral line: certainly they had heard a case of incest, but after all incest was a terrible sin and ought to be punished, therefore, those who punished an act of incest were commendable. Equally, they had after a fashion heard evidence of heresy against Mr Legg the parson of Ampton; but then it was a particularly bad heresy – he had denied the immortality of the soul, and as this was his second offence he really ought to have been burnt.

'About four years since' Jermine and Higham had made 'penal orders or constitutions' for Bury; this refers to 1579 and to the orders already described. In the articles these are not set out in detail, and the mere making of what appeared to be legislation for the church was evidently the gravamen. The reply asserted, with dubious truth, that the orders were based on acts of parliament, and also referred to the fact that Andrews, not named in the articles, was equally a signatory of the orders. (They claimed, wrongly, that Day signed them too.) In the last few articles the justices were accused of trying to enforce the principle that no non-preacher could be a minister. This, in substance, they denied, although they did not seek to conceal their hostility and contempt towards non-preachers.

The leading magistrates of Bury had clearly been stretching their authority as far as it would go in the puritan interest, and of their devotion to that cause there can be no doubt. I think there could have been a good deal of doubt, in that age, whether they were exceeding the bounds of their office as ordinarily understood; whether, for instance, it was unreasonable for them to treat the commissary of a bishop from the next county as an interloper, and to behave towards him with a hauteur that reflected his inferior social rank rather than his spiritual office. They had, at least, invaded the debatable ground between church and state far enough to arouse suspicion which their obvious puritan sympathies encouraged, and when the issue was joined in the open the judges of assize were disposed to think of them as dangerous and headstrong magnifiers of their own powers. As the quite different attitude of the Privy Council shows on this and on other occasions, the line taken by the judges was not the only line with a claim to be called 'official', and the disfavour eventually shown to Jermine and Higham can be regarded, not too absurdly, as bad luck.

The last development was presumably welcome to a large inarticulate number in the town besides Day and the non-preaching clergy, but Bury had not been an unfruitful vineyard under the quasi-Calvinist regime. There were still the zealous Mr Handson and other preachers, and the great Knewstub was still taking an interest. In 1582 (August) upwards of two hundred names had been set to a lengthy petition denouncing the non-puritan faction in general terms for devious and ungodly attempts to undo the Lord's work. This petition was expressly in favour of Handson and a preaching colleague, Gayton (who was then the lecturer in St James'); those against whom it was directed were nowhere named but were apparently numerous, powerful, merciless and unscrupulous; it may be supposed further that they drew inspiration from the Adversary himself, to judge by the kind of language considered appropriate to their dealings: (their object, which had proved temporarily successful, was to make the town so uncomfortable for Handson and Gayton as to induce them to leave.)

The Coninge to conveighe this mischeif of mischeifes unto us, is noe doubte verie deep and secret, for they are wise in their generation, and see to their greate grief, that god himself, hir ma^{tie}, and your hono^{rs} doe maineteigne the cause of the gospell, and punishe everie one y^t opposeth himselfe againste the ministerie of yt, in anie open or knowen action. And therefore are they enforced to retire them selfes, to a more close handlinge of their wicked and ungodlie purposes, for not long sithence, they plotted a moste subtile and dangerous devise utterlie and forever to have beaten the worde and the preachers of yt out of our towne, wch was by wthdrawinge their Contribucon,[1]

[1] SP 12.155.5 (6 August 1582).

that is, their assessment for the maintenance of the lecturers. In this effort they had failed, for the Privy Council had stepped in and ordered everybody to pay their regular amount. It passes my understanding how the withholding a dubiously legal tax could be a secret or under-hand action. Like many who oppose the will of their betters, they seem to have been credited with extreme subtlety on rather inadequate grounds, and I might add that the Gospel, by this account of it, could be rather easily beaten out of Bury. It is true that the malignants, foiled in one device, were soon ready with another. Taught, un-doubtedly, by the Father of Lies, they set out to incriminate the doctrine preached by the godly ministers:

As nowe of late either by falsifieinge the matters, or maners of our preachers Sermons, or by perverting the sence and true meaninge of ye same, usinge the notes taken by children at their sermons, not Conceyvinge the purpose of the Speaker, to bringe them and their true meaninge wth their godlie laboures into question and contempte. . . [1]

Against this diabolical device the petitioners hint as a solution that any enquiry arising out of accusations against the preachers' doctrine should be entrusted by the Council to good party men. This is only a hint; the petition speaks openly of 'suche personnes as yt shall please your honours to appoint', but there hardly needed so long a petition and so many signatures to secure that. When we bear in mind that the malignant party are not named, it is clear that there is no corroboration for the suggestion that the same people who formerly resisted paying their assessment are those who now seek to blacken the fair fame of the preachers. The whole thing looks rather like a precaution in case such an effort is made. Anyhow, it is some indication of the state of feeling among the puritan rank-and-file, and the degree of their organization, at a time when puritan control of Bury was passing through a crisis.

The same crisis, continuing, is reflected in a pathetic letter to Walsingham[2] from a puritan minister, Oliver Pigg, who was in prison in Bury in July 1583. The state of the town was very different from the heyday of Jermine and Higham. They were no longer justices, and in their place one Mr Denry was an open oppressor of puritans – 'O it is a wofull thing to o^r contrie that Mr. Denrie is in the commission of the peace.' Pigg was a nonconformist but in his own eyes a moderate one; he thought it wise to repudiate any connexion with Browne or Harrison; his dispute with Denry was partly a matter of tithe, but the heat was on and there were several godly preachers in prison or in present danger of it.

[1] *Ibid.*   [2] SP 12.161.33 (12 July 1583).

This was not of course the end of Bury St Edmunds as a puritan stronghold. Bancroft's famous and wholly hostile account[1] shows it as a place where preachers of the most advanced doctrine were countenanced in the clearest possible fashion by the local gentry, and where ecclesiastical laws not pleasing to these preachers and gentry were simply of no effect. One point made by Bancroft was that every minister used a different form of baptism. This may well have been a natural exaggeration, but while we are on the subject, Oliver Pigg had got into trouble for tinkering with the baptismal service (or he thought that this was his main offence), and one of the cases where Jermine and Higham had taken it upon themselves to be judges of canon-law matters likewise involved irregularities in that service.[2] As for Bancroft's vivid picture of the Suffolk squires vying with each other for the privilege of inviting a hot puritan preacher to Sunday dinner, it is of course completely believable but unless we know for certain that the preacher's doctrine was seditious, and that the gentlemen knew it was, the picture remains essentially an innocent one, whatever Bancroft may have thought it.

None of the puritan half-way houses, until the founding of Massachusetts, was to remain completely safe. None of them at all, not even Massachusetts, really set forth what Travers and Cartwright would recognize as the public face of a church truly reformed. Either the secular magistrate retained an authority which on Genevan principles he should eventually have given up, or no proper elders could ever be elected, or ministers and elders were never joined in a fully functioning system of consistories, classes and synods.[3] England, as a matter of fact, was to wait till the *nineteenth* century before a church with a fully presbyterian system of government existed on her soil, and when that happened it was a minority church with no power to discipline the stiff-necked.[4] Thus even those puritans who were content to place all their hopes in the future placed them, had they but known it, where no security was to be had. In some respects – on preaching, and for a time at least on sabbath-keeping – the whole national church came round to the puritan way of thinking. On many more matters the movement failed. We can say of the half-measures and local expediencies of Elizabeth's reign as we can of the opinions put forward at the same

---

1 *Quoted* Collinson, *Elizabethan Puritan Movement*, p. 188.
2 BM Egerton 1693, f. 97 (articles 12 of 2nd set).
3 The synodal system was most obviously lacking, both in New England and in the eighteenth-century 'presbyterian' denomination. Efforts to set up a Presbyterian structure in England after the Solemn League and Covenant were incomplete and abortive.
4 The so-called 'Presbyterian Church in England' (now part of the 'United Reformed') which was almost entirely an ethnic church for Scots immigrants.

time by the 'Scotch' or politically quietist school among catholics, that although they may not have looked very impressive, and they have both certainly earned the scorn of romantic historians on their own side, they were pointing the way towards the only future their party was to have.

ENDNOTE — HALF A BANBURY CAKE

Banbury, in Oxfordshire, was another puritan centre of some notoriety. Like Northampton and Bury St Edmunds, there were those who regarded it as the heart of the movement; Zeal-of-the-land Busy, the puritan preacher in Jonson's *Bartholomew Fair*, was a Banbury man and evidently Londoners were meant to catch the allusion (Incidentally, Zeal-of-the-land, and some others by Jonson, are about the only comic puritan names invented by a contemporary writer.) Besides puritans, Banbury was beginning to be famous for cakes; it was ceasing to be famous for Banbury Cross, which was torn down in Elizabeth's reign, presumably by the puritans though this has not been proved.

The reason for the town's eminence was, pretty clearly, the residence near it of puritan landed magnates. Anthony Cope, of 'Cope's Bill and Book', was member for Banbury when he introduced the bill and book in the Parliament of 1587, and for years he shared the representation of the borough with the Fiennes family (later Lords Say and Sele). The landowning interest in the district, although it included these very leading names, was not solidly puritan, and the town was therefore not safely puritan and cannot be regarded as a city of refuge. It was rather a place of sharp encounter or 'confrontation' between puritan and non-puritan, and as such had a value of its own to the true partisan. It would be strange, however, if no efforts were made in such a place to set up the true face of a church godly reformed, and in fact we can find some evidence of such efforts.

The town was just an ordinary borough, subject for most purposes to the authorities of the county but possessed of its own corporate session of the peace – a great advantage to puritans where they held power in a municipality; we have seen the use of it in Northampton and the lack of it in Bury. The corporation must have been pretty puritan, given the absolutely consistent record of the borough in Parliamentary elections, and the destruction of the Cross – never blamed on private vandalism – must have had the countenance of the civic magistrates.

The parish is, at first sight, more interesting. The town used to be in the lordship of the Bishops of Lincoln (who built the castle) and the living was attached to a prebendal stall in Lincoln cathedral. All

Oxfordshire belonged to the newly created Diocese of Oxford, but Banbury, right on the boundary, was disputable between two bishops. On paper, it was a Lincoln 'peculiar'; probably nobody at Lincoln was interested in exercising the jurisdiction, since the prebend and rectory had been claimed by the Crown at the Reformation and granted out to lay rectors. In 1568 a twenty-one years' lease of the rectory was acquired by Richard Fiennes; in 1581 or earlier he bestowed the vicarage on one Thomas Brasbridge, of Magdalen College, Oxford, I suppose presenting him in his capacity as Rector and Patron, and inducting him as Prebendary and Dean of Peculiar. So far as I can see Fiennes must have held this latter office, and although the possession of such offices by laymen was a rock of offence to the puritan party in theory, it seems clear that the peculiar court of Banbury was useful to them in practice. It may even have been accepted in the minds of the brethren as a kind of substitute for a godly seignory.

In 1589 the officers of this court (apparently) exhibited articles against one John Danvers in the court of High Commission, of all places. The records of that court have been destroyed, but these articles found their way into the State Papers because the matter was brought to the attention of the Privy Council.[1] Danvers was a non-puritan gentleman of the neighbourhood, and, as emerged, a personal enemy of Anthony Cope. At least, Cope refers to him as 'mine Adversary', and it is clear that they had been making trouble for each other. The articles mentioned above cover a period from 1581 to February 1589 and open enmity between Danvers and the local puritans broke out, or came to a head, in the following May. In the same set of articles complaints against Danvers are preceded by complaints against a recusant lady, Mary Greene; there is no indication why they were linked together, not even a suggestion that they were friends, and I can only suppose that the complainants had not noticed, or hoped that the High Commissioners would not notice, that there was no connexion between the two cases. Mary Greene need not concern us. John Danvers had not made his communion 'above once or twice' since 1581, and went to Morning Prayer about once a month. His household profaned Christmas Day, 1588, with dancing, 'offending many, and withdrawing some from yᵉ catechisme, and from common prayer'. He and his wife married without their parents' consent, now lived apart, and were both suspected of adultery. Danvers' servant Thomas Horsman had insulted Thomas Brasbridge. Danvers' daughter, who *claims* to be married to one Abell Ruswell,

[1] SP 12.223.47 (? March 1589).

had a child before marriage; it was suspected that this child was begotten in incest; it was baptized in secret by her brother, 'being a young stripling, and no minister: most horribly thereby prophaning yᵉ holy sacrament, contrary to yᵉ law of God, & his church' (a remarkably impertinent line to take in a document intended to convince High Commission).[1] The child died shortly after, 'yt not being knowne when, where, nor by what meanes: being neglected as a thing odious to father & mother; but especially to yᵉ grandmother, wife to yᵉ said Jhon Danvers esquire'. The same daughter had had another child since; the churchwardens had seen no certificate of her marriage, and when they went to look for it Danvers abused them, 'calling them, and all other wel disposed persons, a company of busy headded fooles'. As for Mary Danvers alias Ruswell, she sent for Thomas Brasbridge under pretext of summoning him to a death-bed and then, together with her sister Anne and a woman servant, made a murderous assault on him. This was on 17 February, and is as far as the articles go. But it was not till May that Danvers showed his full hatred to the Gospel.

Early in the month the maypoles went up according to custom in the villages around Banbury. (In the virtuous borough itself it seems reasonable to suppose that it had been done away with earlier, since to puritan eyes the maypole was as pagan as the cross was catholic, and there was trouble about it the previous year; on this point we have no other information.) For Whitsun, which fell on 18 May, the villagers no doubt planned Whitsun-ales, again according to custom. On the twentieth – extraordinarily late for any effective action – the High Constable of Banbury Hundred, Richard Wheatly, sent letters to the parish constables ordering them 'by vertewe of a precept unto me sent' to take down all maypoles, allow no new ones to be set up, and repress and put down all Whitsun-ales, Maygames and Morris dances.[2] *Whose* precept he did not say, but instructed the constables 'yf eny do resist or speke agaynst you in exikewtyng your office' to take the offender before a Justice of the Peace to be bound over for contempt. Wheatly seems to have felt an almost boundless confidence in the persuasive force of authoritarian language. Pressed on the question of where his orders came from, he or somebody came up with the name of Lord Norris of Rycote, one of the Lords Lieutenant for Oxfordshire. Whether he actually had that nobleman's authority

---

[1] The Prayer Book at this date contained instructions for lay baptism in emergencies; Puritans consistently claimed that only baptism by a minister was valid.

[2] SP 12.224.54 (20 May 1589).

may be doubted, and it may also be doubted what authority that nobleman had. A Lord Lieutenant's province was national defence, not law-enforcement, even supposing there had been a law to enforce; Norris was only joint Lieutenant; it was and remained a touchy question whether a Lieutenant outranked a sheriff, and to make it touchier, the sheriff of Oxfordshire was John Danvers.

He lived in the hundred and must have heard of Wheatly's efforts immediately. On Thursday 22 May (Market day at Banbury) he fired off a counterblast: a letter addressed to the justices of the county and all inferior officers, ordering them to disperse any crowds that might collect 'under yᵉ coolor and pretence of yᵉ takynge downe Maijpoles, for yᵉ correccion whereof, beinge well used, and yᵉ tyme of devyne service keapt, no lawe dothe touche'.[1] He also wrote to Archbishop Whitgift and the Lord Chancellor (Hatton), complaining in particular of Cope and alleging that the constables claimed to have authority for their proceedings from Lord Norris, 'which authoritie notwithstandinge they refuse to shewe'. Of the bad proceedings in Banbury

I finde Anthony Cope esq. originall under colour of religion to the great disturbance of the Countrie aswell in maintayninge suche Preachers in his owne howse, as have benne deprived for their disordered speaches, and sermons and also fostering the wives of the same persons, with such continuall meetinges & conferences as this parte of our Countrey doth much mervaile at.[2]

He is also prepared to put in a good word for maypoles, at least until they are suppressed by law or by genuine orders from the government.

Wheatly got a subordinate, William Long, to sign a paper on 25 May to the effect that the two of them had taken Danvers a letter from 'my Lord Lefetennauntes debyttie', and that Danvers after reading it 'with grett out ragus speches' demanded to see 'my Presepte', which he then refused to return.[3] This precept of Long's must be the one signed by Wheatly himself on the twentieth, now in the State Papers;[4] it could not be from Norris, whoever the letter to Danvers was from. Already, on 24 May, the Council had written to Norris,[5] in very polite terms, about the possibility of disorders arising in Banbury, and taken the opportunity to suggest indirectly that maypoles were good things and unlawful assemblies were bad. From this letter we learn that there had been some sort of fracas in Banbury on the same subject in May of 1588. We do

[1] SP 12.224.57 (– May 1589). [2] SP 12.224.58 (22 May 1589).
[3] SP 12.224.65 (25 May 1589). [4] Above, n. 232.
[5] SP 12.224.61 (24 May 1589).

not learn what, if anything, the Council believed Lord Norris to have done, and the letter looks to me as if it was carefully phrased to avoid finding out.

Lord Norris was an old and close friend of the Queen, a man of Burghley's generation who had served Henry and Mary as well as Elizabeth. He may, like Burghley and like many of the Queen's older courtiers, have entertained a respect for puritan zeal without sharing puritan party spirit. It is also possible – since we do not have his end of it – that his name was taken in vain. If so, Anthony Cope was quite impenitent about it when he wrote to the Council to refute what Danvers had said about him, and also apparently what some other people had said: 'as allso the Lyke reportes made unto your honours of my Resystance to your aucthorities with manye men with swordes & Bucklers'[1] This was not in Danvers' letter and Cope does not name the accuser. Against Danvers he is very haughty, evidently hoping to persuade the Council to regard both of them, not Cope alone, as equally persons accused of being responsible for the present situation in Banbury, whatever it was. In this interest he suggested, in indirect but confident-seeming tones, that he could tell a tale or two about Danvers if he was so minded:

ffor myne adversarye: yf I should search into his proceedinges, his resystance of aucthoritie withowt warrant from your honors, anymatinge the people to great disobedience agaynst the L. Livetenant, the ryotous assemblys that therbye have ensued, their proceedings in their pastymes with diverse sortes of weapons never used before, endaungeringe the places to which they have resorted, his neglect of all Religion, And the vicious lyves & infamous reporte of himself & his famylye, I doubt not, but as he amongst us is accounted both symple & wyllfull so I should manifestlye prove him to abuse your honours altogether with untrewthes.[2]

It may be noted that Cope is still trying to get the sheriff in trouble for not accepting, as binding upon him, the instructions he was supposed to have received from the Lord Lieutenant, but is not quite saying in so many words that the Lord Lieutenant gave the instructions. He is bringing one serious accusation not against Danvers in person but either against 'the people' in general or a villainous 'them' with no antecedent. Both of these may be camouflage but both have something to do with the original charge against Cope, of promoting riotous assemblies. The further effort to blacken his opponent's general moral character has nothing to do with it but it alone has corroboration (at least among the material that got on

[1] SP 12.224.66 (25 May 1589).   [2] *Ibid.*

the file and is preserved to us). I am referring, of course, to the articles in High Commission. It is plain that whether Cope 'searched into' Danvers' neglect of all religion and so on or whether he did not, somebody did. The content and enclosing dates of the articles point to Thomas Brasbridge as the main informant; they range back to the year of his appointment, 1581. They include things that only a puritan could object to, but they also include an insinuation of infanticide, a felony, and incest, a really major ecclesiastical offence. That the peculiar court should choose to act at just this moment (against Danvers and a couple of other old offenders) is stretching the arm of coincidence. It is plain that Cope, Brasbridge and presumably Fiennes the lay Rector were in partisan collusion against Danvers whose position in the county made him a menace to the puritanism of the Banbury district. The constables, churchwardens, and official and apparitor of the ecclesiastical court were instruments and Wheatly, the High Constable, perhaps something more. There is no real reason to suppose that Lord Norris was involved at all; it looks rather more as if he had expressed a quotable opinion that maypoles and Morris dances were relics of the bad old days and ought to be put down, and that this had allowed some vanguard spirits to take him at more than his word. The uncertainty of whatever warrant the constables had is obvious from the whole episode and may help to explain why they acted so absurdly late.

The attempt was a failure. It did not shake the puritan political grasp on the borough, which Cope continued to represent and the Fiennes family after him. It may have influenced the Queen to make other arrangements for the parish. Fiennes' lease of the rectory ran out in 1589, and it was granted to the Bishop of Oxford, thus in effect ceding the peculiar back to the diocese and tidying up the ecclesiastical situation. Next year, 1590, Brasbridge got into trouble for non-conformity and was deprived. It would seem on balance that if the episode had any result at all it was a setback for the puritan cause.

What it looks like is a feeble and ill-planned piece of 'adventurism'. In the language of the contemporary Left, 'adventurism' is when someone who has an emotional need to be in the forefront of the movement tries to go faster, in the desired direction, than is politically realistic. It frequently involves pretending that a hoped-for future state of affairs is the present state of affairs; it usually involves springing an idea on people without preparing their minds for it. The business of 'Cope's bill and Book' shows that Cope was that kind of person.[1]

---

[1] Neale, *Elizabeth I and her Parliaments* vol. 2, p. 148f.

It is possible, however, that he and the other Banbury puritans were pushed into this piece of bravado not only by their own psyches but by the situation they were in. Maypoles and Morris dances were objectionable to puritans in their own right anyway. In addition, once the issue had been raised – and apparently it was raised in Banbury in 1588 – it became a test of strength, and a test that a party which had almost won control of the community could not afford to refuse. This it would have been whatever the nature of the issue. But maypoles and Morris dances and so on, by their nature, were a very public defiance of good rule and religion wherever they were done in defiance of it. Such occasions of revelry were natural occasions for mocking at dignities, and Cope had probably suffered from this; in his letter to the Council he claims credit for forbearance: 'As for whitsonales & morisdaunces (beinge in all the townes about me) I have restrayned none, althoughe they have used their sportes in my presences' – which was evidently very ill-mannered of them.[1]

On the whole, a movement must either expand or contract; everything except steady progress from one position to a further position is failure. In particular, any movement that takes up a stance of *denouncing* the society around it no longer has any choice at what pace it will go. It is committed to action, and every action must produce results, because anything else is ignominious. Milder movements can philosophize, 'you win a few, you lose a few', and settle down at peace with their neighbours to build up themselves as institutions, and perhaps this is what the Oxfordshire puritans should have done, but in that case they should have started earlier and learned to live with Banbury Cross. It was specially difficult for puritans to be moderate, though, because the one thing above all else that singled out the party was extremism on moral questions. It is hard to be conciliatory, or a friendly neighbour, when the whole bent of your rhetoric is towards righteous wrath.

Sooner or later, the Banbury puritans had to try to make Banbury puritan. What if they had succeeded in 1589? If Danvers had failed to save the maypoles, if the sheriff had been more sympathetic to the cause or the Lord Lieutenant more forceful (after all, sheriff was an annual office; Lord Norris himself, before he became a peer, had been sheriff of Oxfordshire), if Fiennes had renewed his lease, with these and a few more 'ifs' the district might have been made a shining example of reformation, and one place where there was no need for the sincere sort to tarry for the magistrate. Of course, if it was

[1] SP 12.224.66.

made comfortable for the sincere sort it would have to be made uncomfortable for everybody else. There would be no more dancing instead of catechism on Christmas Day. Worldlings with rings on their fingers, Morris-men with bells on their toes, would have to take their fooleries elsewhere, and when the puritan party had finally achieved the success it sought there would be nowhere else for them to go. The puritan demands on society were ultimately totalitarian. Wherever puritans were organized enough to form a party they could hardly be satisfied with local arrangements that allowed the godly to live in peace without interfering with others. In theory, catholics and 'Anglicans' also believed in reformation of morals for everybody, but to puritans it was the central thrust of their movement. One thing that this incident brings out is that it was difficult in practice even for people with such a universally respected purpose to know what the rules were, who made them or how they could be changed.

10

Legal devices

The puritans, as I have mentioned, found allies among the common lawyers. The alliance plays a very conspicuous part in general English history in the age of the Long Parliament and Civil War. Historians of that age have traditionally overstated it, and found it hard to tell the issues apart.[1] This is highly ironical when you consider what a contempt the good calvinist must have for the 'works of the law'.

The liberty of the gospel which the reformers proclaimed was meant to liberate men from bondage to the works of the law, to legalism. Legalism, in the reformers' eyes, was a characteristic of the old church, and of the Pharisees before it. The accusation of Pharisaism, of tithing mint and cummin and cleaning the outside of the cup, was one that was freely used in both directions; Cartwright called the bishops Pharisees for their legalism in ritual matters, and Whitgift as we have seen returned the epithet on the puritan party.[2] Everybody was against Pharisaism. But no important school of reformed theology has driven the rejection of legalism as far as the calvinist school. Its critics regularly accused it of 'antinomianism', of abolishing all respect for law and for established norms of behaviour to the point of encouraging an anarchic permissiveness; this is supposed to be the result that naturally follows from putting the stress the calvinists did on predestination. True, an Anglican can hardly say so; the seventeenth article, which looks 'calvinist' to many people, is not calvinist but it is about this problem and what it says is that belief in predestination does not lead to antinomianism but to something different.[3] But when Elizabethan defenders of the establishment had

---

[1] Although most twentieth-century historians tend to argue that S. R. Gardiner over-stressed the religious aspect of the 'Puritan Revolution', that term itself has been favoured and the importance of religion strongly reaffirmed by, esp., Christopher Hill.

[2] Above, p. 128.

[3] Namely, 'mortifying the works of the flesh, and their earthly members, and drawing up their minds to high and heavenly things', article XVII. Those who believe themselves irrevocably *damned* are, indeed, drawn into 'wretchlessness of most unclean living', and

to defend it against puritans, they had to defend it on the grounds that it was legal; they had to show the puritans, theology apart, as bent on a course that subverted law and order. The puritans, for their part, sometimes used the rhetoric of liberty and toleration, but the rhetoric that was truer to the essentials of their position was that of a higher law, the law of God, whose demands overrode the mere regulations of the State.

This does not really conflict as much as it seems to with the rejection of 'legalism' or 'works', because the error of the legalist is to rely on the law to get him to heaven, to measure his righteousness by works. The predestined child of grace has no need of such a reliance, and he knows that compared with God's glory all his righteousness is filthy rags. He is all the more conscious of a duty to walk in God's ways for their own sake, irrespective of rewards and punishments. This makes sense, and many a supporter of the establishment – Whitgift, for instance – would acknowledge the principle.[1] You can assert a duty of obeying a higher law, or any law in its proper context, while denying the efficacy of obedience as a means to justification. What is harder to square with the puritans' theoretical position is tactical resort to the devices of secular law. Against the bishops, the Geneva party became 'erastian'.

By the word 'erastian' I hope I need only mean the actual doctrine taught by Thomas Lieber or Erastus.[2] He taught that the church's sentence of excommunication, and all lesser means of discipline that depended on the power to excommunicate, were subject to appeal to the (Christian) civil magistrate. He was defending the ecclesiastical polities of Zurich, the Rhineland Palatinate and (as he believed) England, against strictures made originally by Oecolampadius; the classic instance of a non-erastian polity, however – apart from Rome – was Geneva. Those who held that Geneva was the best model of a church sincerely reformed, and that England was hardly a model of a reformed church at all, held among other distinguishing notes of reformation that the consistory's power to control the magistrate, and not the magistrate the consistory, made Geneva what it was. In an ideal Christian commonwealth it would not be possible to invoke the authority of a secular court to defeat the intentions of

the doctrine is a dangerous one for that reason and also because God's promises are 'general' and not particular.

[1] On Whitgift's 'Calvinism' see Harry Porter, 'The Anglicanism of Archbishop Whitgift', in *Historical Magazine of the Protestant Episcopal Church* vol. 31 (1962).
[2] See *Encyclopaedia Britannica*, s.v. Erastus.

a church court. In the sub-ideal Christian commonwealth where they lived, the puritans did this without hesitation.

All the elements of delay and inefficiency in the legal system, which I have already mentioned as working in favour of threatened catholics, could of course work in favour of threatened puritans as well. In addition there was the chance of exploiting the old rivalry between the canon-law and common-law jurisdiction. The rivalry went back to the Middle Ages and lay behind the original statute of *praemunire*.[1] What had changed since the breach with Rome was that the lay system was clearly winning. Perhaps the neatest illustration of this is the way in which, during the seventeenth century, the common-law courts managed to annexe into their purview all cases relating to tithe. Even in the Middle Ages they had captured advowson,[2] but tithe lay very close to the heart of the consistory jurisdiction, and the obligation sprang theoretically from the Mosaic code. More to the present purpose, however, is the question of 'prohibitions' – the power of King's Bench, in effect, to stop all proceedings in any ecclesiastical court at its discretion if it elected to believe that the case more properly belonged in some other court. Prohibitions had existed before; what was new was that they had become irresistible by ecclesiastical judges, and also that the King's Bench, by James' reign, had got in the habit of issuing them very freely. Chief Justice Coke, in particular, needed no persuasion.

The argument about prohibitions that arose in the early seventeenth century was an argument between the judges of the two systems, not between judges of either and puritan clergy. It benefited puritans often enough but only incidentally and therefore I shall not pursue it; in connexion with puritans it has been examined by S. B. Babbage.[3]

Elizabethan puritans had professed to have a high respect for the Queen's authority, though in doing so they must have taken advantage of the theory of the Queen's two bodies.[4] The Admonitioners of 1571 were appealing to Parliament against the bishops, and political lay puritans continued to do this. In this period, Queen and Parliament, separately or together according to the circumstances, was what most people meant by the phrase 'Christian Prince' or 'godly magistrate'. Around the time of the Hampton Court Conference there comes a

---

1 The writ '*Praemunire*' forbade appeals to Rome. From 1353 repeated statutes, seldom enforced, confirmed its authority.
2 By the writ *Darreyn Presentment* (from the reign of Henry II). Advowson is the right to nominate a parish priest.
3 S. B. Babbage, *Puritanism and Richard Bancroft*, e.g. pp. 272–4.
4 E. Kantorowicz, *The King's Two Bodies, passim.*

switch. I do not know if there was an increased readiness to apply the phrases to the judges of a court like King's Bench – this would certainly be a departure from the earlier meaning, which referred to the supreme power in the State and not to its particular subordinate officers or agencies however virtuous – but there was an increased interest shown in the chance of using that kind of court as a refuge. Elizabethan puritans had had no skill in playing legal games; Jacobean puritans were interested in developing such a skill.

The great occasion for this seems to have been the promulgation of the *Canons and Constitutions Ecclesiastical* of 1604, after the failure of Hampton Court. The canons were largely a codification of existing law, but they were drawn up in an anti-puritan spirit and were therefore a challenge. They were enacted by the Convocation of Canterbury (later accepted by York) without Parliamentary approval, which was becoming a bone of contention to constitutional lawyers, and that suggested a way the challenge could be met.

The situation produced a document, first printed by R. G. Usher (it was also used by Babbage) and called by him *The Puritans' Directions to Avoyde the Proceedinges of the Byshopps*.[1] It presents an interesting parallel to the catholic *Brief advertisement* of 1581, noticed above.[2] Like it, it is a mixture of legal advice how to do the best for yourself and political advice how to do the best for your party. Like it, it tends to digress into abstract indignation at the arbitrariness it imputes to those in authority. It is mercifully much shorter. It takes a very high view of the sovereignty of statute, particularly the Henrician and Elizabethan Acts of Supremacy, and concludes that bishops, as bishops, had no authority at all beyond their powers of order (i.e. to ordain clergy and so on). They could only claim to exercise jurisdiction as members of High Commission. This sounds very remarkable language for anyone who claimed to know any law, and it seems downright astonishing that a puritan should so exalt High Commission. But in fact that is not what he is doing. Still going by the letter of statutes, he argues that High Commission was set up to enforce the legislation of 1559 and the canons, and is limited to what the legislation actually said and what canons (which of course in his eyes are inferior to statute) *can* say. By a fascinating echo of the debate about recusancy, he urges that the Act of Uniformity laid down no penalty for not wearing a surplice and therefore there can be no penalty. The Act referred by name to the Edwardian prayer-book with two changes;

---

[1] R. G. Usher, *The Reconstruction of the English Church* vol. 2, pp. 362–5 and cf. BM Add. 28571.205, BM Add. 38492. [2] Above, p. 60.

so a prayer-book with any other changes from the original of 1552 could not be enforced by High Commission, and *a fortiori* not by the bishops. If, impervious to these reasons and relying on mere canons unsupported by statute, the bishops try to deprive a beneficed minister, they run up against the common law, because the parson's benefice is his freehold and none but common-law proceedings can take away a freehold.

The writer probably thought his own legal logic was unanswerable, but he was realistic enough not to expect that the bishops would be persuaded by it. If, in spite of it, the bishop or the commission tried to deprive him, the puritan minister was advised how to stave off the execution of the ecclesiastical sentence until the common-law court could intervene. He was to arrange that some member of his household should be physically present both in the church and in the parsonage house night and day, to establish possession and prevent another minister being inducted. If evicted by force he was to apply at once to a neighbouring magistrate for redress, and make a deposition. At this point the writer is unfortunately vague; he does not, as he would if he had been a real lawyer, name the form of action that the aggrieved parson was to ask for. He may have had something like *novel disseisin* in his mind, but for that you would have to go to Chancery and sue out a writ. If the bishop sequestered the living, he says, 'the law hath a verie direct remidie', but he does not tell us what it was. He ends with a number of purely political considerations, intended to persuade wavering ministers to refuse their subscription to prayer-book and articles – considerations over and above the moral issue that the book was repugnant to the word of God. The argument here is entirely in terms of the bad effect that it would have on Parliament, the bishops and the King if many subscribed, and the good effect if many refused. Once again we are not talking about the problem facing the individual under the threat of economic disaster, but the golden opportunity he has of being serviceable to his party.

In the imagined circumstances, the puritan's final earthly reliance was that King's Bench would intervene to save him, and in the years after 1604 this was a reasonable expectation. The parson's benefice *was* a freehold, though a freehold of a very peculiar kind, and the protection of freehold could almost be called the main purpose of the common law. Common lawyers were always ready to see tyranny in the procedures of the church courts, and they may sometimes have been right. They could point, for instance, to the oath *ex officio mero*.

Puritan ministers were always complaining about the *ex officio* oath. Few of them ventured to refuse it. Cartwright did so in High Commission in 1590; his determination was stiffened by the hope that Burghley would back him up.[1] For lesser men, the consequences of refusing an oath in a prerogative court might be drastic. It could be classed as contempt, and involve imprisonment if nothing worse. John Lilburne, the later Leveller, was publicly flogged as a young man for refusing to swear in Star Chamber. Lilburne, an inveterate amateur lawyer, had discovered what he thought was a valid legal ground for refusal, namely that the oath was strange to him and of a nature he could not understand. The objection was (and is) a well-established one, for children too young to understand what swearing an oath means; it is hard to be sure whether Lilburne had failed to grasp this, or whether he knew it perfectly well and was merely being perverse, as the court probably thought.[2] His case made history, in that it was the first time anybody drove a legalistic exception to compulsory swearing to the point of flat refusal. The legal discussion about the propriety of the oath *ex officio*, and the grounds for objecting to it, seem to have been almost totally barren of result. The government in James' reign, however, took the debate sufficiently seriously for some official person, probably Salisbury, to put together a collection of tracts on both sides.[3]

The first of these is really mainly concerned with the right of King's Bench to intervene in any case in a church court by writ of Prohibition. The common lawyers had been claiming, on general principles, that this writ was capable of infinite extension, and if it could be used to hold up any action in church courts it could of course be used for the protection of harassed puritans. While he was about it, the author showed that pretty well all authority claimed by bishops involved them in a *praemunire* and was practically treason, and this was especially true of the *ex officio* oath. On this he argues very ingeniously from

the lawe of lawes, that is the great charter of England, touchinge the oath now unlawfully used by the Clergie, and sought to be mainteyned by the overthrowe of the authoritie of the lawe, and discredit of the authenticall bookes, and reverent Judges of o^r lawe.

Magna Charta in the 28, or 29 chapter hath these wordes *Nullus Balivus de cetero ponat aliquem ad legem manifestum nec adjuramentum simplici loquela*

---

[1] A. F. S. Pearson, *Thomas Cartwright*, pp. 317, 328.

[2] Pauline Gregg, *Free-Born John* (London, 1961), cap. 4.

[3] BM Lansdowne 421.

sua sine testibus fidelibus ad hoc inductis. wch in the English statutes is translated thus. Noe Bailiffe from henceforth shall put any man to his open
lawe, not to othe upon his owne bare sayinge, wthout faithfull witnesses
brought in for the same.

This clause of the charter refers to the medieval procedure of 'compurgation', which allowed a man to clear his name by swearing to
his own *innocence*; it had nothing to do with the problem being
discussed, but the writer made up in eloquence what he lacked in
cogency:

...it was thought meete that the same custome should be taken away
whollie, for that it was a tyrannicall custome, and therefore it were a great
pittie that a lawe that was debated by the space of an hundred yeares, wth
the losse of the lives of moe English subiectes, then be at this day livinge in the
land, soe sollemlie made and soe often confirmed in sondrie parliamentes,
and corroborated by the oth of all the kings, and Queens and subiects should
be nowe overthrowne, and made voyde by revivinge of that tyrannicall
custome wch the Clergie seeketh to bring in againe. But seeinge by this lawe
Magna Charta the Judge was prohibited to proceede, to the puttinge of
a man to his open lawe, or othe, soe I doubt not but the accuso^r, or informer
was bound to the like, and therefore doe assure myselfe that I may lawfully
according to the said lawe of Magna Charta inferre, that in an accusation
upon the bare information of any man Judge, or accuso^r wthout other lawfull
witnesses none ought to be put to his oath, or proceeded against wthout
better proofes.[1]

The author, who would appear to have been writing in Elizabeth's
reign although this copy is later, is really rather early to be quoting
Magna Carta out of context. He is already using it, in the phrase
of his own day, as a nose of wax; but he has still not quite established
that a man cannot be required to testify on oath against himself; that
is good Common Law but the charter does not say so. A little later,
'I doubt not but I may lawfullie inferre' that the restraint here
imposed on the King's bailiffs was meant to extend to the bishops,
which would have surprised Stephen Langton.

The procedure of compurgation did in fact survive in canon law,
and might be associated with the oath *ex officio*. A later tract in the
same collection, signed by a number of Anglican divines, explains it
by way of justifying it:

if the partie deny the Cryme obiected then he is by lawe inioyned his
purgation, at wch tyme of purgation he must directlie answeare in clearinge
or convicting himselfe...and his Compurgato^{rs} are to sweare *de credulitate*

[1] *Ibid.* f. 28v, 29.

(weighinge his feare of god, and conversacon in former tymes) that they beleeve his hath taken a true othe, wch if they all doe then he is cleare... [1]

but the argument mainly relied on here to establish that the oath is not an oppressive imposition is the theory, already mentioned, that the concern of the ecclesiastical courts was with the spiritual benefit of the accused person, and the penances imposed to 'reform' him should be regarded not as *penae* but *medicinae*.

Another and more legally-minded contributor to the collection was more downright: 'And they that hold opinion that the Ecclesiasticall Court cannot give othe but in matrimoniall, and Testamentarie Causes, take away the life, and soule of the lawe for the execution of the lawe is the effect the spirit and life of the lawe.'[2] At this point it would seem that both sides were trying to prove too much. The enemies of the oath had suggested that no oaths at all could be imposed by ecclesiastical judges except in the two types of case where the Common Law itself happened to recognize the right explicitly. Its defenders, in pouring scorn on this position, seemed to be saying that without the oath no court could function at all, but obviously the Common Law courts got along quite happily, certainly not without the power to administer oaths, but without the power to administer them to the accused. As in so many questions where the spheres of Church and State were intermingled, both sides might have their reasons for avoiding perfect ideological clarity.

The line of demarcation was unclear between the two court systems, and the lay one was in an empire-building phase. It could be induced to take umbrage at almost anything a spiritual court did. It could not quite go so far as to deny that the spiritual court had, somewhere, a legitimate function and could exercise some kind of jurisdiction. Thus, for the puritan clergy who were in danger of the spiritual court, an appeal to secular justice was always worth trying but it could never be banked on to succeed. Like all other legal games, it might succeed and if it did not it would at least delay matters. Like all legal games, it would have the effect of counter-harassing those who were harassing the accused, and that might or might not be a clever thing to do.[3]

[1] *Ibid.* f. 84.   [2] *Ibid.* f. 92v.
[3] On this whole subject of Puritan danger from the law, much work of a quantifying kind remains to be done. As with the sufferings of catholics, the material is abundant – enough for a stream of doctoral theses – but far from complete. In particular, the 'harrying' of puritans after Hampton Court requires detailed examination. Preliminary observations by my former student, Mr Ogbu Kalu, relating to Essex, suggest that there was in fact very little harassment of puritans for acts of puritanism, even under the eye of the Bishop of London; but we might get a different impression if we had the records of High Commission.

11

Puritan casuistry and
internal debate

The puritan party was behind the catholics, but ahead of the conforming Anglicans, in building up a body of systematic moral theology.
The great name is William Perkins whom I have already mentioned.[1]
His fullest work on the subject, *The Whole Treatise of the cases of
conscience, distinguished into three bookes*,[2] finally achieved publication
in 1608, after his death which took place in 1602. In his lifetime
he produced *A Discourse of Conscience*: *Wherein is set downe the nature,
properties and differences thereof*: *as also the way to Get and keepe
good Conscience*, published in 1596.[3] *A Reformed Catholike* (1598)[4]
bears on the subject only because it involved him in attacking catholic
casuistry, apparently summed up for him (as I have indicated) in the
single person of Molanus. Perkins' work as a popular expounder
of calvinism won him fame but does not concern us. Of Perkins'
contemporaries, Richard Greenham the puritan parson of Dry Drayton
acquired a considerable reputation as a man skilled in the art of
resolving moral scruples, but he did not publish any work of case-
divinity, and his reputation, like that of Richard Baxter later, remained
largely a matter of oral transmission. A younger contemporary,
William Ames, was proud to regard himself as Perkins' disciple; his
De Conscientia et eius jure vel casibus libri quinque (1630)[5] is the
most solid work of case-divinity by any puritan of the age except
Perkins. Ames has some light to cast on the spirit of the school,
though he is late for my purpose and since he spent most of his active
career in Holland he cannot be expected to apply himself directly
to English problems.

The high regard in which these names were held is a fair indication
that they truly represent the mind of their school. In all probability
Perkins was giving, and his admirers were passing on, much the

---

[1] Above, p. 93.   [2] Cambridge; *Short Title Catalogue* 19669.
[3] *S.T.C.* 19696.   [4] *S.T.C.* 19736.
[5] I have used the Amsterdam edition of 1643.

same kind of advice that his published works contain before they came to be written. Would this advice help a peace-loving member of the party to stay out of trouble?[1]

In the ordinary way the commonest problem to beset a puritan conscience was that which faced a minister who was uneasy in his mind about wearing the surplice or performing the various objectionable ceremonies enjoined by authority. To comply was to help perpetuate the rags of popery and delay the day when the English church could be called truly reformed. To refuse, and to be deprived for refusing, was to lose all chance of feeding that particular flock and to jeopardize your chances of ever preaching the gospel again, and in your absence it was only too likely that the flock would be entrusted to the worthless care of some hireling shepherd or 'dumb dog' who read the book of homilies and actually approved of bowing at the name of Jesus. Could a man with any sense of responsibility, and one who knew that he had been divinely called to the office of a preacher, leave his helpless people to that kind of risk? In a less acute form the same question arose over specifics – how bad was the surplice? admitting that sponsors were wrong, could you pretend to yourself that god-fathers and godmothers were merely deputizing for real fathers and mothers? Assuming that you did not have to make a stand on each and every occasion that could conceivably give rise to any offence, how were you to tell when the right occasion had arisen?

On general principles, Perkins and Ames were reasonably helpful; at least you could find in their writings, and presumably in their counselling by word of mouth, some guidelines, some criteria for making up your mind. On specifics they were not helpful. They remarkably seldom descend to details at all, and when they do they are concerned to argue why the other side's practice is wrong, rather than what the individual on our own side is supposed to do about it. On this they are reminiscent of catholic writers we have already noticed on the subject of attendance at common prayer. Moreover, to both Perkins and Ames the other side whose bad practices are really worth arguing against is still the Roman side, and the argument is beside the point. The godly preacher who was awkwardly caught in the rules of the Anglican establishment and wanted some guidance on his own conduct would hardly find that his problem was treated at a deep level of seriousness by either of these oracles. They were more eloquent on the kind of behaviour that befitted a child of God

[1] It remains uncertain whether Perkins himself subscribed to the articles. See below, p. 191.

in this world – on 'puritan' behaviour in the broad vernacular sense – and even on the nature of conscience in the abstract.

Perkins did go into the question of conflict between divine and human laws. It is immediately obvious that we have left behind the teachings of the earlier reformers, back to Martin Luther, who emphasized the duty of obeying constituted authority in all matters that pertained to them; the actual teaching may not be very different but the emphasis is all the other way. In the *Discourse* he begins moderately enough to illustrate the principle on which we choose which law to obey when two appear to be in conflict: 'Example 1. God commandes one thing, and the magistrate commaunds the flat contrarie: in this case which of these two commaundements must be obeyed, Honour God, or Honour the Magistrate?'[1] Put that way, nobody could be in much doubt, but Perkins obligingly explains that the conflict is between the first and fifth of the Ten Commandments, and as a general rule (later he notes some exceptions) the lower the number of the commandment the more it matters: 'the answer is, that the latter must give place to the former, and the former alone in this case must be obeied. Act. 4. 19. *Whether it be right in the sight of God to obey you rather than God, iudge ye.*' – where the rhetorical nature of the question in the quotation suggests that the previous argument was unnecessary, and may suggest that Perkins was only equipped to unravel rather easy tangles. But not everything he has to say about civil obedience is an elaboration of the obvious. Like Walter Travers earlier,[2] he takes issue with the Romans on the question whether a secular law can bind the conscience, and he says it cannot. Citing Gerson as an authority, he affirms that there can be no power to bind the conscience without a power to punish the soul, which is the exclusive prerogative of God; therefore, such binding power belongs only to the laws of God. If this principle is accepted it becomes more than ever necessary to know what laws fit into which categories. Perkins as a puritan is inclined to draw the distinction not between the lay and spiritual jurisdictions – the positive laws of the church are just as man-made and contingent as those of the State – but between the laws of God as expressed in the Bible and all other laws whatsoever. This leads him to include among the laws of absolute and unconditional authority anything that can be classed in the 'moral' part of the Mosaic code. Thus, he firmly states that the death penalty for murder is God's law, though he

---

[1] *Discourse*, p. 12.
[2] Walter Travers, *An Answere to a Supplicatorie Epistle of G.T.*, p. 234f.

actually argues this on non-scriptural lines: 'without it a common-wealth can not stand'. On the death penalty for adultery, equally scriptural, Perkins weakens, and avoids a final conclusion. Of course the ceremonial law of Moses no longer has any status at all; after the destruction of the Temple, 'ceremonies of the Iewes church became unlawfull, and so shall continue to the worlds ende'[1] – a quite conventional view, though we may be meant to extend it by analogy and conclude that the same condemnation covers any ceremonious style of worship or the retention of any customs and traditions from a former religious dispensation.

Perkins will allow that the Christian ought to obey the temporal magistrate in matters of indifference, although he is very unwilling to relate this obligation to the conscience. In Perkins' case the concession is a small one anyway, because 'matters of indifference' were a very small and exceptional category in his scheme of things. Nothing that was enjoined by the catholic church, for instance, was indifferent; obedience to it was positively bad, and the shortcomings of catholicism are in fact the main subject of this whole part of his discourse. He does not seem to be very interested in the commands of the secular state. Luther, who was not either, on that ground would have them obeyed, because they are not important enough to be worth disobeying.[2] Perkins is more libertarian, in effect if perhaps not in intention:

Moreover, in that mans law bindes not but by the authoritie of Gods law, hence it followes, that Gods lawe alone hath this priviledge, that breach of it should be a sinne.
...Therefore humane laws binde not simply of themselves, but so farre forth as they are agreeable to Gods worde, serve for the common good, stande with good order, and hinder not the libertie of conscience[3]

– hardly a revolutionary position today, but remarkably permissive in an authoritarian age. It is hard to believe that a good puritan minister really wanted every individual soul to decide for himself – as this formulation of the problem practically requires – how this or that particular law squares up to the test of 'serving for the common good' or 'standing with good order'. On the other hand if you are looking for a principle that will justify, at need, any act of disobedience you feel inclined to, you could hardly ask for a better. To people who did feel so inclined, Perkins has more words of comfort yet:

[1] Perkins, *Discourse*, pp. 18–19.
[2] *The Liberty of a Christian Man.*
[3] Perkins, *Discourse*, p. 55.

Hence it followeth that a man may doe any thing beside humane laws and constitutions without breach of conscience. For if we shall omit the doing of any law, I. without hinderance of the ende and particular considerations, for which the law was made: II. without offence giving, as much as in us lieth: III. without contempt of him that made the law, we are not to be accused of sinne.[1]

though it is to be feared we shall be accused of plain ordinary law-breaking. We are here the judges of the legislator's intention; of how far we need to avoid giving offence; and (more reasonably) of the inner disposition of our own hearts towards the legislator. Admittedly we are talking about sin and not crime, but even so this is to give a large discretion to the private judgement. If on all these counts we hold ourselves blameless, then our action which might seem, to uncharitable observers, to be a violation of the law, when rightly regarded is nothing of the kind: 'For as there is a keeping of a law, and a breaking of the same; so there is a middle or meane action betweene them both, which is, to doe a thing beside the law, and that without sinne.'[2] If at this point we are anxious to learn about an objective standard whereby we, and if possible our judges, can distinguish between an action that is against the law and one that is merely beside it, Perkins will disappoint us. He never makes it clear how you are to do this. The idea of a middle ground between obedience and disobedience may sound familiar; it is reminiscent of the conception of a law 'merely penal', and Perkins indeed goes on to explain this conception. In spite of his normal anxiety to show that his principles are quite different from those of the catholics, he accepts it into his system. It is hard to see what it could add to the principle just stated, which apparently covers any human and temporal law whatever, whereas only some laws are 'penal' and Perkins is not very good at explaining which. (He seems to think that the *text* of the law ought to tell you.)[3]

The general tone of Perkins' advice as regards civil obedience is to rate it very low in the scale of virtues. Presumably if human laws have no power to bind the conscience they must draw all their force from coercion and the power to punish (though Travers in his controversy with 'G.T.' on precisely this point denied that this consequence followed).[4] Unfortunately Perkins does not deal with the case of *metus justus*. If you are not satisfied with the inherent justice of a law you are under no strictly moral obligation to obey

[1] *Ibid.*, p. 56.   [2] *Ibid.*
[3] *Ibid.*, p. 59.   [4] Travers, *An Answere* ..., p. 234.

it. Having established this, he seems content to let it be inferred that if you have a moral obligation to do something else, and the law stands in your way, you are not to be deterred by any fear of punishment. As there is no real conflict of duties (no religious duty being owed at all to a merely human authority), so it simply follows that there ought not to be a problem. Perkins' advice is fit for heroes.

He does, of course, tell you what laws are higher than human. He makes perfectly plain the proper attitude towards ceremonies in the church. Indeed, he is almost too plain; he hardly seems to leave himself or anybody else room to manoeuvre in a situation where give-and-take might be necessary.

Thirdly, hence it appears ['hence' does not refer back to any previous argument; it merely means 'because conscience is important'] that all things devised by man for the worship of God, are flat sinnes; because conscience can not say of them that they please God. Esay. 29.13. Mark. 7.7.[1]

Did people like Perkins really believe that the kind of church service they preferred *wasn't* 'devised by man'? In any case, there can be no doubt what Perkins thought about the prayer book and the Queen's Injunctions, and after the principle thus broadly stated there could be no point in particular arguments about surplice or cross or ring. Nothing in the *Discourse* bears usefully on the question of questions, whether these ceremonial matters were important enough to risk a man's ministry and livelihood for; so far as it gives any guidance, it says that they are, but this is an inference *ex silentio*.

Conceivably Perkins may have felt, in the *Discourse* which was not trying to be a systematic work, that discussion of this point was unnecessary because in a broad and general way the party line was well known, though this would be a somewhat irresponsible thing for a leading casuist to feel. It was also hard to be altogether explicit about the limits of lawful obedience in a printed book, if you hoped to keep the book inside the law as Perkins plainly did. (It was only scurrilous hotheads like Martin Marprelate who resorted to secret presses.) And Perkins may have felt, though again it would involve something of an abdication of his rôle, that his primary concern was to give counsel to the puritan laity and that ministers of religion if they were truly fitted for that vocation should be their own casuists – this, though psychologically not realistic, would be consonant with the general puritan attitude towards the ministry and the sort of talents it required. For whatever reasons, he never did make himself

[1] Perkins, *Discourse* 81.

wholly plain on the issue. There arose a tradition that Perkins was blamed in his own day for silence or double-talk on the question of whether a godly minister ought to subscribe the book and articles.[1] If Perkins had said that he ought not, then the case of subsequently breaking the church's liturgical rules and regulations would hardly arise. If he had said that he ought, then we should expect some discussion of how far subscription binds, and it would be useful as well to know how far the fear of losing an office or benefice in the church (with all its opportunity to do good) will serve to justify an outward compliance with bad rules. Perkins says nothing about subscription though he does say a fair amount about oaths. (As was customary at that time he regarded an oath as binding even though it was extorted by force or fraud; it is invalid, among other causes, if it goes against the laws of God or the *good* laws of man. The last detail is original, but it is necessitated by Perkins' general theoretical position on human laws.)[2]

Perkins was against separation, of course. He expected the English church to contain a fair number of godly, painful preaching ministers. It has to be inferred that he expected those ministers to make the minimal gestures of conformity that had to be made if they were to get a parish. He may afterwards have wanted them to keep the parish at their peril, by ignoring the inconvenient rubrics and injunctions and trusting to be ignored in their turn. Perkins himself held no ecclesiastical preferment except his college fellowship (at Christ's College, Cambridge) and a 'lectureship' in St Andrew-the-Great in the same town. 'Lectures' were cracked down on in the Canons of 1604 (canon 56), and in the Laudian period this was enforced, but in Perkins' day all they did was preach, they could wholly avoid reading the service book or wearing the apparel and it was no part of their task to minister the sacraments. It is not possible to say whether Perkins ever subscribed or not.

If we turn to his bigger book, the *Whole Treatise*, we will not be much the wiser on this sort of issue. This represents Perkins' mature thoughts on the subject of conscience, as its title indicates it is meant to be a complete coverage, and it is physically a large book. It is rather less good than the *Discourse* at getting down to cases. Perkins, having rejected catholic tradition as completely as all his school did, saw the task in front of him as one of creating a new

[1] Thomas Fuller, *Holy and Prophane State* (London, 1642) contains a wholly laudatory account of Perkins. Fuller is, however, I believe the source of the tradition; I regret I have not run it to earth.
[2] Perkins, *Whole Treatise*, Bk 2, cap. 13, question 3.

branch of theology *ab ovo*. Accordingly he has to work from first principles, and the work remains, throughout, heavily theoretical and abstract. When, in Book II, he does come to consider some of the questions his brethren were likely to be concerned about if they wanted to be, and to stay, ministers in the Church of England, the line he takes is unexpectedly mild. At this stage he is evidently thinking more about the danger to the church from schism than about the danger from superstition. It is lawful to use set forms of prayer, although reading the *Discourse* you might have gathered that it was positively sinful. No particular gestures of prayer are laid down in the law of God; the proper practice – not just a permissible one – is to follow the usage of the church at large, for the sake of unity. It is likely that he was here thinking mainly of laymen, but the principle could be of help to a minister. He was certainly thinking mainly of the scruples of laymen when he turned to the question, 'Whether the Sacraments ministered by Heretickes, Idolatours, and unsufficient ministers, be Sacraments or no?'[1]

He discusses this question without any reference to Article 26 of the Thirty-Nine, or any use of its argument (the unworthiness of the minister is irrelevant, 'forasmuch as they do not the same in their own name, but in Christ's'). Neither does he distinguish between the three classes of bad minister named in the question. Instead he distinguishes three other classes. First there are ministers duly called 'by God and men', who perform their ministry 'keeping the right forme of the Sacrament acccording to the institution'. In this case there is no problem. Secondly there are private persons with no authority who arrogate the office of ministry to themselves. Here there is no problem either; whatever kind of ritualistic performance such people might go through would not count as a sacrament. He does not say so in express words, but this case would surely cover the midwife who baptized in an emergency. All puritans were dead against this practice, but the church at that date officially recognized such baptisms in the most unambiguous way.[2] Thirdly, the sacraments might be performed by those 'admitted to stand in the roome of lawfull ministers by the acceptation and consent of men, or by custome, though corrupt'. These sacraments Perkins will allow to be valid. I think the case he had primarily in mind, and which determined his judgement, is that of baptisms in the unreformed church, in the days of popery; it will stretch to cover unpreaching

1 Perkins, *Whole Treatise*, Bk 2, cap. 8.
2 Rubrics introducing the order of 'Private Baptism' in the Prayer Book of 1559.

ministers in the days of the gospel. The point that he remains utterly evasive about, after unnecessarily introducing it into the discussion, is what importance attaches to 'the right form of the sacrament according to the institution'. There would here be a large opportunity for puritan scruples to arise, after they had been allayed on the matter of the insufficient minister.

Apart from that, I can find nothing in the *Whole Treatise* that is relevant to the actual situation of puritans in England in Perkins' day, as distinct from the situation they might be in under a catholic or pagan government. He does consider the proper conduct of Christians under persecution, but his examples show that he is only thinking of catholic or pagan persecutors. Thus, the closest he comes to the question of outward conformity is: 'Whether it be lawfull for a man being urged, to go to Idol-service, and heare Masse, so as he keepe his heart to God?'[1] where it emerges that he is literally equating 'idol-service' and mass. (The answer is No.)

In both these books Perkins gives a lot of attention – the whole Book III, in the *Treatise* – to the kind of personal behaviour expected of every godly brother, lay or clerical, and it is indeed the kind of behaviour we associate with the word 'puritan'. We may remember what Whitgift had to say about puritans and laughter when we read: '...it is not meete, convenient, or laudable, for men to moove occasion of laughter in Sermons'[2] though many a later high-churchman would agree. It even more clearly recalls Whitgift on the subject of Pharisees when we read:

...we must so make our apparell both for matter and fashion, and so weare it, that it may in some sort set forth to the beholder our modestie, sobrietie, frugalitie, humilitie, etc. that hereby he may be occasioned to say, behold a grave, sober, modest person.[3]

The word 'modesty' may here be taken in a non-modern sense, something like 'decency', but that still leaves us with the problem of making sure that the neighbours notice our humility. It is our duty to do so, under the head of 'Do all to the glory of God' (I. Cor. 10.31). Otherwise, the principle – of not betraying our neighbour into uncharity towards us, which would be bad for his soul – sounds like the one invoked by the catholic author of the *Brief Advertisement* when he urged recusants to avoid letting the protestants suppose that they stayed away from church out of disregard for religion.[4]

---

[1] Perkins, *Whole Treatise*, Bk 2, cap. 12, question 2.   [2] *Ibid.* Bk 3, cap. 4, question 2.
[3] Perkins, *Discourse*, p. 89.   [4] SP 12.136.15; see p. 61.

A Reformed Catholike mentions casuistry among the branches of Christian doctrine perverted by the Romans; in that connexion I have given it as much attention as perhaps it needs;[1] it is not a work of casuistry and says nothing to our present purpose. One of Perkins' polemical tracts was called 'A Case of Conscience', but was not really one.[2] His only other casuistic writing was a fugitive piece against astrology.

William Ames begins his *De Conscientia* with a generous acknowledgement of his debt to Perkins: 'Grata mihi semper illius temporis recordatio quando juvenis olim audivi Cl.D. Perkinsium, in egregia studiosorum corona . . .'[3] and, indeed, the debt is evident throughout his work. One curiosity may serve to illustrate this. Perkins, like Travers before him, made it a point of accusation against catholics that they distinguished between 'mortal' and 'venial' sins, whereas protestants rightly regarded all sins as equally mortal. He was not able to maintain that all sins were equally horrible, and having got rid of the traditional distinction he was put to the necessity of finding another; at least, it seems to have been a necessity in practice, for in the *Whole Treatise* we find a classification into 'crying' sins – sins which are not to be pardoned, which automatically call down the wrath of God – and sins of 'toleration'.[4] He sets up the classification and then makes little use of it, but his theoretical scheme was not complete without it. Anyhow, we must not talk about 'mortal sin' but there are two kinds. Ames does not go into the wrongness of the Roman system of classification, nor does he offer us another, but every now and then he talks as if a category of specially bad sin existed, indeed he almost sounds as if he was talking about *peccatum mortale*, but he will not use the phrase, and instead resorts to *culpa*, or *reatus, lethalis* – which means exactly the same and merely avoids the words.

On outward ceremonies, Ames agrees very closely with Perkins, allowing for some personal difference of emphasis. He says more about gestures of prayer. Notwithstanding the well-established custom in Leiden, where he lived, he is bold to say that it is quite permissible to pray when not sitting down: 'Sessio per se, non est gestus orandi'[5] and, incidentally, covering the face with the hands is more suitable to women than to men.

[1] Above, pp. 93–5.   [2] Perkins, *A Case of Conscience S.T.C.* 19665.
[3] Ames, *De Conscientia*...Sig. A3v. 'It is always pleasing to me to remember when as a young man I heard the noble Dr. Perkins, that outstanding crown among the learned...'
[4] Perkins, *Whole Treatise*, Bk 1, cap. 1, section 5.
[5] Ames, *De Conscientia*, Bk 4, cap. 18. Sitting is not in itself an attitude of prayer.

194

On the question whether human laws bind the conscience, Ames follows the classical Calvinist line taken by Travers and Perkins and denies that they do, giving the orthodox reason (besides others) that men cannot punish the soul; he is however rather more anxious to hedge this around with qualifications and different ways of saying 'strictly speaking'.

Conscientiam proprie, directe, immediate, et per se, nihil obligat praeter legem divinam...Leges tamen humanae observandae sunt propter conscientiam erga Deum. Rom. 13.5.
R[atione] Quia lex Dei constituit hunc ordinem, ac potestatem, et subjectionem ac obedientiam eidem jubet praestari.[1]

When human laws do not simply express and give effect to the laws of God, their authority is merely relative and contingent on their justice or utility – of which Ames leaves the individual to be the judge. Otherwise, the more laws the more traps for the soul, and men living in civilized states would have more occasions of sin than savages – which Ames clearly regards as a *reductio ad absurdum*:

Si enim sic esset, tum quot sunt leges tot essent laquei animarum, et qui sub legibus vivunt, pluribus multo peccatis essent obnoxii, quam qui in barbaris gentibus, vel absque legibus, vel cum paucissimis transigunt vitam.[2]

In giving permission to his reader to make up his own mind how far the obligation of a law extends, Ames urges him to take into account the reasons why the law was made: 'Intentio et obligatio legis non debet extendi ultra causam et rationem ejus; ita ut ratione, vel causa cessante, cesset etiam obligatio legis'[3] – I am free to decide that this or that law need not be obeyed because it is out of date. As we should expect, Ames endorses the idea of a law 'merely penal'. 'Multae leges sunt pure poenales, ita ut ipsis plane satisfiat, si poena solvatur.[4] Like Perkins, he is vague about how we are to tell which laws these are; he does not seem to accept the view of some catholics,

---

[1] Ames, *De Conscientia*, Bk 5, cap. 25, question 4, XVIII and XIX. Conscience properly, directly, immediately and of itself requires nothing besides the divine law.
'Human laws are nevertheless to be observed for conscience's sake, by God's word. Romans 13.5. Reason: Because the law of God set up this authority and power, and ordered that subjection and obedience be payed to it.'
[2] *Ibid.*, XXII. 'For if that were so, then so many laws would be so many traps for souls, and those who live under laws would be in danger of many more sins than those who lead their lives among savages, or without laws, or with very few.'
[3] *Ibid.*, XXVI. 'The purpose and binding force of laws should not extend beyond the reason for them; so that, if the reason should come to an end, the law no longer binds.'
[4] *Ibid.*, XXVIII. 'Many laws are merely penal, so that they are fully satisfied if the penalty is payed.'

that a law is 'merely penal' if it carries a set penalty. He does tell us a little more about this class of laws. The point about a penal law is that it is meant to discourage the frequent or habitual use of an act which might be tolerated once in a way. Breaking such a law involves no sin; there is a kind of unspoken agreement between you and the government (how arrived at is not made clear) – *tacita conventio et pactum* – whereby you are liable for the fine if you transgress. Ames goes on to say, however, that you are under no obligation to co-operate with the authorities, or pay them your fine before you are forced to by due process, *quod esset ridiculum*. Examples of this kind of regulation are game laws and sumptuary laws; he clearly did not have it in mind that this category included laws in the matter of religion.[1]

However, true to his general principles, Ames is no great friend to the secular legislator in matters of religion either. It seems likely that he was thinking of English conditions, and the grievances of his fellow-puritans against the bishops, when he dealt with the question of '*adiaphora*', matters of indifference in religion. The bishops constantly urged that in '*adiaphora*' it was proper to follow the rules laid down by authority, for uniformity's sake (or for the sake of decency and order). It was always an awkward point for puritans, and the usual way round it was to assert that this or that specific detail of the required usage – the cross in baptism, the ring in marriage, or whatever – was not a thing indifferent, but was forbidden by some principle of the laws of God. Often this was very difficult to argue. Ames asks himself whether the category is a real category at all: 'An adiaphora desinant esse adiaphora, cum de iis aliquid certi statuitur ab iis qui authoritate pollent?'[2] A puritan would be tempted to say 'No', with the implication that therefore the bishops' argument falls to the ground – once an issue has been made officially of the surplice or cap, surplice or cap are not 'indifferent' any longer and you cannot justify them by an argument that says that they are. Unfortunately, the answer 'no' could just as well carry the opposite implication: when a thing has ceased to be indifferent because constituted authority has commanded it, it has ceased to be a matter of choice and become a matter of obligation. Ames' answer, like his question, could be taken either way, and in fact he avoids answering the question that a puritan would want to have answered, though

[1] *Ibid.* (whole section).
[2] Ames, *De Conscientia*, Bk 3, cap. 18, question 5. 'Whether "things indifferent" are properly so called when those in authority have laid down definite rules about them?'

indirectly he suggests that disobedience is legitimate where obedience is inconvenient. The authorities *ought not* to command what was not good in itself, or forbid what was not bad: 'Imperari nihil debet nisi bonum: neque prohiberi quidquam nisi malum: quod adiaphorum est, non potest simpliciter...vel prohiberi, vel imperari[1]'. At least it was quite clear that, the English bishops having disregarded this rule, the godly owed only a partial and qualified obedience to them. It even seems that ecclesiastical authorities are not entitled to that favourable construction, that presumption that what they order is wisely ordered, which applies in the case of the secular prince or indeed in the case of an employer. If a domestic servant is ordered to work on a Sunday, which is *prima facie* a breach of the Fourth Commandment and thus of the law of God, he ought to assume that his master has the discretion to tell a necessary work from the forbidden kind of work, and the task he has been given to perform is surely necessary, therefore to be done.[2] That the authority of a master over his servants is closer to the divine order, and more morally compelling, than that of the State over its citizens is an idea that can be matched in catholic casuistry.[3] Ames would almost certainly not allow the Fourth Commandment to be set aside by the Book of Sports. The civil law giver, however, does qualify for a sort of benefit of the doubt; he is to be presumed to have intended his laws for some good and sensible purpose, even if they appear to serve some other end. This principle does the lawgiver no good at all; it merely widens a gap for evasion of the letter of the law, coming as it does in Ames' scheme immediately after his discussion of laws, including 'penal laws', that only bind up to a point and according to circumstances. 'In omni dubio, praesumendum est pro justitia et aequitate legis, et moderata ejus intentione, aut vi obligante.'[4]

Ames gives no example, but one is supplied by the personal history of Thomas Cartwright. When Whitgift, as Master of Trinity College, Cambridge, deprived Cartwright of his fellowship because he had not fulfilled his obligation under the College statutes to take orders by a certain time, Cartwright was indignant, and protested that he had been hardly used. He could not deny that the statute said what it said, and he did not claim to have received orders. All the same, he

[1] *Ibid.*, IX. 'Nothing ought to be ordered but what is good; nor forbidden but what is bad; what is indifferent may not be absolutely...either commanded or forbidden.'

[2] *Ibid.* 264.

[3] See Appendix A.

[4] Ames, *De Conscientia*, Bk 5, cap. 5, xxx. 'In all cases of doubt the presumption is that the law is just and rightful, and reasonable in intention or in scope.'

had obeyed the intention of the statute, and Whitgift had no business to enforce it on him literally, because the only purpose it existed to secure was that there would always be a sufficient number of ordained clergy to run the services in the College chapel. (This argument is accepted by Cartwright's modern biographer.)[1] Actually, nearly every Cambridge college had such a rule or one like it, and the intention was to confine the founder's charity to the class of students it was meant for. The statutes of Trinity had been drawn up for Henry VIII and Mary Tudor and there was nothing protestant about their intentions. Cartwright was simply inventing out of the whole cloth the intention he claimed to read in the statute, according to which reading – although he still hadn't observed the rule – there was no reason to deprive him and Whitgift was thus proven wrong.

Ames has little to say to the English puritans' situation. What he does say, and his attitude to law in general, has a laxist tendency in that it would create an impression that strict, literal observation of the commandments of men does not matter very much to an enlightened soul. I think you could read Ames and take comfort, if what you wanted to do was to stay quiet in a parish living and break the rules, regardless of any subscription you might have made. He would be harder to quote in favour of keeping the rules when it was not safe to break them and when they appeared to conflict with the word of God, but he could be some comfort there also. He does seem to think there is room for leeway in the matter of ceremonies, and although when talking about religious obligations he comes close to setting up an ideal church order of his own he does not ascribe absolute validity to his conduct.

Ames of course was vehemently anti-catholic. Catholics, whom he calls by the curious coinage '*Pontificii*', are firmly described as *semi-Christiani*;[2] reluctantly he allows that their children may be baptized, and in this case he departs so far from English puritan norms as to assert that suitable sponsors, other than the parents, are necessary. As might be expected, he has quite a lot to say about the well-known untruthfulness of papists. On the subject of truth-telling he is actually rather mild. He first affirms that *silence* is permissible when neither piety, justice nor charity requires that we should reveal the truth. But in this case we are not confined to a straight choice of truth or silence: 'Licitum est etiam aliquando, salva veritate, illa verba proferre, ex quibus probabiliter novimus auditores aliquid

---

[1] A. F. S. Pearson, *Thomas Cartwright*, pp. 65–6.
[2] Ames, *De Conscientia*, *passim*, esp. p. 248.

conclusuros falsi',[1] which is as clear a definition of equivocation as anyone could wish, and an endorsement of the practice that would be hard to match among the catholics. All the same, we must recognize that Ames is teaching something essentially different from the detestable principles of the enemies of the gospel: 'Illa tamen occultatio veritatis, quam Pontificii plerique docent vel per mentalem reservationem, vel per aequivocationem verbalem, in variis casibus posse adhiberi...nihil aliud est quam ars mentiendi.'[2] He even quotes Roman casuists, when he can, against mental reservation: 'Inter ipsos Pontificos sunt viri magni...'[3] They include Soto, Covarrubias and Azor, and it seems that when attacking the Roman tradition in moral theology Ames at least knows more about it than Perkins did. He only agrees with these authors up to a point, and is concerned to show that they make all the wrong exceptions to their own rules. From this part of Ames' work it certainly sounds as if the citizen who has broken a law of the State, regardless of the category of law involved, is not free to conceal the violation if he is taxed with it.

From Perkins and Ames, is it possible to say anything about the early history of the 'Non-conformist conscience'? They often seem to be encouraging the reader to regard himself as his own only judge, under God, and to take all mortal rulers, and their rules, lightly. At the same time they urge, in the matter of ordinary daily conduct, a constantly recollected 'walk with God', a graveness and sobriety of habit such as we associate with the name 'puritan'. These two taken together do suggest the godly and unbending individualism of a later generation of protestant dissenters. The whole Calvinist emphasis on the overwhelming majesty and sovereignty of God, contrasted with the 'total depravity' of man, points this same way. It implies that the smallest detail of God's commandments is to be obeyed as an absolute necessity, whereas the highest authority in the world that is not divine can hardly be called an authority at all and its sternest and most categorical command has only a relative, limited and functional force. Given this view of the universe, puritan defiance of High Commission would be easy to understand. It would be explicable if there had been altogether more defiance of High Commission than there ever was, more prophetic denunciations of those who made Israel to sin and less mere hole-and-corner disobedience.

---

[1] Ames, *De Conscientia*, Bk 5, cap. 53, xx. 'It is even lawful on occasion, saving the truth, to use such words as will probably lead the hearers to understand what is not true.'

[2] *Ibid.*, xxi. 'But that obscuring of the truth which many papists teach may be lawful in certain cases, either by mental reservation or by verbal equivocation...is nothing but the art of lying.' [3] *Ibid.* xxvi.

Calvinist thought was very influential in the Elizabethan church. It inspired Whitgift as well as Cartwright and Perkins. Its anthropological assumptions may have been those of a rising mercantile and middle-class world, as some have supposed. Its ideal man – if the phrase can be allowed in such a context – was, no doubt, a staunch and upright individualist, accountable for all his acts to God and to no lesser power. This attitude would belong to Calvinism if Perkins and Ames had never written about it, and it is quite reasonable to see this attitude as typical of the puritan movement. However, this is an anthropology fit for heroes, and many puritans were fallible men.

It is remarkable that neither Perkins nor Ames gives much attention to any of the points of detail on which the puritan clergy of their own day were likely to feel an uncomfortable discrepancy between conscience and convenience, between what puritan principle or the word of God seemed to demand and what the archdeacon demanded unambiguously. Considering how often puritans complained of such ceremonies as the cross and the ring, such ornaments as the surplice, it is strange that the case for and against compliance on such points was not treated in depth. So far as their printed words go, both authors fail to give clear guidance here. You might suppose that this was on principle, that this was the sort of thing that every man ought to decide for himself, except that such a principle is nowhere affirmed by them and almost certainly they would have repudiated it. The individual moral sense is *not* its own sole earthly judge. Perkins, for instance, definitely and in express words recommends the practice of private confession. The puritan in any spiritual perplexity was meant to seek advice, not only from Lord in prayer, but from his discreet and experienced brethren.[1] If the *Whole Treatise* or the *De Conscientia* had been written within the framework of an old, settled penitential system like the catholic, no doubt they would have been written, like most catholic casuistry, for the professional needs of those who were called upon regularly to hear people's confessions and to give them advice. They would be books for the confessor and not for his penitent, and it would be ridiculous to include in them the advice, 'see your confessor about it'. This was the advice, and sometimes it may have been the only printable advice, that Perkins' and Ames' readers were ultimately expected to follow.

Unhappily we must conclude that the earliest bases of puritan casuistry are lost to us because they were a matter of oral transmission.

[1] Perkins, *Whole Treatise*, Bk 1, cap. 1, section 1.

There were men in the movement with a reputation for skill in resolving conscientious scruples. The leaders, men like Cartwright and Perkins himself, must have been constantly applied to. Some odd scraps of counsel on vexed points, from Cartwright's hand, survive.[1] Perkins' big books are presumably the distillation of many years' experience, though he must regret in that case that the experience was so thoroughly distilled. From a later generation we have the familiar picture of Richard Baxter as the chosen moral guide to whom all Kidderminster resorted in any personal difficulty. Unfortunately – and the more so because this picture was drawn for us only by Richard Baxter himself[2] – we know nothing about the sort of cases he handled and the sort of advice he gave. It is extraordinarily difficult to base any judgement, any generalization about early puritan casuistry on the fragmentary evidence before us. People inside the movement did consult their brethren on cases of conscience, they did get answers and to some extent they must have been swayed by them. It is usually not possible to go further than that.

In these circumstances we must be grateful for scraps; we have a monument to the views and activities of one Elizabethan puritan who early acquired a reputation as a man of deep perception on vexed questions, in the shape of a memoir of Richard Greenham.[3] This makes no pretence to be a systematic study either of his teachings or of his life, and rather resembles a collection of 'table talk'. It is the work of a warm admirer and disciple and if the character there represented emerges as a peculiarly repellent example of the 'puritan' of popular mythology the ugliness must be in the eye of the beholder.

Greenham was the incumbent of Dry Drayton, near Cambridge, and it is quite clear that he ruled there in a manner quite unaffected by the wishes or the doings of Bishop or Archdeacon. Undoubtedly he was equally unprovided with the assistance, which he presumably would have desired, of a godly signory; puritan ministers wherever they found themselves seem to have had no success in setting up anything of the sort, leaving aside the wholly exceptional conditions that temporarily prevailed in the Channel Isles. It says a good deal for the respect in which Greenham was held that he evidently played the part of something like a party oracle in a place so close to Cambridge (walking distance to a good walker); it may also be taken as indicating that even in Cambridge the puritans found more perplexities needing

---

[1] See *Cartwrightiana*, ed. A. Peel and L. H. Carlson.

[2] Richard Baxter, *Autobiography* (ed. by J. M. Lloyd Thomas from the *Reliquia Baxteriana*), London 1925, 77.

[3] John Rylands Library English MS 524.

resolution than competent judges to resolve them. Greenham seems to have been particularly successful in persuading members of the puritan party who were dissatisfied with the half-reformation to swallow their frustrations for the time, and find spiritual comfort where they could not have full satisfaction. Thus,

When one complained to him of want of discipline hee said Let us bee thankful for that discipline wee have it is yᵉ lords wil even in this want of discipline to advaunce his own glory in taking yᵗ to himself otherwise wee would attribute to discipline...it may bee, discipline would hide many hipocrites wᶜʰ now are discovered, and cover many christian true harts, wᶜʰ now are knowen. for they that are godly now are godly of conscience being a discipline to themselves. But many may seem godly in discipline wᶜʰ do it for fear not of love.[1]

The argument is a natural one to employ to comfort members of a reforming minority out of office, but it surely makes a rather large admission about the merely limited and contingent desirability of the 'discipline'. It is not to be supposed that Greenham thought people were better left to themselves, or that the parishioners of Dry Drayton were so left. He was free with his rebuke, to those who were subject to his direction and to those who were not, and on occasion he would even urge the brotherly admonition of a carnal clergyman by a godly parishioner. 'When a certain man came to have his children Baptised of him, becaus hee durst not commit them to the ordinary minister who had some defects', Greenham did indeed take the orthodox line that the personal lack of grace of the minister did not affect the validity of the sacrament, and urged the man therefore to have the children baptized in their own parish, but he also suggested that the man might improve the occasion by explaining his decision to his minister, in words proposed by Greenham:

Go to your pastor, and say Sr, wheras your wants in your calling, and (though otherwise I reverence both your person, your calling and your gifts) had almost forced mee from committing my children unto your ministry, yet now having learned out of the word by the spirit of god through Jesus Christ, yᵗ it is rather your sin then myne as I thought good to bee obedient to the ordinance of god, whose blessing only I looke for: so I am to desire you to looke to yourself lest your blood bee upon yourself, how either in this or in other duties, your negligence offendeth the saincts. If you wil hear mee I shalbee glad, if not I shalbee sorry.[2]

Baptism was a subject which concerned Greenham and his enquirers a good deal. He found it necessary to explain that Popish baptism

[1] *Ibid.* f. 3.   [2] *Ibid.* f. 10.

was not actually invalid, since they used water and the triune name. Presumably Anglican baptism was valid on the same grounds, but certain details of it were very hard to justify. Greenham himself was at first prepared to follow the book form in such matters as the promises by the godparents, which all reformers disliked. It was not until he had been invited to preach in another parish against the use of godparents, and did so in very vehement terms, that he felt obliged to insist that the natural parent must personally sponsor the child, though once he had become convinced of this he insisted on it even where the father was sick, and came close to refusing baptism when the mother was a stranger.[1] On the form of words provided in the book, and on forms in the book in general, he was inclined to put up with them 'for the time', and so advised others, though naturally he disliked the ceremonies and would say so publicly on the most unlikely occasions. Thus, when some sinners, apparently adulterers, did penance in white sheets in his church – not of course because of proper discipline, but according to the inferior discipline of the established church – in the course of denouncing them from the pulpit he took the opportunity to criticize the use of white sheets: 'I thinck they [i.e. ceremonies] ought to be such as must humble us, and therefore in the law they used sackcloathes, the basest kind of attire and not sheets, wch rather impart [*sic* for "import"] a purenes and recoycing then impurenes, and humbling', and he goes on to reject the argument that sheets were symbolic of adultery.[2] In urging that white garments were too good for penitents, he did not of course mean that they were suitable for ministers, and I think we may assume that Greenham avoided using surplice and cap. In one instance he did suggest to an enquirer that other things were more important:

Unto one that asked his advice in outward things who as yet stood in greater need to bee instructed in inward hee said, If you first wil confer wth mee and establish yourself in things concerning faith & repentance, then ask mee and I wil advise you freely for ye outward estate. Howbeit beecaus you seem...to bee scrupulouse in wearing a surples et cap: as I will not for al the world wish or advice you to wear them, so I would counsaile you generaly to bee wel grounded ere to leav them, lest that you shaking them of rather of light affection then sound judgement, afterward take them againe to your shame and the offence of others.[3]

The principle here is that an outward act of disobedience is not to be ventured upon by those who are not quite sure that they have

---

[1] *Ibid.* f. 11, 32, 40v.   [2] *Ibid.* f. 19.   [3] *Ibid.* f. 18v.

the constancy to persevere in defiance if the going gets tough. There is no question of the wrongness of wearing a surplice in itself.

As a curiosity I might note here that there was one prayerbook ceremony, and only one, for which Greenham expressed warm approval. This was the 'giving away' of a bride by her father – and Greenham insisted it had to be really her father, and a deputy would not do.[1] To him it expressed the profound and Christian truth that children were the property of their fathers and could be disposed of according to the parental will. He believed this with deep fervour (he would undoubtedly have preferred it if grooms were given away as well as brides), and he proved it out of Job; when Satan was authorized by God to afflict Job, he deprived him of all his goods and cattle, and among the rest his sons and daughters; when God eventually rewarded Job's constancy by restoring his former riches, his compensation included more goods, more cattle and more sons and daughters to replace those he had lost. It is all there in the Old Testament. In adopting Old Testament attitudes so completely for his own Greenham repels the modern man and shows himself the archetypal puritan. This impression could be supported by other extracts:

Hee could not abide to bee crossed in his admonitions because it argued a proud and prefact [?] spirit, not that hee respected so much his private person, as y^t it was a thing against gods glory and truth and would have men swift to hear admonitions, slowe to crosse.[2]

When he had before him two dishes, the one better liking his stomach then the other, hee used that wch lest liked him beecaus hee would controul his appetite,[3]

Though this last principle is one that would appeal to some catholic directors also: as might Greenham's view that marriage was permissible if a man had tried every means to overcome concupiscence first. Sometimes his disciples were almost too successful; there had been one

whom hee knew wonderfully to be moved by marriage, and yet attending some longer time on the lord by fervent and continual praier, hee was delivered even from every inward motion, and titillacon therunto. wch man afterwards marrying had such a feeblenes in his body that hee cold not use the act of generation.[4]

His admiring biographer noted that he never looked anybody straight

---

[1] *Ibid.* f. 45, 49v.   [2] *Ibid.* f. 21–21v.
[3] *Ibid.* f. 16.   [4] *Ibid.* f. 25.

in the eye, but told people apart by their voices. However, little missed him:

As hee was woont to profit much by the judgements of god, so one a tyme one of his people burying his wife, hee used this speach unto him, I feared god wold bury something from you, beecause I saw you often bury mine instructions made unto you.[1]

Those who came to consult Greenham may have included some who wanted to combine a quiet conscience with a quiet life. In that case they were probably disappointed, though in the extracts just quoted his advice on the subject of waiting for the discipline and wearing the apparel is at least temperate. He was not the hottest zealot that could be found. Neither does he sound like the sort of person you would be inclined to call moderate, but he did manage to hold a parish living in the Cambridge district together with a reputation for the puritan kind of godliness, which argues either some sort of balancing act or extreme good luck.[2]

His advice on the surplice and cap was not so much advice to a troubled soul as to a troubled party member. He was schooling his man, I should say rather well, on how to be a principled radical when those things were the badges of radicalism. Another time – on the godparent issue – we see Greenham himself developing as a radical. Having accepted an invitation to denounce one of the corruptions of the establishment in public, he found it necessary to make his own practice fit his words. This must often have been the way individual puritans crossed minor Rubicons, the way that people whose dissent had previously been wholly in the realm of words found themselves committed to acts of disobedience. Another way it could happen, particularly with the very respectable, was to find their bold language being quoted as a persuasive to others to make a bold stand. In these ways people on the fringes of movements get drawn further in. If you want to escape trouble it is not enough to avoid hostile attention, it can be just as dangerous to be admired and looked up to. The fringe of a movement is not an easy place to stay, and the difficulty of keeping one's footing there is part of the situation confronting the would-be moderate man, the cautious reformer, the liberal or the Laodicean. It would be rather unfair to call Greenham any of those names, but he illustrates the principle.

All the puritan leaders I have mentioned in this section, whatever

---

[1] *Ibid.* f. 27v–28.

[2] He later went on to become a lecturer in London, and claimed that he had always managed to avoid subscribing the articles. See Seaver, *The Puritan Lectureships*, p. 193; and D.N.B.

the incidental occasion that they were writing about, or that they were consulted about, were men with a programme for the English church. They were leading a reform movement. As such they were not likely to encourage the absolutely extremest line of conduct that could be imagined. Leadership itself imposes one kind of moderation, and by so doing provokes a challenge to itself from those who regard themselves as the truly dedicated souls. As the whole puritan movement, in Elizabethan days at least, could most naturally see itself as a ginger group within the church, so did people like Browne and Barrow and Penry see themselves, to start with, as a ginger group within the puritan movement. Sectarianism was a natural result of this spirit developing. The later history of puritanism is largely a history of sects. The broad, undifferentiated current of puritan feeling disappears from sight as a single and palpable phenomenon, after which any historian who wants to can claim that he sees it still flowing through the national life and consciousness at a subliminal level. These developments are not my concern. Puritan sentiments, unrelated to politico-religious activities, never got anybody into trouble. When sectarians who had consciously chosen the sectarian way got into trouble for their politico-religious acts they had usually been asking for it.

Separation came in the 1580s. Robert Browne, the first name to become famous in this connexion, had been a friend of Greenham. He admired him, though he talked himself into an argumentative position which forced him to condemn anybody who held an Anglican benefice as being necessarily outside the true Christian fold. Eventually, as is well known, Browne accepted an Anglican benefice; he was an unstable character as well as an extremist; many extremists are.

'Brownism' in its short heyday while Browne was still with it was a major problem for the leadership of the respectable movement. It ought to have sparked its most serious internal debate: the debate over tarrying for the magistrate *versus* separating from the ungodly. I say 'it ought to', because it is a matter of opinion whether a debate on this subject was ever conducted at an adequately serious level. There was a debate. The most famous interchange was between Cartwright, at that time (1584) minister of the lawful expatriate church in Antwerp, and Harrison, minister (succeeding Browne himself) of the unlawful expatriate church in Middelburg, with some final comments by Browne.[1] Cartwright of course was urging the

---

[1] On this whole quarrel, see F. J. Powicke, *Henry Barrow, Separatist, and the exiled church in Amsterdam* (London, 1900).

duty of non-separation, and as a puritan whose reputation stood second to none his opinion on the subject ought to have special weight, which no doubt it did, and to be worth hearing which I am not sure that it is.

Cartwright did not have a deep or original mind, and his treatment of the separation issue is uninteresting. Obviously from his point of view it was a bad thing if small groups hived off from the movement and went their own way, whether or not they did it in the name of greater ideological purity. Such separations subtracted from the total strength of the movement and they suggested that there was something wrong with it. Cartwright did not find any new or compelling way of saying this to Harrison. He did not recognize any difference of principle between himself and Harrison. On the principles which they shared, Harrison's strictures against the official church were largely apposite and justified by the facts, and Harrison's language was not much more violent than Cartwright was wont to employ. An acuter mind might have perceived that a difference of principle was really there, but on the other hand an acuter mind might also have seen tactical reasons to pretend that there wasn't.

As long as no difference of principle was recognized between the two groups the difference between them had to be one of degree. Whoever was championing the cause of unity and co-operation more or less had to take this line, and to minimize the degree of difference that he would admit to exist. Cartwright, pleading with Harrison to stay and work inside the English church like everybody else, had to admit the imperfections of the English church, all the same imperfections that Harrison complained of, or he could scarcely argue that he and Harrison were really on the same side. He had to allow that they were very black imperfections, or it would seem that he and his semi-conformist friends merely differed from Harrison in being less seriously concerned about the need for reform. (Actually, Harrison had given up hope of reforming the English church, but this was part of the logic of the Brownist position which Cartwright could not officially allow himself to see.) Cartwright's line had to be that, granted these imperfections existed and were very bad, they were not bad enough to justify separation from the body. The English church despite its manifold corruptions, despite the malignancy of its bishops, despite the absence of any indication that it was moving in the direction of Geneva, was still by the skin of its teeth a true church and the one that all Englishmen ought to be loyal to. If it had been as corrupt as the popish church, then of course it would have been right to leave it, indeed this would be a sacred duty (on that point Cartwright himself was verbally committed; the *Admonition* and its defenders had been too rude about the bad records of people who went to Mass under Mary). Somewhere, at some point along a measured line between the corruptions of Rome and the corruptions of the Elizabethan settlement, there must come the exact moment when a duty not to separate becomes a duty to separate. Cartwright is sure that this point has not been reached. His line of persuasion implies that it exists. He gives no indication where it is or how it can be known. It would have been most unwise to be specific, even if he had clearly thought it out. He would be committing himself in advance to the position that separation, hitherto wrong, would become right, and incumbent on all true reformers including himself, in 'Circumstance X'. He was arguing in a box already, and it was not the way his talents lay. He was altogether more at his ease in normal controversy, when the task before him was to scarify an open enemy like Whitgift, than when he was called upon to woo and win a doubtful friend.

Cartwright's plea for unity, though, would be soothing syrup to anybody who wanted to be persuaded. The broadest and vaguest ground for believing that separation was not a duty would be enough to convince the great majority in an age when conformity (of a kind) and heroic resistance seemed to be the only alternatives. And every feeble arguments for not breaking the unity of the body had the advantage of being backed up by the personal example of Cartwright and almost every other leading figure in the movement. There is no reason to doubt that most puritans sincerely believed that they belonged to the English church, their duty was to work for its further reformation as occasion served, and that to separate from it on grounds of ecclesiastical preferences and without necessity was schism, and schism was sin. This attitude is seldom clearly stated by anybody, because it was such a deep underlying assumption and entered implicitly into nearly all their other assumptions. Unless churches ought to be national churches, and separation from them except in the last extremities was sinful, there could be no reformation on the puritan plan and there would be no point in the 'Platform'. When national reformation, and a covenanted relationship between the Lord and His new chosen people, are seen as the end, it is Browne and Harrison's choice of a path there that looks unthought-out and illogical.

It is an elementary point but it must be clearly understood that the Elizabethan separatists, the pioneers of independency or Congregationalism, did not favour general toleration or a real separation of Church and State. They had not conceived the possibility of religious pluralism in the modern sense, and if they had conceived it they would have repudiated it with horror. It is true that some of the language used by early separatist writers like Browne can be read as an affirmation of universal religious freedom, but only by reading it out of context. Browne's position was a polemical one; naturally he was against persecution when his enemies were persecuting him.

The theoretical ground on which early sectarian puritans quarrelled with what by contrast may be called mainstream or orthodox puritanism was that they saw membership in the church, and presumably the hope of salvation, as being confined to a tiny minority of 'saints', and mainly on Old-Testament analogies they taught an absolute duty of cutting oneself off from any unnecessary contact with the unrighteous, the reprobate, mass of mankind. This self-isolation of the saints ought to be supported and endorsed by the civil power, and in a truly godly nation it would be. As the saints were the only true church, of course it followed that theirs ought to be the only permitted public worship. Though the state had nothing to do with determining religious matters, which could only be decided by the church of the saints, the secular arm still had a rôle, remarkably similar to the one allowed it by medieval catholicism, to back up the authority of the one true church and to enforce its monopoly.

This is not an appropriate place to go at any length into the question why an emphasis on the duty of the godly to separate from the ungodly led – as historically it did lead – to 'Independency' and to 'Congregationalism', or why these two principles, which are notionally distinct, seem at least in the English-speaking world to have involved each other. Both contradicted the 'Platform' put forward by Travers, Field, Cartwright and so on. This required not Independency but a national pyramid of synods, not congregational rule in a parish but the oligarchy of the 'godly signory'. This was the most fully articulated puritan programme in the early days; later, some were prepared to accept an episcopal system modified in this direction. The kind of church that nearly all puritans had in mind was still a nationally organized church.

Between these two programmes for a reformed church in a reformed nation, these two rival but equally puritan polities, there was a middle position. It has not lasted very well and it does not look very viable, but it has had a remarkable history. This was the position of 'Non-separating Congregationalists'.

The phrase was perhaps invented by Perry Miller.[1] Certainly he gave it its present currency and has amply documented what it means. Possibly not every individual whom Miller described by the term ought to be so described. For instance, an expatriate living in Holland, like William Ames, was living in a situation where the case of separating from the church of England with all its corruptions did not directly arise; such a man, and I believe it was true of Ames, could stay unseparated, could even have moved to Holland in order to enjoy that privilege, and could favour the 'Congregational Way' in matters of church polity, without this combination quite adding up to 'Non-separating Congregationalism'. To believe in non-separation as a principle, and in congregationalism as a principle, and in their full compatibility with one another, was to tread a very narrow path indeed. You could describe it as a tightrope. As is well known, it was a one-way tightrope stretched from Amsterdam to New England. In New England – that is, in Massachusetts and Connecticut – it was the dominant form that ruling and official puritanism came to take. In Old England, those puritans who pointed with pride to Massachusetts as an example of what reformation could do when it had the chance, puritans who were certainly not aware of any important ideological cleavage between themselves and the saints of the American wilderness, who looked upon them as valuable though physically distant colleagues and allies, remained impervious to the attractions of the Congregational way. In the Civil War period the friends of Massachusetts emerged as what that age called, vaguely, 'Presbyterian'; friends also to the Solemn League and Covenant. A minority of more enthusiastic souls, especially during the heyday of Oliver Cromwell, affirmed the superior virtue of the 'gathered church', sometimes against the Presbyterian scheme, sometimes alongside it. Puritanism in Old and New England took strangely different courses. It is really odd that puritans in the two countries, by the middle of the seventeenth century, do not seem to have noticed their divergence from each other or do not seem to have minded. The fact that they diverged, however, is not odd at all. Once the Non-separating Congregational position had distinguished itself from other positions (which it did not do with any clarity until James' reign) there was nowhere it could go except America. Only in a new country could the conditions be met. The church, the only church,

[1] Perry Miller, *Orthodoxy in Massachusetts*, cap. 1.

was to consist of a select company of the saints, the regenerate, whose spiritual qualities would be discernible only to the other regenerate saints. The remainder of the population were fit subjects of the church's outreach in teaching and preaching, they could walk orderly in God's ways and it was the business of the Christian magistrate to see to it that they did, but they must stay outside the church, at least outside its most important ministrations, until God in His good time sent regeneration upon them. Saints, with powers of rule, and non-saints without, formed inner and outer circles in one concentric Christian community.

The church of England was not in the least like this. An English church remodelled on Presbyterian lines would still not be this. The multiplicity of churches in Holland was not like it either. To achieve a church so ordered, you had to construct a Christian commonwealth on new principles round it. It could only be done where the field was open, where there was no existing church to complicate matters. Emigration, not just to Amsterdam but to the wilderness, was the only way.

This explains why the Non-separating Congregationalists went to New England. It does not quite explain how they came to predominate there, in precisely the colonies (omitting Plymouth Plantation and Rhode Island) that had the closest links with puritan political circles in the home country, and which ought, you might have supposed, to have been organized in the interest of the Presbyterian way. There is, however, a simple explanation. The Non-separating Congregationalists went to New England because only there could their conditions be met. Nobody else was in quite that situation, so almost nobody else went.

Massachusetts and its daughter-colonies were planned by puritans. Maryland was a colony planned by catholics. Probably we should think of Maryland as intended to be a place of refuge, and the New England settlements as rather intended to be social experiments, religious Utopias. Whatever the intentions of the founders, one thing is clear in both cases, very few members of the religious group the founders belonged to wanted to leave England in order to take advantage of the new opportunity presented to them. The puritans managed to keep control of Massachusetts, as the catholics did not of Maryland, but in neither place is it reasonable to assume that the typical early settler went out for the kind of motive imputed to him by the planners (or the similar motive imputed to him by romantic historians later). The really outstanding fact about emigration to

America as a solution for religious difficulties in England, at a time too when there do not seem to have been many other solutions within the law, is that it was so unpopular as to be largely inoperative and unused even when special colonies were planned for the purpose.

Very few people seem to have thought of colonization as an option among the range of options from religious conformity to earning a martyr's crown. This is remarkable, since in the seventeenth century the option did actually exist. It means, though, that colonization only comes in for a brief mention here. I have mentioned it in connexion with the internal debates of puritans because what it chiefly throws light on is the subdivisions within the party. There was never any debate on whether emigration to the new world was permissible to a Christian. It obviously was. To the great majority, even of puritan Christians, staying in England was more attractive.

12

Patrons and protectors

The early puritan movement was a movement of clergy. In theory it ought not to have been. The 'Platform' was completely unviable as a programme of reform unless it was going to be possible to find a 'godly signory' in every parish. Not only did the party, like all parties, need to win support in order to have a chance to try out its ideas, but it was the peculiar nature of these ideas themselves that they had to be fairly popular, at least among the governing classes, before they could be implemented even with official authority behind them. Puritanism required the heart's assent; it could not be simply imposed. It was, after all, a programme not only for the organized church but for men. Plainly this is even more true of the congregational way than of the older Geneva pattern; it implies, it necessitates, a puritan-minded congregation. There seem to have been very few of these. Of course it was one object of the movement – the ordinary object of the ordinary godly preacher – to puritanize the population at large or as much of it as could be reached. This was the duty of ministers anyway, for the people's own benefit; it could also be looked to in time to build up a basis of popular support. In the meantime puritanism did not have much of a lay base.[1] What it had instead was lay patrons.

The word 'patron' is ambiguous in the context. Both senses apply. Patronage in the general sense, *patrocinium* in its various guises, permeated Elizabethan society. Nearly everybody in that society stood in a client-to-patron relationship to somebody above him. Most men were servants to a master, and in the lower orders the 'masterless man' was assumed to be a delinquent. In the upper orders the relationship was less formal and legal, but perfectly well understood, and it extended through the ranks of middle class and aristocracy to the highest in the land, to those great noblemen who

[1] For some qualification of this view see Richardson, *Puritanism in North-West England*, cap. 3.

paid court only to the sovereign, and who, when they did that, were quite often suing for a favour on behalf of their clients.

Patronage in the narrower, technical sense which the word had and has in church matters was something of the most vital concern to puritan clergy. Patronage right or 'advowson' over parish churches was very widespread in England (much more so than in most of Europe) and deeply embedded in the secular law, which continued, and continues to this day, to protect it, reformation or no reformation. The power involved consisted (virtually) of one thing only – the right to present a suitable candidate to the benefice when vacant. This was and remained an enormous limitation on the effective authority of the bishops. As such it worked the puritans' way, although they cannot have approved of it.

Neither kind of patronage fits very well into a puritan scheme of things. If the ultimate reformation had ever come, it is safe to say that the private right of appointment to the office of preacher, enjoyed all up and down the country by great noblemen and petty squires, would have had to be abolished. The godly minister ought to be called by his people; there was no guarantee that the patron would even be a member of the local church whose parson he nominated. In a more general way the dependence of one supposedly free citizen on another by ties of a traditional and quasi-feudal nature did not fit the puritan attitude to individual responsibility, though the party never had any quarrel with the master-and-servant relationship. The point is perhaps not very material. It borders on the vexed question of the connexion, if any, between puritan morality, or puritan ideas about man in general, and the 'modern', urban, individualistic spirit. Puritanism certainly can be seen as conflicting with the hierarchical conception of society that was still dominant and fully respectable in our period, but this is a matter of reading between the lines of what puritans actually said and wrote. None of them would willingly be quoted as an opponent of due subjection in the commonwealth.[1]

In any case, they could not do without patronage. It is in the rôle of patron that laymen first played a prominent part in the movement. The preacher who wanted to have an opportunity to follow his calling normally needed a patron in the ecclesiastical sense in order to do so, and his livelihood as well as his chance of exercising a useful ministry would remain wholly precarious until he had one.[2] The

[1] Max Weber, *The Protestant Ethic and the Spirit of Capitalism* (trans. Talcott Parsons); R. H. Tawney, *Religion and the Rise of Capitalism*; Christopher Hill, *Society and Puritanism*.
[2] R. G. Usher, *Reconstruction of the English Church* is still the fullest account of puritan dependence on lay patrons; I think it would now be generally held to overstate the case.

man who attracted hostile attention by his puritan zeal needed to find favour in high places if he was to escape persecution; against one kind of authority, incensed by his insubordination, he could perhaps set up another kind. For this purpose he needed the countenance of some great protector, a man of prestige and influence enough, with luck, to overawe a mere bishop.

It was notorious that leading puritans were so protected.[1] Indeed, some of them were able to attract the sympathy of patrons so highly placed that it begins to look, deceptively, as if the movement had an unbeatable formula for success, and we have to ask why success did not follow. Walter Travers enjoyed the favour and friendship of Burghley, and had been an inmate in his household. Cartwright was publicly honoured, and enriched, by Leicester. Even after the rise of High Commission, after the Hampton Court Conference and new repression under James, the shaken and disarrayed puritans were able to gain the ear of George Villiers, Duke of Buckingham.[2] Throughout Elizabeth's reign, Privy Councillors and men in high secular office seem to have felt kindly disposed towards the preciser brethren, and prepared at most times to back them up against the bishops.

There is, however, an obvious difference between the kind of patronage that great men were pleased to extend to those whom they regarded as exceptionally able and zealous clergy, and the total identification with the movement of the few odd lay supporters one can name in Elizabeth's day – Job Throckmorton, Peter and Paul Wentworth. It is the difference between the man who scatters largesse and the man who makes sacrifices; between the man who adds to his own temporal prestige by demonstrating his power to protect a suppliant, and the man who takes risks in his own person. The puritans could not do without their great protectors, but their great protectors were not puritans. The names of Leicester and Buckingham show that clearly enough.

If you think of what went on in Elizabeth's parliaments, it is possible to see the activities of a lay wing of the movement, of men whose own convictions were puritan.[3] It is also possible to see, in parliament and out of it, in the Privy Council and in the country, a disposition within the political nation to give the puritans a chance

---

[1] On Leicester as a puritan patron, see Patrick Collinson (ed.), *Letters of Thomas Wood, Puritan 1566–1577* (London, 1960). See also Claire Cross, 'Noble Patronage in the Elizabethan Church', in *Historical Journal* 3 (1960).

[2] Irvonwy Morgan, *Prince Charles' Puritan Chaplain*.

[3] Neale, *Elizabeth I and her Parliaments, passim*.

and to deal with them mildly when they needed correction. This vague sort of sympathy from outside, from people who only imperfectly understood what the zealots wanted, in its day and age may have been more useful than a large and devoted popular following could be. In any case the puritan party did have to rely, for its chance to put across any of its intentions and even for its chance not to be ruthlessly suppressed, on a source of support that was external to itself. It was not inevitably external because lay. Nothing in puritan principles forbade a layman from participation in the innermost life of the movement. The movement was never going to achieve a really satisfactory measure of success unless this happened. There simply was not enough participation, of the useful kind of laymen, to be had.

This comes out very clearly in the history of the 'classical movement'.[1] If ever there was a need to recruit laymen into the ranks, it was here. If the classis, besides being a convenient machinery for co-operation between godly preachers in a locality, was also to be a demonstration model of synodical church government in action, this prototype of a presbytery required some 'elders' besides preachers. If the model of the Discipline was to exercise any discipline, it required the active collaboration of leaders of the secular community. If it was to do any moral good, it must win the people over. If it was to further any political plan it must gain political allies. On the whole it may be said that the classis did none of these things. If anything, by making the godly ministers and their problems better known to each other, it revealed more clearly than before how lacking in a lay base the movement at grassroots level, the movement in the parishes, still was in the 1580s. Yet every minister who became a member of a classis and brought it the tale of his troubles, every minister who came himself but failed to bring his churchwardens or any other substitute for a signory, had himself been presented to his living by someone, some patron who presumably had nothing against puritans and might be regarded as an ally. In some cases these patrons would not be laymen. The odd preacher was appointed to a benefice by a bishop or a college, and one way that great courtiers could show how great they were was by using their influence to get a client clergyman into a Crown living. There was a patron of some kind behind every preacher. Such patrons, by that mere fact, cannot be identified as puritans themselves. The sort of favour that Burghley or Leicester might be prepared to do, not to the party but to one of its

[1] Collinson, *Elizabethan Puritan Movement*, Pt. 7.

members, was very like the sort of favour that might be shown to an individual, though hardly to the movement, by a thorough-going protestant bishop like Grindal in Elizabeth's time or Abbot under James. Cartwright himself as a young man was in the service of Archbishop Loftus of Armagh. That fact in itself does not prove very much – Irish conditions were peculiar, and when Cartwright was a young man there hardly was a puritan party – but it illustrates the point that puritans could be patronized from time to time by non-puritans.

Many puritans depended on patronage by non-puritans. Many can have had nowhere else to set their worldly hopes. This need not have been a particularly bitter pill to swallow, it need not have involved any very ignominious compromising with a man's principles, but it did face the movement with a dilemma which in our period remained wholly unresolved. In the true church sincerely reformed the exercise of this kind of temporal lordship could have no place. It is true that the example of the best reformed churches abroad, that habitual criterion for condemning the English church settlement, did not tell decisively against aristocratic intervention in church affairs. There was plenty of it in the Huguenot church in France, and a really uncomfortable amount in Scotland. Yet nobody could doubt that ideally these things should not be.

In happier conditions, somebody like Peter Wentworth would doubtless have been a Ruling Elder and had a regular public career in the church. Somebody like George Villiers in those conditions would never have had a public career at all. The arts of the courtier were not arts that a puritan could admire, or willingly practice. It must have gone heavily against the grain for John Preston to pay court to Buckingham, in order that Buckingham in his turn might pay court to James for the preachers, and it was something that only happened, with that kind of favourite, in the dark period after Hampton Court. Preston naturally would feel no qualms at all about living on the bounty of a benefactor like Sir Walter Mildmay, founder of Emmanuel College, even if Mildmay had been still alive and dispensing his bounty in person. Mildmay was a man of outstanding gravity and high, God-fearing reputation whose support of the puritan cause was entirely compatible with his life and character. To all intents and purposes he *was* a Ruling Elder. One could feel the same sort of way about a nobleman like Lord Saye and Sele. Even Saye and Sele had to be resisted by the brethren when he wanted to set up temporal lordship, on the English plan, in New England.

The whole system was one that might be suffered for a time. It was naturally easier to suffer it when the people who enjoyed its advantages were, on the whole, good people; easier to accept patronage from a patron whom you could personally admire. But the only practical alternative to a patron whom you could admire was a patron whom you could not admire. The situation was not one which a sincere reformer could regard as tolerable indefinitely. As for the patronage system being a thing that might be 'suffered for a time', there were not lacking men in England and men in the party itself who said the same about surplices and the cross in baptism. There was no corruption in the English church that did not find its defender, even among the brethren, who would gloss it over by invoking the same phrase. If suffering for the time was a principle of universal application, life would be very much simpler for party men with moral perplexities. On the other hand, the principle would be fatal to the party programme, to the Platform. If anything and everything could be suffered for the time, nothing needed to be done. A man might develop within himself special qualities of patience and long-suffering. There might be some gain, as well as certainly some danger, to the soul. But the movement would cease to move; puritanism would be dead.

Conclusions and comparisons

Catholics and puritans experienced the intolerance of the Elizabethan church and state in different ways. The moderates among them, who hoped to stay out of trouble so far as was consistent with conscience, were hoping to stay out of different kinds of trouble. Their militants hoped to achieve quite different things by their militancy. There remained some features common to both situations, and they can be summed up in the fact that both catholics and puritans referred to bishops as 'bite-sheeps'. If the similarities were wholly superficial there would still be something to be said about them, but the two situations touch at a deeper level of personal motivation. Eventually, for people of sincerity on either side, there came a point where an other-worldly standard required them to go against the grain of this world. Temperamentally this was more of a problem for moderates and I find them more interesting for that reason.

In comparing the two it must always be remembered that Elizabethan puritanism was a movement whereas Elizabethan catholicism was a resistance. I suppose you could call a resistance a reluctant movement; if it is at all serious it is bound to take on movement-like qualities, but it springs from another kind of impulse, and the difference this makes is fairly obvious. The catholic opposition to the pro-testantizing state brought together people who shared a common detestation of what was going on but who never at any time had a common purpose to replace the government's policy with any specific other policy. Co-operation in the catholic ranks did not involve any agreement about an ultimate programme. It could bring together people with widely differing aims and outlooks. Puritanism on the other hand started out as a close-knit body of like-minded enthusiasts with a definite programme and a great deal of *koinonia* within the group, a high expectation of mutual warmth and brother-hood. Splits over fine points of philosophy developed later. Con-temporary models are convenient to hand, although their attraction, as ever, is dangerous. Marxism is like puritanism; the movement against the Vietnam war was more like recusancy.

If these parallels are accepted, for the time being and for what they are worth, they will serve to show that the resistance does not have to be underground, nor the positive movement above it. A resistance can be quite overt and conspicuous, although it is likely to become illegal. An instance from our period, and from catholicism in our period, would be supplied by the activities of the *Ligue* in the French wars of religion. A movement that aims at a fundamental change in society, and not merely some remedial adjustment like (say) abolishing the death penalty, will probably have to work very largely underground because it is bound to stir up that society's defence mechanisms, official and psychological.

In the case before us, catholicism was of course more of an underground than puritanism. It had, because of the state of the laws and the nature of the change that the government itself was trying to bring into effect, more to be underground about. The government's own programme of change was related to the puritan one, and it was not plain to contemporaries and it still is not plain to us where precisely the two parted company. This certainly could be a reason why puritanism initially lacked the appropriate psychology for an underground movement. In my own opinion, it never developed one, although it also was pushed by circumstances into illegalities. This need not be a reason for failure, and assessments of ultimate success or failure are not my main concern, but at least on the face of it the puritan movement did not achieve its aims, ever; the common purposes that made it a movement were not brought to fruition on English soil. This provides a point of contrast with catholicism, because the catholics did achieve the one purpose on which we must suppose that the whole body was united, namely the survival of the catholic faith in England. Of course this was a more limited aim than the kind of thing the puritans had their sights set on, which brings us back to the presence or absence of an underground mentality. With an underground mentality your aims are bound to be limited.

The lack of such a mentality can be seen in the lack of mental preparation for tough moments, and the lack of contingency planning even where the movement showed planning of some kind. There was no widespread discussion in puritan circles of the point at which compliance with what the hostile state commands becomes sinful, the point where principled disobedience has to start. Yet this was absolutely crucial in a situation where the need for some such disobedience could be foreseen. The catholic resistance was built up around the symbolic act of not going to church, of defying the Act of Uniformity and publicly avowing, if it had to come to that point, that you meant to go on being defiant and that you did so on grounds of conscience. All catholics who had been brought to accept the discipline of the movement were schooled in what they were to do and say. On this point at least the Seminary priests and the Jesuits were completely in accord, and the main thrust of the mission (from which some missionaries diverged to plot rebellion) was to organize this united stand. Among the puritans it was up to every individual, of those (mainly clergy) to whom disobedience was a live issue, to make up his own mind where his personal disobedience was going to begin, and there was an almost total absence of theoretical discussion of the subject. This may be explained in part by the different *ethos* of catholicism or puritanism, different attitudes to authority and obedience in a religious context, but if we argue that way I think we shall argue unhistorically. In Elizabeth's England it did not at all follow because you liked the latin mass, or disliked married priests, that your belief in catholic ecclesiastical discipline was very strong or that you were ready to undergo it, although to protestants who could manage to forget that the Queen liked ritual and disliked parsons' wives you would look like a 'catholic' or what they called a catholic. Conversely in the early days of puritanism it did not put the sort of emphasis on religious individualism and the rights of the private judgement that we have come to associate with the 'non-conformist conscience'. After all, the puritans did nothing else but talk all the time about the need for 'discipline', to stress that this discipline was ecclesiastically ministered, by the body to the body, and to assert that the worst thing about the English church was that it did not have any discipline. If puritans did not know how to preserve solidarity within their own party, and induce the membership all to see and observe the same moral imperatives in a matter that concerned the future of puritanism itself, then puritans did not know much about discipline, and in that case they ought to have talked less about it.

The lack of contingency planning is evident in the aftermath of the Hampton Court Conference. There was no lack of planning ahead of time. The Millenary Petition showed such plain evidence of forethought that the government was thoroughly alarmed. There was careful consultation, careful drafting of papers, careful briefing of spokesmen.[1] All the leading names were involved, divines and

[1] S. B. Babbage, *Puritanism and Richard Bancroft*, cap. 2, and cf. BM Add. 38492 f. 46f.

sympathetic laity. A high degree of organization was revealed. At the Hampton Court Conference, rigged as it was against them, they came near enough to winning to scare Whitgift and Bancroft. After it, when Bancroft came into his own and the High Commission went to work with the hauteur and uncompassion typical of authority in the Stuart age, there was, for the first time, present danger of a purge; the king's irate words, that he would 'harry them out of the land', looked like being fulfilled.[1] This danger, which must have been foreseeable, struck the puritan movement into such disarray that for a time it becomes all but invisible. This ought not to have happened, and surely would not have but for the fact the puritans were so used to looking upon themselves as the best-conducted of men that they could not readily grasp the implications of being looked on by others as deviants.

Puritan planning was not flexible in a crisis. To a lesser extent that had been demonstrated earlier by the classical movement, the most ambitious of puritan efforts at organization and a very impressive one in its way, but which disintegrated before its intended structure was ever completed. How flexible was the puritan individual in a crisis? The popular picture of such a man shows him dour, rigid, austere and unbending. Leaving aside the separatist martyrs like Barrow and Penry it would be hard to find a clear example of a puritan standing firm on a point of principle and outfacing his persecutors come what come may.

By comparison, the catholic who was actively engaged in the mission whether as a priest or as a lay accomplice was on the run and knew it. Whether they were the political kind of recusant or not, whether they were Jesuits or not, they developed the skills of the fox, of the specialized escape-artist. The word 'accomplice' of course has a bearing. If you helped a priest of the mission in any way you were breaking the law, and unless you were most remarkably ignorant you knew which law you were breaking and what the consequences were likely to be. In a situation where the conspiracy was what was needed, catholics reacted conspiratorially.

With an underground mentality, as I said before, your aims are bound to be limited. There are very strict limits to the amount you can hope to accomplish by underground methods, if your aim is to change the face of society. This was the puritan aim. A wholly secretive movement would have been wholly inappropriate to it. Perhaps a more militant movement, a movement more schooled and

1 Babbage, *Puritanism*...caps. 5, 6.

tutored in militancy, might have had a more spectacular quantity of achievement to show. When, briefly, in the 1640s, puritanism of the old, 'Geneva', 'Platform' kind, the 'good old cause' as it came to be called, actually came within hailing distance of what looked like success, this was the result of civil war, of a downright military alliance between the forces of righteousness and the armed forces of the Parliament. Would it have been wise for them to have resorted to force earlier? Anybody can see a dozen historical reasons why they *did* not. If it had not been for tactical and prudential considerations – they were most unlikely to win – there seems to be little in the theory of puritanism, as there is little in the Old Testament, to suggest that victory for righteousness accomplished by the sword should be a victory unpleasing to God. They were most unlikely to win.

But there are other kinds of militancy besides outright armed rebellion. There was the kind of 'reformation without tarrying for any' that Browne advocated. Browne's advocacy would hardly recommend anything to a sane mind, but the possibility might have been worth exploring. The reason why it found no favour is plain enough; to Browne and to his opponents alike, 'reformation without tarrying' meant separation. If, instead, it had meant a concerted refusal, across the board, to have anything to do with the idle ceremonies and a concerted insistence, across the board, on recognizing the excommunications carried out by godly ministers and not recognizing any other kind, it would rapidly have forced confrontation with the bishops and in all probability the Privy Council as well, and that would have been very uncomfortable for everybody, but it is an unhappy fact that you cannot seriously challenge the existing state of things if you are always avoiding confrontations. Sometimes they are necessary, sometimes not. The catholics in our period seem to have taken this much more thoroughly into their calculations than the puritans. Once again, of course, anybody can see several reasons why.

Actually, the proposal sketched out above or something like it was hinted at from time to time. So Snape, in Northamptonshire, at the height of the classical movement (1590) had said: 'How say you... if we devise a waye, whereby to shake of all the Anti-christian yoke and government of the Bishopps: and will ioyntlie together erect the discipline and government all in one day?'[1] and his words were duly reported back to the government along with a description

---

[1] BM Lansdowne 64.16. Item 12.

of the 'classical' organization in those parts calculated to show that the party did not lack the means for such direct action if it wanted to use them. And it is probably true that if ever there was a moment when the puritans had organization enough for such a venture, then was the time. In general they did not have a tight enough control over their own membership to make a policy of direct action practical, or thinkable except to hotheads. Such organization as they did have was not geared to that kind of function. The 'classis' was not a revolutionary cell. It bore a misleading resemblance to the earlier 'prophesying', and a resemblance which was perhaps intentionally misleading to a harmless sort of clergy dining club. Part of its purpose was to give the brethren a foretaste of the synodical government that should be hereafter. Part of its purpose was to put heads together in a regular way, not to plot any specific subversion but to evolve a corporate wisdom for the practical needs of present painful ministers and future ruling élite. There was quite a lot in this for nervous authorities to complain of, and the authorities of the day were nervous about any signs that their subjects were capable of independent organization for any purpose at all, but this organization was only secret and a conspiracy for accidental reasons which the members themselves were not in love with but sincerely regretted. There was nothing conspiratorial about the essence of what it was trying to do. The line of action that seemed to be laid down for puritans by the historical situation was the line of normal political process. They had friends in the Council chamber and many friends in Parliament. Their task was to educate the political nation, and through it the country, to appreciate the need for a thorough-going reformation. The appropriate methods were the ordinary methods of publicizing a point of view, so far as these existed in the sixteenth century. The puritans grew up in a world already familiar with the printing press, and they took to it naturally.[1] It cannot be claimed that they used the press in a particularly clever way, but nor did their opponents, who took to it equally naturally. What is natural is without art. The Anglican–puritan debate eventually produced two masters of contro-versial writing, in absolutely opposite modes – Hooker and Martin Marprelate – but the majority of pamphleteers on both sides were tedious, or waspish, or tedious and waspish. (Cartwright, for my money, heads the last class.) Very little that any of them wrote was

[1] On occasion they took to it illegally, though secrecy was never as necessary for them as for catholics. On this subject see Leona Rostenberg, *The Minority Press and the English Crown: A Study in Repression, 1558–1625* (Nieuwkoop, 1971).

well calculated to win over an opponent, and you could say that about what catholic spokesmen wrote as well, people like Parsons. The age, like the middle ages, saw discussion in terms of disputation, of defeating an opponent. The sour or bullying tone that resulted may be uncongenial to us but to contemporaries that would hardly have seemed to matter – such a tone was what you used in the political arena, and the political arena was where you were. In the protestant world, throughout Europe at this time, a mass of literature was dedicated to the purpose of winning debates and demolishing errors. Some literature was addressed to the religious enquirer by way of instruction. There was almost no devotional writing, addressed to the soul. For that, protestantism had to wait till the seventeenth century – early in the century, in the Anglican case – and then it borrowed from catholic sources. But the catholics themselves were mainly writing polemic in our period, as how should they not?

The puritan pamphleteers were writing for the needs of the political arena. They were seeking to convince politicians, to recruit political allies. They assumed that that was what they needed, and given the nature of their programme the assumption was valid. They were pinning their hopes of reformation on an improved scheme of ecclesiastical discipline, to be imposed on the nation from above. Plainly it had to be imposed by Queen, Lords and Commons in Parliament. So parliamentary action was the device that always had to be tried first. The position of the *Admonition to the Parliament* of 1572 in this process is hard to assess; appearing anonymously right at the end of the session, and very tactlessly phrased, it is hard to look on it as a serious attempt to do what it said it was trying to do – to instruct the members of parliament in their christian duty by pointing out to them what needed to be done, and what only they could do, to give England the benefit of a true and sincere reformation. It looks rather more like a gesture for the sake of a gesture, not to let it be said that the brethren let a golden opportunity slip by and did nothing. On the surface, however, the *Admonition* is the clearest possible illustration of how the puritan party went about things, of what picture they entertained of their own situation in their own society and how they expected things to work out their way. The circumstances in which a godly reformation would eventually be brought in – the right sort of way for it to happen – were the circumstances that the Admonitioners implicitly assumed to exist and those further circumstances that they tried to call into being. An upright and enlightened body of secular magistrates (holding an authority, as secular magistrates in a Christian commonwealth, that came directly from God) would receive the new light of the Gospel from the dedicated ministers and preachers of the word; taught by that light, interpreted by those ministers, they would see the corruptions of the half-popish establishment, and would powerfully and wrathfully intervene to purge the dregs of popery out of the national temple. Once this necessary catharsis had been effected the magistrates would have no more to do, as principals, for the church reorganized along the lines stated in the *Admonition* would be adequately governed by the ministry and the godly signory. Under such care, the nation would prosper henceforward as a people well pleasing the Lord. This was what was supposed to happen and this was the way it was supposed to happen. If the *Admonition* was actually expected to trigger the process, the expectation was naive. There was, indeed, a suitably puritan bill in that parliament, and it may have been prepared in conjunction with the *Admonition* and as part of the same strategy, though that can only be a matter of guesswork.[1] But the *Admonition* itself despite its title was not delivered to either house of parliament, nor yet distributed to the individual members. This last, which seems the most elementary technique today and which would surely not have been beyond the capacity of people who had proved their capacity to improvise a secret press, was not attempted with any literature of the puritan party, ever, so far as I know. If *Admonition* and bill were planned together, probably the bill was thought of as the main thrust and the *Admonition* as its support. In the upshot, however, the *Admonition* won a central place in public attention and the bill was forgotten. The attention it received and the controversy that sprang from it entitled us to treat the *Admonition* as the manifesto of the puritan party, summing up its theoretical position, and also to regard its publication as the party's first major bid for success, its open challenge to the establishment. Seen in this light, the fact that it claimed to be addressed to parliament, even if it really was not, is significant. If the authors themselves did not literally expect that parliament to do their work, they intended that their readers should have that kind of expectation, of that parliament or (given the time factor) more likely some other parliament. Of course the 'open letter' format can be a mere literary device – that is probably all it was when Father Parsons addressed his *Reasons for Refusal* to Queen Elizabeth. More usually, if you write somebody a politically motivated

---

[1] Neale, *Elizabeth I and her Parliaments*, vol. 1, 297f.

letter and publish its contents to the world without bothering to make sure that he has received it, your object is to put pressure on him (unless it is to show his past conduct towards yourself in an unfavourable light, which does not apply here). In any case, the puritans always did want, and try, to work through parliament. This could have, probably did have, a braking effect on their extralegal activities.

There is a widespread belief among respectable people that as long as the regularly constituted means of political persuasion remain open, they and they only ought to be used. As long as there remains a chance that constituted authority will eventually come around to the right side of its own accord, constituted authority should be left to do that, and only importuned in the most acceptable and conventional way. Approaches should always be made through the normal channels, and change should come about in a constitutional manner and, at the fastest, at all deliberate speed. This attitude appeals to responsible people inside government and out. It appeals to those who identify themselves with the establishment, to those who see themselves as natural rulers even if they happen to be out of power for the moment, and this of course included the early puritans, at least the more typical and representative among them. It was an attitude that appealed very strongly to those who wanted to keep out of personal trouble. The only thing wrong with this attitude is that it encourages a choice of strategy which often does not work. The world can be convinced by your eloquence that the existing laws are bad, and those in whose hands the power rests may be brought to agree, quite sincerely, that the laws are capable of improvement, but they still do not necessarily feel any urgency about improving them.

The puritans did not in fact get to this point. They did not convert the nation, they did not convince the governors, although they were never without friends at court. As long as that point was not attained, it continued to be something to strive for, a legitimate goal for everybody's efforts and thus an outlet for zeal. If zeal had run more generally than it ever did into other courses, less legitimate and more dramatic, nobody can say what might have happened to the puritan cause but the puritan image might be less stodgy. When natural activists like Prynne and Lilburne did let zeal outrun discretion they captured the popular imagination and built a following, though it is hard to say that they advanced the puritan cause: their personal acts of defiance, gutsy and effective in their way, were practically unrelated to any programme. Much more typically, the puritans looked to the politicians to be their salvation, and their optimism was not at all unreasonable but ultimately they looked in vain.

The catholic situation was totally different. The catholics' immediate aims could not be attained by political means and could not possibly await the convenience of parliament in any case. They had to put their first reliance on direct action. When they were political, they were political in a different way. The normal channels were almost complete closed to them. They had, in fact, their parliamentary spokesmen,[1] but after 1559 the occasional raising of a voice in protest was all that they could do. Catholic political hopes and plans lay in another direction. The émigrés lived in a constant atmosphere of plots: the competing plots of exiles which might as well be incompatible with each other since they were utterly unrealistic anyway, and the serious, but still unco-ordinated plots of real spies and real assassins. The majority fed their hopes and soothed their frustrations with dreams of better times. Better times were to be brought in by the intervention of Providence, perhaps using the King of Spain as its instrument but preferably not. All that was needed was something very simple, the succession to the throne of a catholic-minded monarch. Even the activists, even such an ultimate activist as Robert Catesby, thought that the relief of catholic distresses could be achieved by means almost equally simple – by little more than the removal from the throne of a protestant-minded monarch. Until James actually succeeded, even for some months later, many pinned their hopes on James. If he was not a catholic at heart, and many believed him to be that on the strength of the fact that his mother had been, then he could be easily terrorized into it; these alternatives were offered together in the first uncertain days of the reign.

A conversation, apparently among prisoners, was reported to the government in 1603. It was mainly about the chances of a successful rebellion, but – as was natural enough in that year – the king's attitude was the point to which all speculations came back.

Nay said Mr Bluets kinsman we are stronger in England and wee may force the k. to graunte a tolleracon if that all Catho: wold ioyne together... The residue thought that the k. wold be mercifull and w^thall was a grave wise and sage prince. Mr. Raufe of the Klinke said, what will not any prince

[1] The very occasional voices in the Commons are noticed by Neale, *ibid*. There was no law against the election of a catholic, though it was naturally rare, until 1606. The catholic representation in the Lords had by then sunk to one, but there has always been the odd catholic peer. (Their right to attend Parliament was not abolished, but put in doubt, by the act of 1606.)

doe to gaine a kingedome soe though he be a protestant in shewe yet he is a Catho: in hart and mynde[1]

Interestingly, although this group (who disliked the Jesuits) would on the whole rather trust to James' mercy and good feeling than to rebellion, the chief obstacle they saw to a successful rebellion was the lack of a great catholic nobleman to lead it. Another prisoner, interrogated about speeches of his that had been reported, forgot and then, under pressure, remembered having said 'if the king were not a papiste he should not live 5 yeres nor 5 monethes nor 5 weekes for that there were in the kinges own bozsome that would cutt his throate'.[2] From first to last, and whether they were talking about Elizabeth or James, Mary Queen of Scots or Philip of Spain or the Archduke of Austria, catholics of all degrees of fervour and all levels of sophistication seem to have seen politics in simplistic terms of kings deciding everything, according to their royal whim or as they might be manipulated by shrewder politicians than they.[3] This was what they thought had happened in 1559, and on earlier occasions. It was what they expected to happen in the future. To those who did not ascribe to the monarch a god-like power to determine the course of events by his own will, politics were a game of chess in which the king moved at a player's bidding but what happened to the king determined the game.

This was quite far from the realities even of seventeenth-century politics, although looking at the age from the standpoint of our own we are perhaps inclined to underestimate the real power the king enjoyed. James was the most important man in James' England, though we can see that he was not as important as the catholics thought, nor anything like as important as he thought himself. The catholics were wrong about his religious opinions if they thought that he took after his mother. They were not wrong in supposing that in a general sort of way he favoured toleration, possibly not wrong in thinking that he could be influenced by the threat of violence. In any case he could not oblige them. In all their political calculations the catholics seem to have been misled by a distorted view of their own society, a view entirely proper and suitable to traditionalists because it exaggerated the importance of traditional authorities, the visible greatness of kings and noblemen, to the point where kings and noblemen seemed to occupy the whole stage to themselves.

[1] SP 14.1.7 (n.d. ? March 1603).   [2] SP 14.1.31 (31 April 1603).
[3] This is brought out in T. H. Clancy, *Papist Pamphleteers*, cap. 2.

The catholics did realize that any political action within their grasp had to be underground. They did not expect the normal political process to work their way, as the puritans were always tempted to do. They did not understand what the political process of their day was all about, and they were quite powerless to manipulate it had they been tempted to. The puritans with all their valuable contacts and their well-informed modernity were not good at manipulating it, not good enough to produce the effect they wanted. While the two movements approached the political scene from opposite ends and adopted plain contrary styles, they were both destined to be disappointed by the results of political action.

Both dissentient groups were thrust into illegalities – different illegalities with different consequences. It was not really a question, for either, of choosing a road that would lead to success and finding that it lay through disobedience. It was rather that they had the alternatives of doing something illegal or doing nothing. We have to bear in mind that undoubtedly many individuals, potentially catholic or puritan but only just, opted to do nothing and were thus lost to the movement. Some, presumably, had the kind of temperament that finds the idea of defying authority positively attractive. The majority of those who stayed with the movement must have been reluctant heroes. How does the catholic reluctant hero compare with the puritan?

In drawing any such comparison it is necessary to reiterate the point that at this early stage of puritanism it and the catholic body are asymmetrical with one another. The early puritan movement was mainly a movement of clergy. What is more, until puritans got to the point of forming separatist conventicles (and most puritans in the time of Elizabeth I and James I believed it was their religious duty not to form separatist conventicles) the illegal acts they might be driven to were almost exclusively acts performed, or omitted, by ministers. We do not hear a great deal about the rank-and-file layman in early puritanism, and it is possible that in many places the movement got started without any. The laymen we do hear about are fanatics or politicians or occasionally both. No doubt the plain, painful preachers of the word had eager hearers, but their rôle was a passive one. There was nothing much, legal or illegal, that the common puritan parishioner was asked to do, or able to do, for the sake of the cause.

Here we have at once a major contrast with catholicism. Every catholic had a clear duty to his cause, and one whose performance was likely to attract hostile attention and incur temporal loss if it did not run him into actual danger. Circumstances could arise that were well within the reach of anybody's imagination, in which a true catholic would have no honourable course except to run into horrible danger, and this even if he was fully loyal to the national government and had no intention of getting himself involved in plots or rebellions. The catholic resistance was thus largely a lay movement, even if it was stimulated and held together by the activities of the clergy. There could be no guarantee of a constant supply of clergy, at least not in any given place. Resistance had to sustain itself, keep itself going among the laity of a district whether the district was ever visited by priests of the mission or not, and for long periods some districts could not be. When priests did come, their visits involved the local catholic laity in more illegal actions than usual, with heavier possible penalties; the business, itself, of keeping a priest housed and fed undetected, or of speeding him on his way, called forth exceptional efforts of a conspiratorial kind. It committed people quite definitely to an undercover organization. If they were not already in contact with such an organization they had to invent one. Secrecy was of the essence. No catholic could be in touch with the movement or even know about it without being, and knowing that he was, an accomplice in what was officially guilt. And if he was not in contact with the movement he was not in contact with his church; it would become a question, eventually, whether you could call such a man a catholic.

At first sight it is very odd that the catholic resistance should be largely a resistance of lay people, and the puritan movement hardly at all a movement of lay people. Surely one would expect the opposite, if you think of their two attitudes towards the rôle of the laity in the church. However, no very complicated explanation is needed for the apparent anomaly. The catholic church in England had its laity ready-made, it only needed to be organized to its new task. The puritans might believe in lay participation but they first had to find and educate their laity, and that process was considerably slowed down by the adverse conditions in which they had to operate.

Of course it is also true, and in a sense basic, that the Act of Uniformity, 1559, imposed a duty on every layman which a catholic could not conscientiously perform whereas most puritans could. There was no comparable law which it would have been easy for catholics to observe and difficult for puritans. Perhaps there might have been, if the puritans had early achieved a large lay following and this had come to be seen as an obstacle in the way of the government's religious policy. After all, the Act of Uniformity was not passed by accident, and it was deliberately designed to change the religious habits of people who were catholic at that date. It is also a question which may be asked whether compliance with the act was inevitably by a foreordained necessity bound to be conscientiously impossible to catholics, or conscientiously possible to puritans. If we think we know the answer to that question, I do not believe Queen Elizabeth did in 1559. Indeed we know that both in the catholic and in the puritan camp it remained an open question in the eyes of many for several years, or at least a question which could still be debated.

In any case, the people who were confronted in this age by the problem how to resolve the conflict between their scruples about the official religion and their desire to live at peace included the laity on the catholic side and on the puritan side they did not include the laity to a significant extent. This must weaken the effect of any comparison that can be drawn, since the two groups have one element of incomparability built in.

For a decade after the Act of Uniformity the Queen and her advisers trusted to time to make their reformation complete. They expected popery to wither away and were in no hurry to force religious conservatives into line. Religious conservatism, by itself, was not a problem that the government took a serious view of; it did not have a persecuting temper, nor any particular reason to feel its own authority threatened by the survival of popish sentiments here and there. As for the Roman authorities, their attitude towards Elizabeth and her reformation was at first open or at least cautious. They expected something to happen, such as Elizabeth's marriage to a catholic prince, which would make the problem go away. There was never any wavering on matters of principle. The English church was of course plain wrong. There could be no question of seating its representatives at the last sessions of the Council of Trent, or negotiating a compromise formula private to England, or allowing English catholics to attend and take part in protestant ceremonies as a matter of civil obedience to their sovereign. Rome was in no doubt that the English church was what it called 'calvinist'; it was in no doubt about the sinfulness of *communicatio in sacris*. But it, also, was in no hurry to bring on a crisis. In time both official bodies were jolted out of their inactivity by the march of events, by William Allen's private enterprise in founding the college at Douai, by the public excitements that centred around the arrival of Mary Queen of Scots, by the rebellion of the Northern Earls. There had been a run of years, about a decade, when no pressure was being exerted on the English catholics by their protestant government and no lead was being given them by their overseas church. If anybody bothered to write to Rome and find out, they would be told that it was their christian duty to have nothing to do with the new religion. If they followed that advice, or if they happened to come to the same conclusion on their own, they incurred a regular fine of one shilling a Sunday which the churchwardens might or might not collect. We do not know and cannot find out how often the churchwarden did. It is safe to assume that many catholics went to church at this stage who stayed away later because they later came to feel that it was wrong. It is clear that there were those who stayed away in the early period with impunity or almost, and were cracked down on later; that was the situation that the later, tougher laws were designed for. In the first class we know of the case of Edmund Plowden – a highly intelligent man and a public figure, who for years saw nothing wrong in attending Anglican worship and who drew the line at making a verbal declaration in its favour, when he was pressed to by the government and obviously without any seminary priest having reached him to instruct him in his duty as a catholic. Plowden, the incident itself makes clear, was not a man whose conscience sat lightly upon him. He refused, for a scruple, to do what was demanded of him; he was then at the height of his career in the law, and was cutting off the chance of further official favour. This example should warn us against assuming that all catholics who complied in the early reign of Elizabeth were ignorant or slack, and against assuming that it was the coming of the seminary priests that made all the difference.

Their coming did make a considerable difference. They brought the sacraments where but for their coming the sacraments might never have been brought again. They sustained the undercover church with what it needed to stay alive as a church. More to our purpose, they taught the duty of public and avowed recusancy. Their teaching it did not end all argument on the subject. Indeed, it is more reasonable to suppose that the teaching started the argument. But from henceforward there is a characteristic catholic party position on going to church. It becomes usual for catholics not to go, and that is how you know that they are catholics. The movement's own literature was largely designed to bring this end about. Although there was debate within the movement on the question whether recusancy was an absolute moral duty, the consensus and the official line was that it was. The opposition view attracted little attention and was not widely known. Arguments by catholics that it might be permissible to go to church survive, in a few instances, in manuscript. Refutations of these arguments sometimes got printed. But the typical printed argument why catholics must not go was addressed to the waverer who was merely deterred by weakness in his own character, not to the controversialist with reasons on the other side.

If a catholic refused to go to church, and did nothing else to offend the government, the consequences of refusal could be very serious indeed financially, they might easily amount to total ruin, but the full consequences possible under the law were most unlikely to happen. That is to say that hardly anyone was regularly charged the very heavy fines that became possible after 1581. This was partly because the law was cumbersome and difficult to enforce, and partly it would seem because it was administered with a good deal of partiality, not only at the grassroots level of local justice (which was always a problem for central government) but right from the top down. In any case only a very few catholics could pay the heaviest fines, in sixteenth century money values they were truly enormous and that cut both ways: to the odd unlucky or unpopular catholic who had to pay the full rate they were crippling, from the majority of catholics it was not worth trying to collect. Whether because he had favour at court or because he was too obscure to matter, the typical recusant had a very good chance of not being fined £20 a month. He had a poor chance of escaping scot-free. The whole catholic community lay under a heavy economic burden. In the long run this helped to bind it together, because the burden of one had to be in a measure the burden of all. Poor catholics could only survive as dependents on rich catholics, who in consequence became poorer.

The catholic who was ready to declare himself a recusant, and who was able to pay such fines as were imposed upon him, but who hoped to stay out of jail, had a fair reason to hope. It could not be counted on. Certainly at times the catholic prison population was alarmingly high. A man might be jailed because he had not paid a fine, or because he was suspected of dangerous political activities especially in the war years, or because he was involved in something more positive than recusancy alone, something like harbouring a priest. The risk of being suspected of subversion was one which, of course, nobody could completely avoid, he could only guard against it so far as not to be guilty. The majority of catholics were not guilty of subversion by ordinary standards, but in a time of war and rebellion that is very little security for the government and no protection for the individual. The government may know, as Elizabeth's government apparently did, that most of the suspect class are harmless, but unless it can tell which members of the suspect class belong to the harmless majority it has to suspect them all.

The moderate, peace-loving catholic could keep himself free from guilt in the matter of political subversion. I suppose that as long as Mary Queen of Scots was alive every catholic, however non-militant, must have hoped that somehow she would eventually succeed to the throne, and afterwards they had remoter hopes of less likely successions – that the Archduke would succeed instead of James or that James would turn out to be catholic. These things were hoped, we know, and even then there was no punishment for hoping. Actual complicity in a crime against the state you could avoid. It was less easy to guarantee that you could stay out of all kinds of trouble. If the necessity arose it must have been an inescapable duty for the lay catholic to help in concealing a priest, to carry an incriminating message or in some such way to give positive assistance to the under-ground. For most of the time, no doubt, that sort of thing could be left to the dedicated militants, the people who had a talent for subterfuge or who got emotional satisfaction out of running risks. But the time could always come when they were not there or there were not enough of them and the thing still had to be done. In these circumstances the peace-lover was really in no position to opt out, and the risks he ran were the same that the militants ran. Nobody who was in the movement at all could measure out beforehand the depth of his own involvement; it was not in his power to determine the limit beyond which he would not go.

Old catholic priests, left over from Mary's reign, were in a situation not wholly unlike that of the laity. They had all the same problems as the laity and – on paper – one or two more. They could break one law which a layman could not break, since they could say Mass (though hearing Mass said was illegal too), and it must often have been their moral duty to break it. Also, it was difficult for them to earn a living in any legal way; deprivation of a benefice did not wipe out the effect of ordination and such clergy were still in the power of the bishop's official and not supposed to practise a secular trade. In both these ways the old clergy who could not accept the settlement of 1559 were open to harassment. If such harassment occurred to any great extent the evidence certainly ought to survive in the records of the church courts; it does not, in those known to me. The situation of the deprived clergy was not an enviable one by any standard, their livelihood was precarious and their opportunities for falling foul of authority were extensive. Authority does not seem to have been very interested in them. Theirs is a more extreme case of what can be said generally about peaceable catholics – that their safety consisted in not attracting notice. In a society where persecution could never be systematic, and where the uniform and automatic application of rules was only beginning to be an accepted value for governments, the chance of simply not getting caught was quite a high one, and that was almost the only consideration that made the plight of the papist at all tolerable.

The later, more draconian legislation of the Elizabethan age did not put new burdens on the old clergy as such. Insofar as it concerned priests, it was directed against new priests, the missionaries who entered England surreptitiously from the Continent. These last, of course, were the catholics who ran the most ghastly danger. They included nearly all, not quite all, the recusant martyrs. The handful of laity who suffered death in the cause were single-hearted enthusiasts who committed themselves very deeply by their own choice. In one or two cases – notably Margaret Clitherow – they may be suspected of seeking martyrdom. The priests all had to accept the chance of martyrdom; the situation required it and the fact was emphasized in their training. For them – ideally – life and death were merely two ways of serving the ends of the mission, two ways of glorifying God. A priest had a duty, if he could, to avoid capture; it was his business to stay alive and at large in order to continue his missionary work. To avoid capture, in that sense to stay out of trouble, was his legitimate hope, not that he might lead a tranquil life but that he might labour longer and more profitably in the vineyard. Thus, shifts and evasions on his part are not necessarily proof of a lukewarm zeal. This applies especially to those verbal evasions, those equivocations and mental reservations, which protestants found so dishonest. 'I am not a priest', or 'I was not ordained beyond the seas', or 'I was never at the college at Rheims', with the unspoken qualification, 'in order that I might tell you about it'; very shocking that anyone should be so unstraightforward, but it was true after all that the examinate was a priest, and had been ordained overseas, and was at the college, for quite another purpose and one which would be defeated if he tamely allowed himself to be hanged, drawn and quartered at the first challenge he met.

The seminary priests and the fathers of the Society were human beings, not angels or machines. They had ordinary human motives, apart from the functional needs of the mission, for preferring not to be hanged, drawn and quartered. It occasionally happened that these human motives got the better of one of them. Men who must have had considerable courage to get into the business in the first place, who had passed the screening process at the Douai end which was not negligible, might find some of their courage ooze away over the long haul of years, the loneliness and frustrations of the mission might wear them down or the internal animosities between seminarian and Jesuit. A personal compromise between zeal and discretion might come to look attractive for ordinary human reasons. All the same, taking this body of men as a whole, they were no ordinary men. Neither was there any way they could lead an ordinary life. The choices before them, once they had accepted their vocation, were to behave heroically or to behave dishonourably. They could, of course, betray their associates. Short of that, almost anything else they did to save their skins could be a legitimate tactical evasion in the long-term interests of the cause. Some, no doubt, were more wholehearted than others, but this is not the place to look for moderates.

Protestants believed that the moral teachings of the catholic church would justify any baseness, any breach of common morality, if this served the political ends of the church. Protestant controversialists of this period do not seem to have been as obsessed about the confessional as their successors in recent times, but the spirit of the times encouraged paranoia; it was easy to feel that every papist was a mindless and unprincipled cog in a great machine, whose levers were manipulated by the Pope. Protestants were quite wrong, in their conscious beliefs and in their nameless fears. Catholic moral teaching was no more unanimous then than it is now, but the standard of behaviour usually held up for imitation was a stiff one. In the Elizabethan underground, lay catholics were taught an uncomfortable line of duty, with increasing clarity and definition as the years went by. There was more debate in the catholic world about the duties of priests than about the duties of the laity. This was undoubtedly partly because it was priests who did most of the debating, and the questions that interested them were the ones that confronted them in their vocation. It was also true, and it would be a good enough reason, that the duties of priests were more complicated. The church laid more definite duties upon priests than upon laymen, and the need to reconcile conflicting demands was more likely to arise. Upon all catholics, in one way or another, the church in this age imposed a duty which it could hardly help imposing, that of suffering for the faith; or, at least, of being prepared at all times to suffer for the faith. The church succeeded, to a very remarkable extent, in persuading the faithful to perform this duty. Popes, and such Englishmen as had the ear of popes, tried in addition to enlist them in political attempts against the government of Queen Elizabeth. This latter effort was almost entirely unsuccessful.

The bull *Regnans in excelsis* was a political and legal document, not a moral precept. It was intended to produce results in the fields of politics and law. The English catholic community showed clearly in the outcome that they looked to Rome and to nowhere else for the means of sacramental grace, but for political leadership and for law they would look elsewhere if they chose. To conspire against Elizabeth was the choice of some, and the Pope and several missionaries would have been content if many more had conspired, but catholics as a whole did not feel that this was their moral obligation. They were right; it was not. In this strictly limited sense most catholics did seek a middle path between pleasing the Queen and pleasing the Pope: they obeyed the Pope in matters of religion, and did not rebel against the Queen. This was the only middle path that was fully open to them. Any other compromise led direct to one or the other extreme, to the abandonment of catholicism or to treason.

Compromise, of any kind, tends to get a bad press. It is more inspiring to contemplate the Jesuit fathers suffering at Tyburn Tree, or the Pilgrim Fathers braving the hardships of a new world in search of their Promised Land. Many compromises, moreover, fail. Whoever gives up too much in order to stay out of trouble may end by giving up everything. The 'church-papist', for instance, was despised by both sides; he put himself outside the pale of catholicism and only earned a cold and suspicious reception among the protestants. He saved himself some money in fines, but both seminary priest and parson thought that it was at the cost of his soul. It is hard to find a close equivalent on the puritan side, but that may be because it was only too easy for a timid puritan to camouflage himself as an Anglican. All he had to do was conform, and he *became* an Anglican. When men have perfect disguises they disappear from our sight in any case; in some cases, the disguise becomes the man.

Compromise, in cases like these, is a concealed form of surrender. Anything that is not bold defiance will look like surrender in some eyes. All the same, compromise may be right. It may be the only answer that has a future. The catholics who refused to obey the Act of Uniformity and equally refused to rebel were adopting a compromise, a middle position, which was in no way ignoble or a soft option. The future of English catholicism lay with them, not with the zealots of the 'Spanish party'. The puritans who settled for as much puritanism as they could have within the establishment were wise in their generation and still had a chance of doing some useful work. All that lay the other way was the endless futile bickering of competitive radical splinter groups. Those whose purity or 'preciseness' was such that no church could content them unless it exhibited all the details of the 'discipline' and every plank of the 'platform' were destined not to be contented on this side the grave. It is arguable that Cartwright and Perkins and their school have had a profound influence on English protestantism. To this day, there is no church in old or New England that corresponds in all respects to the kind of church they wanted.

Would bolder defiance, by more people, have brought about a different result? Of course it would; but the people concerned would have had to be differently constituted people. People respond to their circumstances as their natures allow them to respond. There is no point in recommending extremism or moderation as if they were two alternative lines of action, more or less likely to produce the desired result. To any given individual they are not real alternatives. The field within which the individual exercises a choice is limited in one direction by his nature, and if it is his nature to avoid extremes then that rules out the extreme courses whether good or bad. The limit of what is practically possible and the limit of what is morally permissible are other landmarks of that field. These are marks that he may transgress, by stupidity or by sin. They remain part of his total situation, and unless they appreciate the total situation the moralist, the politician and the historian are in a poor position to be judges.

Naaman continued

In 1606 the question of church-going, as far as England was concerned, was officially dealt with, and one might have thought disposed of, by a *motu proprio* of Pope Paul V, which flatly forbade English catholics to obey the laws on the subject. While nothing new in itself, since the same line of conduct had been urged from Rome consistently as long as the laws had been in force, it was the first fully authoritative pronouncement to become generally known outside England. It would seem that continental casuists were aware of no earlier authority for recusancy, and some assumed that prior to 1606 it had been the practice of English catholics to attend church. On this point of course they were simply misinformed. The *motu proprio*, it would hardly be too much to say, was a greater practical inconvenience to the casuists than it was to the church-papists, who had long since adopted their stand and were unlikely to change it. The casuists however now had the task of fitting into their scheme of things a ruling which they could not venture to contradict but which did not always fit very easily.

Like any other papal pronouncement, this one was a relief to some and a disappointment to others but did not end the argument as a protestant might suppose it would. There were still impressive authors to be quoted on the lawfulness of bowing in the House of Rimmon. The *motu proprio* applied only to England; was England in some sense a special case? In fact we do find from now on what we might well have expected to find earlier, that moral theologians are sharply aware of the necessity of taking English conditions into account when treating the whole subject of obedience to heretical governments, of the duty of confession of the faith and the permissible bounds of dissimulation. Unfortunately they do not now begin to give attention to England in order to discuss the proper direction of troubled English consciences. That had become a question on which no further discussion was possible. The foregone conclusion, that Englishmen must not go to church when commanded by a heretical ruler, might have to be reconciled with a general rule which was easier to men of other nations.

Azor remained a much-cited author. Another who became available about this time was Thomas Sanchez. Sanchez in his lifetime was chiefly famous for his work on matrimony,[1] a subject on which he was perhaps the leading celibate authority of his day, although his name was not entirely free from some suspicion of error. He had maintained, until put right by another papal *motu proprio*, that the desire for sexual pleasure for its own sake was merely venial and not mortal sin. A recantation, in a posthumous work, was perhaps inserted by the editors, his brethren in the Society of Jesus. Fortunately no such suspicion attaches to his other great posthumous work, the *Opus Morale in Praecepta Decalogi*,[2] which, however, got nowhere near the seventh commandment. The two large volumes completed by his death reached only to 'Thou Shalt Not take the Name of the Lord thy God in Vain'. They did include his discussion of the duty of confessing the faith, which is the part that now concerns us.

The obligation to confess the faith in times of persecution is in principle absolute. (On this pretty well everybody was agreed, and it was, of course, the oldest of all casuistic debates, going back to the persecutions under Diocletian.) Confession was only not required by the divine law when it was not genuinely demanded by the persecutor. Thus Sanchez cites an incident on shipboard when a drunken unbeliever with a sword demanded to know who were 'catholics' in order that he might slaughter them. This would be a ridiculous occasion of martyrdom, and those catholics who concealed themselves were entitled to do so. It was also possible for words like 'christian' or 'catholic' to refer in the mind of the hostile questioner to something other than a man's religious allegiance. In some countries 'christian', doubtless for excellent reasons, had become a term of abuse (we may think of the word 'cretin', though this was not Sanchez' example): 'Ut apud Indos delictis Christianorum irritatos nomen Christiani odiosum erat, atque eo nomine insignem malefactorem significabant: si quis ergo ab Indis rogatus, an Christianus esset, id negaret, non peccaret in fidei confessionem.'[3] Similarly when

---

[1] *Dictionnaire de Théologie Catholique* s.v. 'Casuistique'.
[2] I have used the Paris edition of 1615.
[3] Bk 2, cap. 4.7. 'As among the Indians, offended by the crimes of Christians, the name "Christian" was hateful, and they called the worst criminals by it; thus if anyone was asked by Indians whether he was a Christian and denied it, he would not sin in the matter of confessing the faith.'

'christians' were one side in a war, or when the word was used by the interrogator to refer to a nation, a man might deny it with safety since his denial would be true in the interrogator's sense; and even if it was false in the interrogator's sense he would only be denying his party or nation, not his faith, and would come under the ordinary rules for simple lies (in which, as we have seen, fear of death is an acceptable excuse).[1] Sanchez will go so far (I doubt if Parsons would) as to allow a priest to deny that he is a priest when a persecutor asks it for the purpose of persecuting. As the faith is common to priests and laymen alike, the duty of confession does not extend to confessing the clerical character; and here he refers explicitly to England and claims the support of Azor, who 'optime ait hoc etiam esse verum, etsi haeretici haec perscrutentur (ut in Anglia passim sit) ad indagandum, an interrogatus fidem Ecclesiae Romanae amplectatur,'[2] which seems to be a departure from the rule previously stated, that what matters is what the persecutor means by asking. (Sanchez himself seems to feel this; there is no other possible relevance to his comment: 'Secus tamen ego censerem, si rogatus, an sit Papista':[3] since this is what heretics call catholics, catholics must not deny the name.) On the same principle a priest can deny having performed priestly functions, even though the persecutor asks it with the intention of driving him to a confession of faith, because to deny it is still not to deny the faith, though (presumably because it is all the same a thumping lie) Sanchez at this point suggests resorting to Mental Reservation: 'Immo, & iudici haeretico ea sub iureiurando interrogati [i.e. when required to swear that one has not performed sacred functions] liceret respondere negando, retento in iurantis mente, ita ut teneatur illi aperire.'[4] So far Sanchez has been talking about the duty of confessing the faith when directly asked. The duty of not attending heretical services, complicated in England by the civic duty of attending them, is closely related. (Both stem historically from the Roman obligation of Emperor-worship.) Sanchez on this subject is in no way original or interesting except that he is writing after the Pope's pronouncement and with knowledge of the situation in England. He agrees, with everybody, that catholics may sometimes

[1] Above, p. 86.
[2] Bk 2, cap. 4. 10. [Azor] 'well said that this was even true if heretics asked it (as constantly happens in England) to discover whether the person questioned has embraced the faith of the Roman Church.'
[3] *Ibid*. 'But I would think it would be otherwise if he was asked, "are you a papist?".'
[4] *Ibid*. 12. 'Indeed, even to a heretical judge asking this under oath it would be lawful to reply in the negative, the swearer reserving mentally "none that I am obliged to reveal to you".'

have lawful occasion to hear heretical sermons, for the purpose of checking on the errors they contain, and subject to the duty of avoiding scandal. As for going to the heretical church because the prince commands it, it all depends on why he commands it:

licebit catholicis obedire, si solus principis iubentis animus sit, ut omnes suis praeceptis obtemperent. [James was now on the throne; it was a principle that might have been of some help to laxists under Elizabeth.]...Si autem eius animus sit, ut eo tanquam haeresis symbolo, catholici eam profiteantur, & ut haeretici discernantur a catholics, non licebit obtemperare...magnaque offensio aliis catholicis datur, nisi catholici adeuntes protestentur publice se non adire causa haeresis profitendae, sed parendi principi.[1]

He here seems to be introducing, probably without meaning to, a possibility of half compliance which nobody had seriously explored but which at some times and places might just have been acceptable as a compromise. It remains unclear who is to decide that the government is imposing a civil rather than a strictly religious test, or how I am to make it clear that, at any rate, it is as a civil and not a religious test that I am prepared to take it. Sanchez at this point brings in Naaman only to deny that the case applies, and at last comes down squarely on the side of heroic virtue:

His tamen minime obstantibus, dicendum est id nullatenus licere, sed potius mortem obeundam. Quod unanimi consensu [a slight exaggeration] multi viri doctissimi ab Anglicanis catholicis consulti subscripsere: & tandem Paulus Quintus de hac re tanquam maximi ad religionem momenti ab eisdem consultus definivit suo proprio motu.[2]

In this passage it becomes quite clear how the English example is forcing the casuists away from the more moderate position where their own arguments seemed to be leading them.

Even the Pope allows that catholics can enter church buildings for the discharge of secular business, and Sanchez now claims that this is all that the example of Naaman will serve for. As for the limitations previously admitted by himself, they cannot be made to

---

[1] *Ibid.* 27. 'It will be lawful to catholics to obey, if the prince's only object is that all men should obey his laws...But if it be his object that thereby catholics should profess an heretical creed, and distinguish themselves as heretics rather than catholics, it will not be lawful...and great offence is given to other catholics, unless those catholics who attend protest publicly that they do so in order to obey the ruler, not in order to profess heresy.

[2] *Ibid.* 'But despite these examples, it must be said that it is no way lawful to do so, but rather to suffer death. Which by unanimous consent many learned men have maintained who were consulted by the English catholics; and more recently Paul V settled this matter, of such high religious importance, in the same sense by his *motu proprio*.'

apply to England. No adequate public protest by a catholic of his real intentions – so he rather airily states – would ever be allowed by the heretical rulers, while as to the intention of the law it is plain that more than a purely secular obedience is demanded by it. This he proves from some words of the appropriate act that he quotes in latin: those attending are not only to attend, but: '*Modeste etiam, atque sobrie, dum preces persolvuntur, se qerere, & usque ad finem dictarum precum, & concionum ibi manere teneantur.*'[1] Some who thought to get away with a bare presence have been deceived, 'ubi primum catholici templa illa adierint, iubendi sunt cantare, orare, genu flectere, instar aliorum haereticorum, ac proinde in ritibus cum illis communicare. . . Quod iam in Scotia, atque alibi factum fertur.'[2]

Actually, in Scotland in Sanchez' day, a quite different kind of compromise had been found possible – namely the proffer by admitted catholics of a special oath of secular allegiance. This is not to say that Sanchez' information was wrong, or that pressure such as he describes did not take place, though I do not know where he got it from. As for England, the status of the catholic community as a church 'under the Cross' was by this time firmly established. Sanchez makes one more allusion to it, when he lays down that recognition of the Royal Supremacy in England is absolutely unlawful. It would seem also to be on the strength of England's example that the case of Naaman fell from favour as a precedent among casuists, though oddly enough I know of no later writers who urged the example of Eleazar instead. The eventual fate of the Syrian commander-in-chief was a strange one. He became the precedent for a permission that might be reluctantly extended to household servants, to take service under a heretical employer and attend him, if required, in his heretical church.

An anonymous manuscript in the Sloane collection sums up the argument; its original can be dated internally to 1666, the evidence for the author's nationality is conflicting but suggests he was not English.[3] The case which is his starting point sounds as if it happened in France, or anyhow a country where both religions were openly practised.

A poor midwife, herself a catholic, was employed by a protestant

---

1 *Ibid.* 'To behave themselves modestly and soberly while prayers are said and to remain the whole time of the said prayers and preaching.'

2 *Ibid.* 'When catholics first went to the "temples" they were ordered to sing, pray, bend the knee, along with the heretics, and so to join with them in their rites. . . as now happens in Scotland and elsewhere.'

3 BM. Sloane MS. 1582.

family and carried an infant to the 'temple' to be baptized. She did
nothing but carry the child, and although presumably she must in
some sense have witnessed the sacrament itself, the point is made
that she did not stay to hear the protestant service ('nam infantis
teneritudo moram tam longam non patitur').[1] Some priests thereafter
denied her the sacraments while others considered she was admissible.
The anonymous supported the midwife. Citing Naaman on one side,
and the ruling of Paul V for England on the other, he considered
the crucial question was whether the servant was discharging her
regular duty to her master, to whom her religion might be supposed
a matter of indifference. The distinction between this woman's
problem and that of an English catholic resides in the nature of the
obedience required, so that once again we are driven to decide somehow, as a matter vitally affecting our own moral decision, what was
passing in the mind of another when he put an inconvenient command
upon us. It is quite clear that in this author's mind an English catholic
of the domestic servant class who has the dubious luck to be employed
by a heretic is free to go to church if his master orders it, although
by the effect of the Pope's brief and of all previous discussion of the
case he should refuse when commanded as a matter of law by the
magistrates. By this distinction it is possible to save Naaman and
Pope Paul and keep them both in credit, a result that the author
hails with relief:

Dei providentia erat, ut Breve Pontificium, ex Petri cathedra, non contra-
diceret sacrae scripturae, et eius expositoribus, nam lex divina immutabilis
est, nec variatur secundum locorum diversitatem vel consuetudinem, sicut
lex ecclesiastica...sed hoc de Elizeo et Naaman, pertinet ad legem divinam,
et ad fidem, quae simul sunt immutabiles...[2]

The pope, it seems, had had a narrow escape, though the upshot is
that so far as the vast majority of cases are concerned the English
catholics are no better off than before and the duty of recusancy,
whatever the penalty, has been reaffirmed.

The anonymous obviously thought the case of servants to heretical
masters was an important one, to be treated with caution, and that
the effort of reconciling his view with the papal pronouncement was
considerable though worth making. He relied most heavily on Cardinal

[1] *Ibid.* f. 3. 'For the tenderness of the infant could not endure so long a stay.'
[2] *Ibid.* f. 7. 'By God's providence it was that the Papal brief, from the throne of Peter, did
not contradict sacred scripture and its expositors, for the divine law is unchangeable, and
cannot vary according to places or customs as the law of the Church can...but this
case of Elisha and Naaman belongs to the divine law and to the Faith which are alike
unchangeable...'

Giovanni de Lugo, who as a recent curialist was an impressive person to be able to quote and of whom he speaks as his personal instructor. He also uses Azor and Sanchez, and two other Jesuits, Becanus (Martin Van der Beeck) and Hurtado (de Mendoza).[1] His reliance on as many writers as possible, oblivious of the fact that for the most part they quote each other, marks him as a 'probabilorist', and indeed he enunciates the principle. After making it clear that of course he thinks it safer for catholics to serve other catholics, and not heretical masters, and without a doubt that would be the advice that all his authors would give if they were consulted, he emphasizes that it takes more than a rejection of good advice, or a departure from the spiritually safest line of proceeding, to put a man into a state of sin that would justify denying him the sacraments; and when so many authors say that a thing is lawful, due weight has to be given to their opinion:

Ratio est quia nemo sacramentis privandus est, eo quod non incedit in via tutiori, nisi simul faciat aliquid directe illicitum (sed licitum est tale debitum [i.e. the servant's secular duty to his master] secundum dictos auctores) et hoc totum credo esse mentem summi Pontificis[2]

– though he prudently goes on to say that if he was wrong about the mind of the Pope he is ready to retract.

In the meantime, he was prepared to allow rather more than a grudging permission to servants to serve heretical masters if they would not be better advised. He could quote one author (Hurtado) for the opinion that you could take your hat off in a heretical church, as a matter of mere ordinary politeness (a larger concession in the seventeenth century than it would seem today). The anonymous, without actually suggesting that protestants were christians, did feel that in some ways they were better than idolaters, or at least less dangerous to guileless catholics, because they only preached, whereas idolaters performed false miracles (he got this idea out of some Jesuit relation: 'hoc...legi in quodam libro epistolarum Patri societatis ...').[3] As for the danger of protestant sermons, those who feared their effect ascribed to them a most unusual efficacy: 'Si qui catholici tantam vim tribuant concionibus haereticis, ut catholici absque perversione non possint eis interesse, plus tribuant haereticis quam

---

[1] His references to these are general and I have been unable to trace them.
[2] *Ibid.* f. 9. 'The reason is that nobody is to be denied the sacraments because he did not follow the safest path, unless he also did something plainly unlawful (but such an obligation is lawful according to the said authorities) and I believe this was all the Pope meant.'
[3] *Ibid.* f. 15.

catholicis concionibus, multi enim haeretici audiunt conciones catholicas, non tamen convertuntur,'[1] which is neat, though I imagine a competent apologist for the official line would make short work of the argument.

The souls of servants, then, were not intolerably endangered by their mere presence in a protestant church in attendance on their masters, however much they would have done better to have found a catholic master instead. It remained to convince the priests of the English mission. The author claimed to have discussed it with them, and to have found many of his opinion. It was, naturally, a question to which they had had to give a good deal of thought. But, alas, not all were convinced:

sed in hac quaestione Presbyteri Angli non fuerunt semper eiusdem mentis, doctiores tamen omnium iudicio, licet numero pauciores, semper dixerunt licitum esse [for servants to go to church. The less learned majority at first relied on Pope Paul's *motu proprio* until this was better explained to them, when] hoc clypeo nudati, quo se vertant, plane nesciunt, in angulos confugiunt, et ex his, scandalum, scandalum clamitant...[2]

It was claimed by some that English servants were in greater danger of apostasy if they went to church than other servants, but proof was lacking for this remarkable suggestion. The anonymous could recall no case of a servant, English or other, abandoning the faith because of the attractions of heretical worship, but he knew of a case where a servant had abandoned catholicism because he was denied the sacraments after he had been inside a protestant church while attending his master. (It happened in Durham, in a countryside full of catholics where it could not have been too difficult to find a catholic master.)

It was claimed by others that the rule for other nations might be as Lugo or the anonymous stated it, but in England another rule applied as a matter of local custom. This would not have been a very good argument in casuistry anyway, and our author had already made the point that the case of Naaman belonged to the universal law of God and the papal brief for England belonged to the mutable, and less august, ecclesiastical law which could not set the other

1 *Ibid.* f. 11v. 'If catholics ascribe such force to heretical sermons that no catholic can attend them without losing his faith, they ascribe more to heretical sermons than to catholic ones, for many heretics attend catholic sermons and are not converted.'

2 *Ibid.* f. 15. 'But on this question the English priests were not always of one mind, though the more learned, if perhaps fewer in number, always said it was lawful.... Stripped of this shield they know not where to turn, but flee to holes and corners from which they cry out "Scandal! Scandal!".'

aside. However, he was prepared to say that there was no such English custom. Many English priests agreed with him, it had been reported to him that his doctrine was taught in the English college in Rome, and Father Barnsley, of the Jesuits of Lisbon, might be supposed to know the customs of his own native country and nevertheless plainly expounded the case of Naaman in Cardinal Lugo's sense, in teaching intended primarily for his fellow Englishmen. Moreover (and here, did he but know it, the anonymous by trying to prove too much nearly destroyed his own case) there couldn't be any such English custom because it was only fifty-seven years since Paul V's brief, and before that all classes in England (so he supposed) had gone to the protestant church without a care in the world. So anxious was he to back up his opinion with English authorities, and thereby show that England was no exception, that he actually achieves the *tour de force* of citing Parsons on his side of the question. Parsons indeed had distinguished between going to church for a religious purpose and the mere physical being there for some other reason, and his words could be taken to mean that the permission extended by Elisha to Naaman might be extended to catholics who were not fully free agents. When all is said and done, after all the debate, this was all that the concession amounted to, and the anonymous himself thought that servants should try by some means to make their own religious position plain.

APPENDIX B

Conscience before Hampton Court

A collection of documents put together, apparently, by puritans in preparation for the Millenary Petition and Hampton Court contains one or two items that look at first sight like 'cases of conscience'. In fact they are draft arguments, drafted with debate in mind; rejoinders to anticipated questions that brought conscience in. The questions are unstated, but by implications they were expected to take roughly the form: 'Are you not obliged in conscience to obey the regulations laid down for you by lawful authority in matters indifferent?' and, 'Why should your conscience enjoy more privilege than a catholic's conscience?'

The first is much more fully treated. Probably, at James' first coming into the land, it was hoped that such a godly prince would never ask the second at all. The first argument is set out like an academic disputation, with numbered propositions proved syllogistically. Probably their author did not expect a formal disputation to take place; the syllogisms are surprisingly sloppy if he did. They would never have got past a university examiner of that date, and would have been a sore temptation to a pedant like James.

1. proposition.
The indifferent things of the church command(ed) by the christian magistrate, for order, decencie, and edification (to which ends they evermore tend) do not simplie bind the conscience as if they were absolutely necessarie, but may with godly wisedome be omitted, when the strict observation of them frustrateth the ends for which they were ordeined, and when the omission of them without any contempt of authoritie, or scandal given, atteineth the ends proposed[1]

– where it will be noted that the user of the argument, like Thomas Cartwright over the question of his ordination and the Trinity College statutes, is taking it upon himself to say what the intention

---

[1] BM. Add. 38492. f. 44.

of the legislator was, if it was not to have his commands obeyed; and also, like Perkins with his actions 'beside the law', to decide for himself whether his disobedience involves contempt of authority. The first proposition is proved by five syllogisms, between which a certain declension can be observed. The first is moderate in language and acceptable in reasoning; slightly rephrased, it would be a valid syllogism in *celarent*;

That which is ordeined for an other thing, and not simplie for it self, is not absolutely necessarie.
Indifferent things are never ordeined simplie for them selves, but always for some other thing, that is to say, for order, decencie, and edification.
Therefore indifferent things ordeined in the church are not absolutely necessarie.

Compare the fifth:

That which maketh a man to sinne is not to be ordeined as absolutely necessarie.
The necessarie imposing of these things upon ministers maketh them to sinne, in that they offend the godly, and confirm the papist in their old superstition.
Therefore these things are not absolutely necessarie.[1]

The second proposition – that the ceremonies of the English church are unlawful – and the third – that they are not expedient – are proved with similar or mounting vehemence, by four syllogisms each.

All monuments of idolatrie are unlawful deut: 7.5 & 12.2
Our ceremonies are monuments of popish superstition and idolatrie, as all men know, and the papists declare in their writings
Therefore our ceremonies are unlawfull...
That which being retained trobleth church and common wealth, but abolished pacifieth both, is not expedient.
Our ceremonies if they be reteined, troble church and common wealth, but if they be abolished pacifie both
Therefore they are not expedient.[2]

By this time it is clear that any pretence of talking about scruples of conscience, and almost any pretence of following formal logic, has been given up in favour of straight polemic. Everything depends on unproven minors which, if they could be proved, would leave no further room for moral doubt; the one just quoted, for instance, or

---

Ibid.   [2] *Ibid.* f. 44v–45.

(the shortest): 'Our ceremonies cause much contention but no edification.'

The next, related, document is less formal; it consists of arguments drawn up by somebody else but intended for the use of Sir Edward Lewknor, if he got a chance to put them to the king. This comes back to conscience, and makes a very interesting point.

... If anie shall suggest that yᵉ Papists may pretend yᵉ like colour & scruple of conscience, for their recusancye, treason &c. because their consciences doe doubt that in going to church, & yeilding obedience to Princes, they should sinne, when the Pope commaunds the Contrarye; we doubt not but that out of your princely wisdome you discerne yᵉ difference, considering that going to church, & obeying Princes are thinges so expresly commaunded, that none ought to pretend conscience to the contrarye, or if they doe, such a palpable erronious conscience is not to be regarded.[1]

It is greatly to be wished that some puritan casuist had developed this distinction more fully. So far as I know none did. It would be convenient for governors, then and now, to have a certain rule by which to tell which scruples of other men's consciences should be respected as virtuous and which could be dismissed as palpably erroneous.

ENDNOTE TO APPENDIX A

Francisco Suarez (cf. note 2, p. 101 above) is another casuist who makes a very odd use of the *Motu Proprio*. His *Defensio Fidei Catholicae et Apostolicae adversus Anglicanae sectae errores* (1613) was mainly a contribution to the debate over the Oath of Allegiance, but one chapter (Book 6, chapter 9) deals with the question of church-going in England. His object seems to be to prove that taking the oath is even more unlawful than going to church, and to that end he actually constructs an argument, explicitly 'probabilist', showing that going to church at the bidding of the Prince is lawful. He then gets out of this by invoking the *motu proprio*; the Pope has discerned evil *per se* in the action, which had seemed intrinsically innocent to earlier Catholic writers. (He goes on to say how thoroughly he agrees with the Pope, and brings in the case of Eleazar for good measure.) It is a curious performance; he seems to be playing an intellectual game rather than seriously considering the case. It should be remembered that, though he is using casuistry at this point, the book as a whole is controversial and is addressed not to confessors but to James I.

[1] *Ibid.* f. 46.

BIBLIOGRAPHY

MANUSCRIPT SOURCES

State Papers (in the Public Record Office, London) series 12, 14, 15
British Museum
  Additional Manuscripts 28,571; 26492 (Townshend Papers 1); 48039
    (Yelverton MS 44); 48064 (Yelverton MS 70); 48085 (Yelverton MS
    92); 48096 (Yelverton MS 105)
  Cottonian MS Titus B III; Titus C VII
  Egerton MS 1693
  Harleian MS 358; 1576; 3795
  Lansdowne MS 8; 27; 33; 37; 64; 72; 73; 97; 413; 421
  Sloane MS 1582
Cambridge University Library MS Ee. 11.34
Ely Diocesan records (in Cambridge University Library)
  Books B/2/4; B/2/5; B/2/6; B/2/18; B/2/22; B/2/25; B/2/31; B/2/32;
    D/2/5; D/2/8; D/2/10; D/2/10a
Lambeth Palace MS 577; 595; 206
London Diocesan records (in Guildhall Library) MS 9537/2, 3, 4, 5, 6
  (in London Record Office) DL/C/7, 210, 211
John Rylands Library (Manchester) English MS 524
Salisbury Diocesan Record Office Act Book 1, Act Book/Office 1
Dr Williams's Library (London) MS Book: Morrice, 'Chronological Account
  of Eminent Persons', 3 vols.
Winchester, County Record Office
  Diocesan records: Visitation Book B/1/A; Court Books 59, 64, 66A
  Hampshire Quarter Sessions Recognizance Book 1607–24

CONTEMPORARY AUTHORS

Ames, William (Amesius), *De Conscientia et eius juris vel casibus libri
  quinque*, Amsterdam, ed. of 1643.
— *Bellarminus Enervatus*, n.p., 1628.
Azor, Johannes, *Institutionum Moralium In quibus universae Quaestiones ad
  conscientiam Recte, aut prave factorum pertinentes breviter tractantur*, Lyons,
  ed. of 1610–16 (3 vols.).

254

Azpilcueta, Martin de, called Navarrus, *Enchiridion sive Manuale Confessariorum et Poenitentium...iampridem sermone Hispano compositum*, Antwerp, 1581.
— (Original Spanish version, Salamanca 1557).
Bellarmine, Robert (Cardinal), *Tractatus De Potestate Summi Pontificis In Rebus Temporalibus, Adversus Gulielmum Barclaium*, Cologne, 1611.
Cartwright, Thomas, *A reply to an Answere made of M. Doctor Whitgift againste the Admonition to the Parliament*, London, 1573.
— *The second replie agaynst Maister Whitgiftes second answer*, Zurich, 1575.
— *The rest of the Second replie agaynst Master Vuhitgifts second ansvuer*, n.p., 1577.
Cecil, Robert, Earl of Salisbury, *An Answere to certaine scandalous Papers scattered abroad under colour of a Catholike Admonition*, London, 1606.
Earle, John, *Micro-cosmographie. Or, a peece of the world discovered; in essayes and characters*, London, 1628.
Fuller, Thomas, *The Church History of Britain*, London, 1655.
— *The Holy and Prophane State*, London, 1642.
Molanus, Johannes (Jan Vermuelen), *Theologiae Practicae compendium, per conclusiones in quinque tractatus digestum*, Cologne, ed. 1590.
Perkins, William, *A Discourse of Conscience: Wherein is set downe the nature, properties, and differences thereof: as also the way to Get and keepe good Conscience*, Cambridge, 1596.
— *A Reformed Catholike: or a Declaration shewing howe neere we may come to the present Church of Rome in sundrie points of Religion: and wherein we must for ever depart from them, etc*, Cambridge, 1598.
— *The Whole Treatise of the cases of conscience, distinguished into three bookes*, Cambridge, 1608.
Persons, Robert (or Parsons), *A Brief Discours contayninge certayn reasons why catholiques refuse to goe to Church* ('Reasons for Refusall'), 'Douai', 1580.
— *Quaestiones Duae De Sacris alienis non adeundis*, n.p., 1607.
Sanchez, Thomas, *Opus Morale in Praecepta Decalogi sive Summum Casuum Conscientiae*, Paris, 1615.
Sayrus, Gregorius, *Compendii Clavis Regiae, pars prima* (no more published), Venice, 1621.
Suárez, Franciscus, *Defensio Fidei Catholicae et Apostolicae adversus Anglicanae sectae errores, cum responsione ad apologiam pro iuramento fidelitatis, & Praefationem monitoriam Serenissimi IACOBI Angliae Regis*, Coimbra, 1613.
Taylor, Jeremy, *Ductor Dubitantium or the rule of conscience in all her generall measures; serving as a great Instrument for the determination of cases of conscience*, London, 1660.
Travers, Walter, *An Answere to a Supplicatorie Epistle, of G.T. for the pretended Catholiques; written to the right Honourable Lords of her Maiesties Privy Councell*, London, 1583.

255

Whitgift, John, *An Answere to a certen Libel intituled, An admonition to the Parliament*, London, 1572.
— *The defense of the aunswere to the Admonition*, London, 1574.

UNPUBLISHED THESES

Burke, V. *Catholic Recusants in Elizabethan Worcestershire*, Birmingham, M.A., 1972.
Davidson, Alan, *Roman Catholicism in Oxfordshire*, Bristol, Ph.D., 1970.
Kalu, Ogbu U., *The Jacobean Church and Essex Puritans*, Toronto, Ph.D., 1973.
O'Dwyer, Michael, *Catholic Recusants in Essex c. 1580–c. 1600*, London, M.A., 1961.
Paul, John, *The Hampshire Recusants in the reign of Elizabeth I, with some reference to the problem of the church-papist*, Southampton, Ph.D., 1958.
Walker, F.-X., *The Implementation of the Elizabethan Statutes against Recusants, 1581–1603*, London, Ph.D., 1961.

MODERN WORKS AND REPRINTS

Allen, William, *A True, Sincere and Modest Defense of the English Catholics*, ed. Robert Kingdom (with William Cecil's *Execution of Justice in England*), New York, 1965.
Allison, A. F. and Rogers, D. M., *A Catalogue of Catholic Books in English Printed Abroad or Secretly in England 1558–1640*, London, 1964.
Anstruther, Godfrey, O. P., *The Seminary Priests: A Dictionary of the Secular Clergy of England and Wales 1558–1850, vol. 1, Elizabethan 1558–1603* (only vol. yet published), Ware and Durham, 1968.
Arber, E., ed., *The Troubles at Frankfort*, London, 1908.
Arénilla, L., 'Le Calvinisme et le droit de résistance à l'Etat', in *Annales Economies Sociétés Civilisations*, 1967.
Aveling (Dom), J. C. H., *Catholic Recusancy in the City of York 1558–1791*, London, 1970.
— 'The Marriages of Catholic Recusants, 1559–1642', in *Journal of Ecclesiastical History* 14 (1968, 3).
Babbage, Stuart B., *Puritanism and Richard Bancroft*, London, 1962.
Batho, G. R., 'The Finances of an Elizabethan Nobleman: Henry Percy, Ninth Earl of Northumberland (1564–1632)', in *Economic History Review*, 2nd series, IX (1957).
Beales, A. C. F., *Education under Penalty: English Catholic Education from the Reformation to the Fall of James II*, London, 1963.
Beesley, Alfred, *The History of Banbury*, London, 1842.
Blatcher, M., 'Touching the writ of latitat: an act "of no great moment"', in S. T. Bindoff *et al.* eds., *Elizabethan Government and Society, essays presented to Sir John Neale*, London, 1961.

Bossy, John, 'The Character of Elizabethan Catholicism', in *Past and Present* 21 (1962).

Caraman, Philip, ed. and trans., *John Gerard: The Autobiography of an Elizabethan*, London, 1951.

— ed. *The Other Face: Catholic Life under Elizabeth I*, London, 1960.

— ed. *The Years of Siege: Catholic Life from James I to Cromwell*, London, 1966.

Catholic Record Society Publications especially:

Record series 10, 11 *Douay Diaries* I and II [i.e. Diaries 3, 4 and 5] (1911) ed. E. H. Burton and T. L. Williams.

18, *Recusant Roll 1* (1916) ed. (Miss) M. M. C. Calthrop.

34 *London Session Records 1605–1685* (1934) ed. Hugh Bowler.

51 *The Wisbech Stirs* (1958) ed. P. Renolds.

57 *Recusant Roll 2* (with important introduction) (1965) ed. Hugh Bowler.

60 Recusant Documents from the *Ellesmere Manuscripts* (1968).

61 *Recusant Rolls 3 and 4* (1970) ed. Hugh Bowler.

Cecil, William, *see* Allen.

Clancy, Fr Thomas H., 'English Catholics and the Papal Deposing Power, 1570–1640' in *Recusant History* Pts I and II, vol. 6 (1961–2), Pt III, vol. 7 (1963).

— *Papist Pamphleteers: The Allen-Persons Party and the Political Thought of the Counter-Reformation in England, 1572–1615*, Chicago, 1964.

Collinson, Patrick, *The Elizabethan Puritan Movement*, Berkeley, 1967.

— ed. *Letters of Thomas Wood, Puritan 1566–1577*, London, 1960.

— 'The Authorship of *A Brieff Discours off the Troubles begonne at Franckford*', in *Journal of Ecclesiastical History* 9 (1958).

Creighton, Mandell (Bishop of Peterborough), 'The Excommunication of Elizabeth', in *English Historical Review* 1892.

Cross, M. Claire, *The Royal Supremacy in the Elizabethan Church*, London and New York, 1969.

— 'Noble Patronage in the Elizabethan Church', in *Historical Journal* 3 (1960).

Devlin, Christopher, S.J., *The Life of Robert Southwell, Poet and Martyr*, London, New York and Toronto, 1956.

Dickens, A. G., *The English Reformation*, London, 1964.

Dictionnaire de Théologie Catholique.

Douay Diaries 1 and 2, edited by Fathers of the London Oratory, London, 1878.

Elton, G. R., *Policy and Police: The Enforcement of the Reformation in the Age of Thomas Cromwell*, Cambridge, 1972.

Finch, Mary E., *The Wealth of Five Northamptonshire Families, 1540–1640*, Oxford, 1956.

Frere, W. H. and Douglas, C. E., eds, *Puritan Manifestoes*, London, 1907, reprinted 1954.

George, C. H. and K., *The Protestant Mind of the English Reformation*, Princeton, 1961.

George, C. H., 'Puritanism as History and Historiography' in *Past and Present* 41 (1968). (This article uses the word 'puritan' in a sense I cannot accept.)

Guilday, Peter, *The English Catholic Refugees on the Continent 1558–1795* vol. 1 (no more published), London, 1914.

Hall, Basil, 'Puritanism: the Problem of Definition', in *Studies in Church History* 11 (1965).

Haller, William, *The Rise of Puritanism*, New York, 1938.

— *Foxe's Book of Martyrs and the elect nation*, London, 1963.

— *Elizabeth I and the Puritans*, New York, 1964.

Haugaard, W. P., *Elizabeth and the English Reformation: the struggle for a stable settlement of religion*, Cambridge, 1968.

Hicks, Fr Leo, *An Elizabethan Problem*, London, 1964.

Hill, (Sir) J. W. F., *Tudor and Stuart Lincoln*, Cambridge, 1956.

Hughes, Philip, *Rome and the Counter-Reformation*, London, 1942.

Hurstfield, Joel, 'Gunpowder Plot and the Politics of Dissent', in *Early Stuart Studies*, ed. H. S. Reinmuth, Minneapolis, 1970.

James I, *Political Works*, ed. C. H. McIlwain, Cambridge (Mass), 1918.

Jenkins, Gladys, 'The Archpriest Controversy and the Printers 1601–1603', in *The Library*, 5th series 11 (1948).

Jordan, Wilbur K., *The Development of Religious Toleration in England*, Cambridge (Mass.), 4 vols. 1932–40.

— *The Charities of Rural England*, London, 1961.
(Both the above need to be read with extreme caution.)

Kantorowicz, Ernst, *The King's Two Bodies*, Princeton, 1957.

Klein, A. J., *Intolerance in the reign of Elizabeth Queen of England*, Boston and New York, 1917.

Knappen, Marshall M., *Tudor Puritanism*, Chicago, 1939.

Knox, S. J., *Walter Travers: paragon of Elizabethan puritanism*, London, 1962.

Loomie, Fr A. J., *The Spanish Elizabethans: the English Exiles at the Court of Philip II*, New York, 1963.

Lunn, Maurus, O.S.B., 'English Benedictines and the Oath of Allegiance, 1606–1647', in *Recusant History* 10 (1969–70).

McGinn, D. J., *The Admonition Controversy*, New Brunswick, New York, 1949.

McGrath, Patrick, *Papists and Puritans under Elizabeth I*, London, 1967.

Maitland, F. W., 'Elizabethan Gleanings', in *English Historical Review*, 1900; reprinted in *Historical Essays*, Cambridge, 1957.

Manning, R. B., *Religion and Society in Elizabethan Sussex, a study of the enforcement of the religious settlement 1558–1603*, Leicester, 1969.

— 'Catholics and local office holding in Elizabethan Sussex', in *Bulletin of the Institute of Historical Research*, 1962.

Marchant, R. A., *The Puritans and the Church Courts in the Diocese of York 1560–1642*, London, 1960.

Mathew, David, *The Celtic Peoples and Renaissance Europe*, London and New York, 1933.

Mathias, Roland, *Whitsun Riot*, London, 1963.

Meyer, A. O., *England and the Catholic Church under Queen Elizabeth*, trans. Rev. J. R. McKee, ed. of London, 1967, with introduction by John Bossy (Original German publ. 1911 as vol. 1 of projected work; trans. 1st ed. 1916).

Miller, Perry, *Orthodoxy in Massachusetts 1630–1650*, Cambridge (Mass.), 1933.

Morgan, Irvonwy, *Prince Charles' Puritan Chaplain*, London, 1957.

Mosse, G. L., *The Holy Pretence*, Oxford, 1957.

Neale, (Sir) John E., *Elizabeth I and her Parliaments*, London, vol. 1 1953, vol. 2 1957.

New, John F. W., *Anglican and Puritan, The Basis of their Opposition, 1558–1640*, Stanford, 1964.

Norwood, F. A., 'The Strangers' "Model Churches" in Sixteenth Century England', in F. H. Littell, ed., *Reformation Studies*, Richmond, Va., 1962 (actually deals only with London in the reign of Edward VI).

Opie, John, 'The Anglicizing of John Hooper', in *Archiv für Reformationsgeschicht*, 1968.

Owen, H. Gareth, 'The Liberty of the Minories – a study in Elizabethan religious radicalism', in *East London Papers* 8 (1965).

— 'A Nursery of Elizabethan Nonconformity 1567–72', in *Journal of Ecclesiastical History* 17 (1966).

Parmiter, Geoffrey DeC., 'Bishop Bonner and the Oath', in *Recusant History* 11 (1972).

Paul, John, 'Hampshire Recusants in the Time of Elizabeth I, with special reference to Winchester', in *Proceedings of the Hampshire Field Club* xxi, Pt 2 (1959).

Pearson, A. F. Scott, *Thomas Cartwright and Elizabethan Puritanism 1553–1603*, Cambridge, 1925.

Peck, F., *Desiderata Curiosa*, London, 1779.

Peel, A. and Carlson, L. H., eds, *Cartwrightiana*, London, 1951.

Pocock, J. G. A., *The Ancient Constitution and the Feudal Law*, Cambridge, 1957.

Porter, Harry C., *Reformation and Reaction in Tudor Cambridge*, Cambridge, 1957.

— *Puritanism in Tudor England*, London, 1970.

— 'The Anglicanism of Archbishop Whitgift', in *Historical Magazine of the Protestant Episcopal Church* 31 (1962).

Prest, Wilfrid R., *The Inns of Court, 1590–1640*, London, 1972.

Richardson, R. C., *Puritanism in North-West England: A regional study of the Diocese of Chester to 1642*, Manchester, 1972.

Rostenberg, Leona, *The Minority Press and the English Crown; A Study in Repression, 1558–1625*, Nieuwkoop, 1971.

Salmon, J. H. M., *The French Religious Wars in English Political Thought*, Oxford, 1959.

Sander, Nicholas, *The Rise and Growth of the Anglican Schism (1585)*, trans. David Lewis, London, 1877.

Schickler, (Baron) F. De, *Les Eglises du Réfuge en Angleterre*, Paris, 1892.

Seaver, Paul S., *The Puritan Lectureships: The Politics of Religious Dissent 1560–1662*, Stanford, 1970. (Deals with all lectureships, puritan or not, and hardly justifies its sub-title.)

Simpson, Martin A., 'Of the Troubles Begun at Frankfurt, A.D. 1554', in *Reformation and Revolution*, ed. Duncan Shaw, Edinburgh, 1967.

Toon, Peter, 'Der Englische Puritanismus', in *Historische Zeitschrift* 1972.

Trimble, W. R., *The Catholic Laity in Elizabethan England*, Cambridge (Mass.), 1964.

Usher, R. G., *The Reconstruction of the English Church*, London and New York, 1910.

— *The Rise and Fall of the High Commission*, Oxford, 1913.

Wark, K. R., *Elizabethan Recusancy in Cheshire* (Chetham Society, 3rd series, 19), Manchester, 1971.

Watkins, Owen C., *The Puritan Experience*, London, 1972.

Weiner, Carol Z., 'The Beleaguered Isle: a Study of Elizabethan and early Jacobean Anti-Catholicism', in *Past and Present* 51 (1970).

Zurich Letters I, ed. Hastings Robinson for the Parker Society, Cambridge, 1842.

The journal *Recusant History* contains much related material though not specially concentrated on this period. It was published from 1951 (originally as *Biographical Notes*) in Bognor Regis, Sussex, and since 1965 has been published by the Catholic Record Society.

INDEX